The Lost Manor of Ware

Also by Kathryn Kersey:

A School at Bearsted

'Dutifulness and Endurance' Bearsted and Thurnham 1914-1918, 1939-1945

Edited by Kathryn Kersey:

Bearsted and Thurnham Remembered

Robert Fludd of Bearsted
(edited by Kathryn Kersey on behalf of Bearsted & District Local History Society)

A Brief History of the White Horse, Bearsted
(edited by Kathryn Kersey on behalf of Rosemary Pearce)

The Lost Manor of Ware

Kathryn Kersey

First published in 2007 by Kathryn Kersey

Kathryn Kersey
5 Greensand Road
Bearsted
Maidstone
Kent
ME15 8NY

British Library Cataloguing in Publication Data

ISBN 978-0-9545831-3-2

Front Cover:
Part of an original Court Book page and the first section of a rental for the Manor of le Ware, Thornham from 1390, copied between 1613 and 1637. Reference CCRc M8 164902 Reproduced by kind permission of the Dean and Chapter of Rochester Cathedral and the Director of Community Services, Medway.

An undated photograph showing the lower section, north side of Ware Street around 1900

Back Cover:
The remains of the engine shed at the brick field in Ware Street, 2006.

Digitally set in Garamond and Times New Roman
Printed and bound in Great Britain by Parchment (Oxford) Limited

Dedication

For Stuart and Michael

in affectionate acknowledgment of shared times: past, current, and future

Acknowledgments

This book would not have been published without the help and assistance of many people. I extend massive thanks to Stephen Dixon and Derek Moore together with their dedicated and special team of staff at Medway Archives Centre. In the course of offering assistance with the manor of Ware records they have extended exemplary quantities of patience and helpfulness.

I am conscious of an enormous debt of thanks to Dr Peter Franklin for his very fine Latin transcription and translation services for the Court Rolls of the manor of Ware. I am quite certain that without Peter's assistance, I would still be looking at documents darkly. I acknowledge generous permission to reproduce photographs of the original documents from the Dean and Chapter of Rochester Cathedral and the Director of Community Services, Medway.

I am indebted to Dr Felix Hull for his original work on the manor of Ware which included a direction towards the title of this book.

Once again, further thanks in equal parts must be extended to the National Archives, Stuart Bligh, Julie Gregson, and the staff at the Centre for Kentish Studies in Maidstone in assisting my many document requests, Giles Guthrie and Simon Lace at Maidstone Museum, all the staff in the reference section of Maidstone library, and especially, the Bearsted and Madginford branches of the Kent Library Service. Together, all these magnificent parties have unearthed many obscure documents and dealt with many esoteric requests.

I am grateful to Julian Swift for a wonderfully enthusiastic, accurate and detailed historical appraisal of Chapel Lane farmhouse and to the Canterbury Archaeological Trust Limited for permission to use information from Rupert Austin's survey of the farmhouse.

During the research for this book, I was surprised to learn that information was required from several other continents. I am therefore delighted to acknowledge the assistance of June Fancett in Australia and Judy Corday in Bermuda. Without the generosity and enthusiastic commitment of these fellow researchers, parts of Edward Hart and John Dyke's lives and stories simply could not have been completed. I remain forever in your debt.

I would like to acknowledge the kind assistance, together with most generous permission to quote and use as a source of information/illustrations, the following people and organisations:

Paul Ashbee, Sylvia and Roy Barham, Bearsted Cricket Club, the late Ella Cardwell (née Foster), the Centre for Kentish Studies, Anthony Chadwick, the Churchwardens and Parochial Church Council of St Mary's church, Thurnham, Terry Clarke, Trevor and Jane Cleggett, Lynda Copsey, Martin Elms, Deborah Evans, Audrey Fermor, Avril and Patrick Finnis, Steve Finnis of the Queen's Own Royal West Kent Regiment Museum, Barbara Foster (née Westall), Sheila and the late Tony Foster, Peter Franklin, Evelyn Fridd (née White), Richard Gilbert and the family of the late Thomas Gilbert, Norah Giles (née Pettipiere), Irene Hales, Winifred Harris (née Guest), Christopher Harrison of Keele University, Maureen Homewood (née Rumble), Jenni Hudson, Felix Hull, Chris and Sue Hunt, Images of England, Jean Jones (née Hodges), Kent Archaeological Society, the Kent Messenger Newspaper Group, Ian Lambert, Ann Lampard, Bruce Leiper, Judith Lovelady, Pamela Message (née Pye), James Moore, Nicola and Mark Morgan, Margaret Morris, Dr Martin Moss, Frank Panton, Michael Patterson, David Pearce, Rosemary Pearce, Margaret Plowright (née White), Peter Rosevear, Arthur Ruderman, Bryan and Malcolm Salvage, Janet and Louie Smith, The Thurnham History Group, and Dr Hugh Vaux.

I am deeply grateful to Elisabeth Rackham, Brendan Walton and Martin Weeks at BJW Computers for prompt recommendations and a steady supply of an ocean of ink to replenish my printer when it was most needed.

Professor Eamon Duffy's work on the church accounts of St George's church, Morebath, in Devon, compiled by the idiosyncratic Sir Christopher Trychay must be acknowledged as a thorough inspiration. In countless ways has the path from Morebath to the manor of Ware been shared.

Great thanks to Anne and James Clinch and Roger Vidler for shared companionship and divers discussions about matters historic. Anne's insights into the Jack Cade Rebellion of 1450 were especially illuminating in a dark place. Likewise, I now regard Roger's collection of visual records as a fabled resource of past times.

Once again, I especially give deep thanks to Michael Perring for his special memories of his favourite place and for sharing an encyclopaedic knowledge of all things Thurnham.

Every reasonable effort has been made to contact the copyright holders of a cartoon about George Dibble, and also L Grace Dibble's published memories. I regret that I have been wholly unsuccessful. I welcome the opportunity to contact the copyright holders in order that formal permission may be obtained and would be pleased to insert the appropriate acknowledgement in any subsequent re-printing of this book.

I take this opportunity to thank my husband, Malcolm, and our sons, James and George, for their immense sensibility and observations. They have read, criticised and discussed the early drafts of this book without leniency, but in a way which comes from those who offer innate love and support in their encouragement. Malcolm and James also made their research debuts in the National Archives search rooms on my behalf when Edward Hart's fate became a nagging voice which could not be ignored. 'Thank you' seems two wholly inadequate words for all their endeavours.

I thank and acknowledge an award made by the Allen Grove Local History Fund of the Kent Archaeological Society, which was of financial assistance in the research required, and in the preparation of this book for publication, together with continued positive encouragement from Andrew Moffat and Dr Frank Panton.

Editorial Note

Where there is a particularly helpful description of events or an explanation of circumstances, it has been incorporated into the main body of the text for reasons of greater clarity and ease of reading. Any inclusions are subject to a note to indicate that the source used and that the words should not be regarded as written by the author - by this means it is hoped to avoid all accusations of that particular horror of all writers: inadvertent plagiarism.

Where an original document has been transcribed and translated from the original Latin, the text has been lightly edited for greater clarity and ease of reading.

Spellings of place and property names found in documents often prove troublesome and show great variance. In the manor of Ware, this is particularly evident for Weltighe Crofts: also rendered as Welteghe, Weltye, Weltis and Weltes. For ease of reading, the spelling from the original document under discussion has been used in the text. Likewise, although the current spelling of Thurnham is now more or less regularised, many documents and sources refer to Thornham. Once again, for ease of reading, the spelling given for a place name is that rendered in the original document.

In the transcriptions of the original Latin, all abbreviations have been expanded wherever possible. Additions, clarifications and interlining in these documents have been denoted by parentheses ( ), [ ] and italics as appropriate. Where interlining occurs it has been used to insert information sometimes omitted through error, but there are also occasions where it was used to indicate a course of action taken by the court or to include information reported to it. **** asterisks denote illegible on original document. Words struck through have been indicated ~~thus~~.

All comparisons of historic monetary values have been achieved from the information on the website: www.measuringworth.com. Readers should be aware that this does not give the real 'value' but is indexed to show the difference in purchasing power.

At least one of the articles in this book has a great deal of reference to matters concerning ships. I have therefore followed the established Admiralty convention of referring to ships as in the feminine gender and their names are given in italics.

All place names are in Kent, except where otherwise stated.

Abbreviations Used

CCA	Canterbury Cathedral Archives
CCRc	Medway Archives Centre
CKS	Centre for Kentish Studies
NA	The National Archives, formerly known as the Public Record Office
PCC	Wills proved at the Prerogative Court of Canterbury
PRC	Wills proved at the Archdeaconry Court of Canterbury

Latin

ibid.	In the same place and refers to the previously named publication.
op.cit.	In the publication already named.
passim.	Wording used that is dispersed through the text rather than a direct quote.

Contents

Appendices

Notes

Introduction

I have long since considered Ware Street, to be a fascinating area. As part of my researches, I was lent a paper about the medieval manor of Ware that had been written some years previously by Dr Felix Hull. It was the trigger for five years research.

The contents of this book are organised in two sections. The Early Manor of Ware commences with translations and transcriptions of the written records for the manor. It should be noted from the outset that although presented in this book in a chronological order, the majority of the records do not appear to be sequential, although the manorial court would have been held on a regular basis. The existing records, then, have survived as a matter of chance and serendipity.

The earliest records from the medieval manor, known as Court Roll documents, date from the fourteenth century. They were written in Latin and a specialised form of handwriting known as Court Hand. This evidence of the manor has been included because the bindings of the original documents are now considered so fragile that they cannot be produced for consultation at Medway Archives and Local Studies Centre, Rochester. However, I realise that the manorial documents may bear a limited appeal and so the reader is at liberty to pass over this section. A closer look at the medieval manor follows the translations, using the evidence found in the documents to highlight what can be learned about le Ware, Thornham, before broadening out to a wider discussion.

The second section of this book, called The Later Manor of Ware, examines the slow evolution of the area and the history of various properties and landholdings in Ware Street.

A full version of the excellent Latin transcriptions of the Court Rolls undertaken by Dr Peter Franklin is included in Appendix One for those readers who wish to exercise their classical skills.

Readers should be aware that some of the Later Manor of Ware information; particularly that concerning Sandy Mount, Ware Street in the early years of the twentieth century, and Henry Hodges, has already appeared elsewhere in print. I make no apology for including it here as it is provides valuable information.

Mr Michael Perring has long since regarded Thornham to be the unofficial centre of the universe. Through this book, it is my fervent hope that he realises that he is no longer alone.

Kathryn Kersey

A brief overview of Ware

Ware Street is a small area of Thurnham in Kent and measures approximately 1,400 yards. It is less than three miles from Maidstone and about thirty miles from London in the south east of England. Today there is little that could be regarded as a separate community; the discrete but neighbouring villages of Thurnham and Bearsted have gradually crept together, filling in gaps with housing as the population expanded. It is now difficult for a modern resident to discern where Thurnham ends and Bearsted begins, and yet, once, Ware was a separate manor with its own court.

Until the twentieth century and more recent times, the main area of Ware, or Ware Street, was, at most a handful of houses dispersed in a largely linear fashion along a street. Perhaps this is in keeping with most settlements in Kent which were originally linear. The main access was a route which ran out of Maidstone and which passed by parts of the Vinters estate and settlements at Grove Green and Hockers Lane, Detling.

Today, Ware Street is reached by signed road turnings for Bearsted from the A249 to Detling and the A20 to Ashford.

In 1086, when the Domesday book was compiled, there was no separate entry for Ware. It is curious that although Thurnham was included, both neighbouring Bearsted and Ware were not and that there is no apparent reason for this omission.[1] There are no early maps for Ware which would show details of the manor. However, by using details from the medieval records and superimposing them upon a map which Hasted used as an illustration to his survey of Kent in 1798,[2] it is possible to envisage some of the holdings of Ware. The grey shaded areas in this illustration below provide some indication of the extent of the manor:

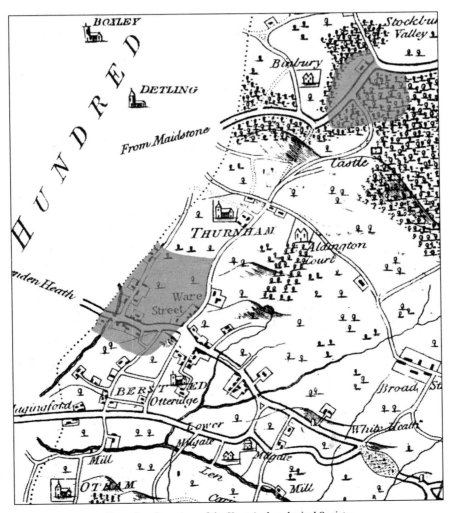

Reproduced courtesy of the Kent Archaeological Society

When Hasted published his book, The History and Topographical Survey of the County of Kent, parts of the parishes of Bearsted and Thurnham remained as separate linear areas but others, such as Roseacre Street, had developed. They all persisted as hamlets which more or less functioned independently, but which were loosely united by the parish church of St Mary's, situated in Thurnham Lane.

Below is Hasted's description of Thurnham: [3]

..The PARISH of Thurnham, though healthy, is yet from the nature of its soil an unpleasant situation, and is rather an unfrequented place, of little thoroughfare; the high ridge of chalk hills cross it, close to the foot of which is the church with the court-lodge and parsonage and at a small distance eastward Aldington court, having a double avenue of trees leading from it, almost to Bersted-green, to which this parish joins southward, near which the soil approaches the chalk, where the inclosures are large and open, having but few trees in the hedge-rows to shelter them, and the land poor and flinty...

From hence, on the hill northward, the country is wild and dreary, lying high and much exposed to the bleak northern aspect; the soil here is very poor and wet, a heavy tillage land of a kind of red earth, covered with quantities of flints...In the north-east part is a large quantity of wood-land, called Binbury wood, near which the high road from Maidstone through Detling leads on towards Stockbury valley and Key-street. Through this part of Thurnham, on the west side of this road, just before you descend to the low country is Binbury manor pound, and at a field or two distant behind it, the house itself...

It is significant that Hasted did not separately mention Ware, Ware Street, or the manor of Ware. His book was published less than a hundred years after the last remaining written record of the manor of Ware. Already the process of assimilation into Thurnham, and the disappearance of the manor as a separate entity from living memory, had begun.

The Court Roll entries
for the Manor of Ware

Document One [1] **- Court held 17 May 1380**

A Court of the Prior and Convent of Rochester Cathedral, held at Ware on the Thursday next before the Feast of Saint Dunstan in the third year of the reign of King Richard

Simon Sucenor comes and [blank] his relief for land bought [blank] of Sheller

And his relief is [blank]

He was ordered to raise from (Thorneham) Thomas [interlined] Whyce, for the lands bought of John [blank] and of the heirs of Richard [blank]

And his relief is [blank]

John Burbache, Roger de Cynton, William de ([blank], are in the Lord's mercy for default of court.

[blank] was ordered [blank], William [blank], for lands bought of William Suconer,

Hamo Mors, James Monk, Robert Arnolde, Roger de Chelisfeilde, William Bedell, for proper reliefs and fealties.

[blank], John de Northwoode and Thomas Whyce, for proper reliefs [and] fealties.

(The Names of) The Suitors [interlined] of the Court of Ware

John Sherstede
John Springe now John? Meggys
Richard Burbache
Joan Dunne
Simon Sucener, now Robert Morrell
Thomas Whyce
Joan Chapman

These are the tenants mentioned before, who are holding the tenements that [written in error for 'once'], of Hugh de Thorneham aforesaid, pertaining to the Chapel of St Mary at Rochester, namely

The Lady of Northwode for the Cynton tenement,
Roger de Syntoner
William Heyes
Hamo Mars
James Monek
Robert Arnolde
Roger de Chelesfeild
William Bedell.

These are all tenants who hold four acres of land in parcels, besides the Lady of Northwoode, and they owe between them, 4s 3d, besides 9d from the Lady of Northwoode for the same.

(end of document)

Document Two [1] **- Court held 1389-1390**

In the thirteenth year of the Reign of Richard II of England

[In margin] <u>Essoins</u>[2]

John Bracok
John Barstede ⎫ by John Spring
John Burbache ⎭

John Gy, the beadle, was ordered to distrain[3] John Wrecocke that he should be at the next court to answer the Lord concerning fealty and relief for one rood of land (of John F) bought of John Fleg.

The beadle was ordered to distrain John Clyve, Hamo Maas, Roger Chelisfeild, William Bedell and Alice Cyntone (concerning relief), that they should be [interlined] at the next court to answer the Lord concerning fealty and relief for the land and tenement bought and fallen due to them (from the Lord) and to remedy defaults of court.

And Alice is in mercy to answer the Lord, for fealty and relief for the lands of John Maas, John Beneyt

And John Roo for land [blank] the son of Roger Cynton.

The beadle was ordered to distrain John Clyve, Robert Morrell, the Lady of Northwood, Hamo Maas, James Monke, Roger Chelisfeild, Robert Arnolde, esquire, Alice Cynton and William Bedell, that they are [written in error for 'they should be'] at the next court to answer the Lord for default of suit of court.

<u>Total of this court</u>: [blank]

[heading blank here]

At this court [blank] to do fealty to the Lord for lands bought of William Cynton and of Roger Chelisfelde   2d

(For) **** not come to fealty to the Lord for land bought of William Cynton and that he raise of William Bedell   2d

And assigned to distrain the aforesaid Hamo, Roger and William Bedell for doing fealty, against the next court

And to remedy their defaults of suit of court.

At the preceding court, the beadle was ordered to distrain John Bacheler and Alice his wife to do fealty to the Lord, for five roods of land which have fallen due to the same Alice after the death of John Beneyt, her father.

And the beadle [blank] has done nothing to carry it out, so he is in mercy and assigned at another time to distrain for the same, against the next court.

The beadle was ordered thus, at another time, to distrain Joan, Lady of Northwoode, John Clyve, they have not come, and William Bette for many defaults of common suit of the court.

And the beadle is in mercy [blank] because he has not distrained Alice Cynton for doing fealty to the Lord, etc.,

And assigned to distrain for the same, against the next court.

The beadle was ordered to distrain Hamo Maas, Roger Chelisfeild, Robert Arnold, Alice Cynton, William Bedell, Roger Cynton, against the next court, for many defaults of common suit of the court.

(end of document)

A Rental of the Rents of le Ware in Thornham 1390-1398

[margin] 5 *(folio 1)*

A Rental of the rents in the Parish of Thornham pertaining to the Chapel of St Mary the Virgin in the Cathedral Church of Rochester, renewed by all the tenants there in the time of Brother Roger de [blank], monk and warden of the said chapel in the year of our Lord 1390 and in the twenty (five) third year (truly [interlined]) of the reign of King Richard, the second after the Conquest.[2]

Paying at the Feasts of the Annunciation of St Mary the Virgin and St Michael the Archangel by equal portions

First concerning the same Rent at the aforesaid Le Ware in Thornham   2s 6d

From John (Spring) [interlined] of Berghestede for one plot of land called Welteghe Croftes, containing five acres of land, lying (next to) between the lands of John Sharsted and of the heirs of Richard Burbach, towards the south, and the king's highway towards the north and the land of the said heirs and of William Wrecok towards the east, and towards Northrokesacrestrete, towards the west

At the same terms   20d

From the heirs of Richard Burbache, for three messuages, containing three and a half roods of day works land, once of Robert Beneyt, Peter Roksacre and Robert ate Welle, lying between the lands of John (Spring) [interlined] towards the south and west, and the king's highway towards the north, and towards the land of William Wrecok towards the east

At the same terms   3d

From the same, three roods of land lying in the place called Ferrays, between the lands of John Sharsted, towards the north and west, and the land of the aforesaid heirs, towards the south, and towards Northrokesacrestrete, towards the north

At the same terms   3d

From Robert Morrell (Elizabeth Cokir?), for three roods of land, lying in the place called Ferrays, between the lands of John Sharstede towards the west, and north, and towards Northrokesacrestrete towards the east

At the same terms   3d

From John Sharstede and John Meggyll, for one rood of land once of William Wrecok, lying at Le weltighe between the lands of the heirs of Richard Burbache, towards the south and west, and the land of William Wrecok towards the east, and towards the king's highway, towards the north

At the same terms   1d

Also concerning the same rent at Thornham street, under the hill

From the heirs of John Clyve, for two acres of land lying at Le Slede and Stuper, between the land of Robert Arnold, towards the east, and the land of John Wookherste, towards the west, and the land of the Vicar of Thornham, towards the south, and towards the land of William Bedill towards the north

At the same terms   6d

From the same, for one acre (of land [interlined]) lying at Berne, otherwise called Le uphouse, between the land of the aforesaid heirs, towards the south and the lands of the Vicar of Thornham, towards the north and west, and towards the lands of Alexander Birland and William Bedill, towards the east

At the same terms   3d

From Edmund Arnolde, for two acres of land lying at Forhell, between the land of the heirs of John Clyve, towards the west, and the lands of William Bedyll and John Broune, towards the east, and the land of the Vicar of Thornham[3], towards the south and towards the king's highway towards the north

At the same terms   6d

From the same for three roods of land lying in Le Eastcombe, between the lands of Margaret[4] Maas, towards the south and east and the land of William Bedyll towards the west, and towards the land of Alice de Ayntone, towards the north

At the same terms   2¼d

From the same for one croft called Littlecroftes containing one rood of land, lying below his messuage towards the west, and lands of Roger Chelisfeilde and (Ha) Hamo Maas, towards the east, and the land of John Broune towards the north, and towards the king's highway called Dunstrete towards the south

At the same terms   ¾d

From the same, for half an acre of land lying at Le Hunost[5] otherwise called Lewente

At the same terms   1½d

From James Monk for one acre of land called Joseacre, once of Hamo Maas, lying next to Dunstreete, towards the south, and the land of Roger (Colisfeild? Chelisfeld? [interlined])

[in margin] Chelisfeild[6],

towards the north, and the croft of Robert Arnolde, towards the west, and towards the land of William Bedill, towards the east

At the same terms   3d

From the same for one acre of land lying at Degherislond, between the land of William Bedill, towards the north, and the king's highway, towards the south, and between the lands of Gilbert Braunch, towards the west and east

At the same terms   3d

From the same, for three roods of land of the lands of Hugh de Thornam, once of John Beneyt, lying in Berashcombe, between the land of the aforesaid John Beneyt, towards the north, and the land of John Bedill, towards the south, and the land of the Vicar of Thornham, towards the east, and towards the land of Richard Bushe the elder, towards the west

At the same terms   2¼d

From Simon Cotev, otherwise Cotebie, for two roods of land, once of Hamo Maas, lying at Breche, between the land of Roger Chelisfelde, towards the west, and the land of William Bedyll, towards the east, and the land of the Vicar of Thornham, towards the south, and towards the land of the aforesaid Roger Chelisfield, towards the north

At the same terms   1½d

From the same, for three roods of land, once of Hamo Mass, lying in Le Eastcombe, towards the land of Margery Maas, towards the south and the land of John Chelisfeilde, towards the north, and the land of Edmund Arnolde, towards the west, and towards the lands of the aforesaid Margaret Maas towards the east

At the same terms   2¼d [altered from 2½d]

From Roger Chelisfelde, for one acre of land lying in Le Eastcombe, the ends towards the land of William Bedyll, towards the south, and the land called (Ga…latelond) Ganelatelond, towards the north, and the land of the aforesaid Roger, towards the west, and the land of William Bedyll towards the east

At the same terms   3d

From the same, for three roods of land lying in place called Le Chermer, otherwise called Shottfor, between the land of John Bedyll towards the south, and the land of the said Roger, towards the north, and the land of William Bedyll, towards the west, and towards the land of Alexander Dirland towards the east

At the same terms   2¼d

From the same, for one and a half roods of land lying at Le Breche, between the lands of the aforesaid Roger, towards the north, and the south, and the land of Simon Cotev otherwise Cotebie, towards the east, and towards the land of Alexander Dirland, towards the west

At the same terms   1d and ½ a farthing

From John Chelisfelde, for one acre and one rood of land, once of Alice de Ayntone, lying in Le Eastcombe, between the land of William Bedyll, towards the west, and the land of the aforesaid John, towards the east, and the land of Robert Arnolde, towards the south, and towards the land of Roger Chelisfeild towards the north

At the same terms   3¾d

From John Bacheler, for one acre and one rood of the lands of Hugh de Thornham, once of John Beneyt, lying in Berashcombe, between the lands of the aforesaid John Bacheler, towards the north and south, and the land of the heirs of John Clyve, towards the east and towards the land of John Foxe, towards the west

At the same terms   3¾d

From William Bedill, Edmund Arnolde and Margaret Maas, for twelve half day-works and the eighth part of one day-work of land, where the messuage of Hugh de Thorneham had once been built, lying at Thornehamstreete, towards the west, and the land of John Broune, towards the east, and the messuage of William Whytewonge, towards the north, and towards the messuage of the aforesaid Margaret Maas, towards the south

At the same terms   1d

From Alexander Dirland, for one plot of land where the barn of John de Aynetone (~~was~~) had once been built, containing one rood of land, lying between the lands of the heirs of John Clyve, towards the south and west, and the land of William Bedyll, towards the north, and towards the king's highway, towards the east

At the same terms   ¾d

Also concerning the same Rent, upon the hill at Ainetone

From Lady Joan, the Lady of Northwoode, for one garden[7], where the messuage of Roger de Aintetone was once built, with one plot of land adjacent in the croft called Ayntonscroftes, otherwise called Eastbynne, once of Roger and William de Aynetone, containing in all three acres and three roods of land, lying between the land of the aforesaid Lady in the aforesaid croft, towards the south and the way leading towards Aynetone Daue, towards the east and Ayntonstreate towards the west, and towards the croft called Northaytonescroftes and the wood called Yppintonswoode towards the north.

And for one plot of land called Aldiflonde, containing three and half acres, once of the aforesaid Roger and William de Aynetone, lying towards the king's highway, towards the north and west, and Le Brome (and Skelkisdale interlined]), otherwise called Cokkisdaue, towards the east, and towards Eastdowne towards the south

And for one and half acres of land once of Robert and John de Aynetone, lying in Skelkisdale, otherwise called Colkisdale, next to the way, towards the north, and towards the lands of the aforesaid Lady, towards the west, east and south

At the same terms   15d

Total of this rent, 10s 2½d and one farthing and a half

(end of document)

A Court of the Prior and Convent of Rochester held there on the Thursday next after the Feast of Saint Luke the Evangelist in the fifteenth year of the reign of King Richard II

John Spring of common suit ² by John Sharstede.

The Beadle is in mercy for (not) not [blank] John Wrecock to answer the Lord for fealty for one rood of land bought of John Flegg, and assigned to distrain for the same against the next court

Order the Beadle that he should raise from John Clyve for the relief for land bought of William Synton

And the relief is   4½d

And assigned (for fealty)to distrain for doing fealty, against the next court.

And from Hamo Maas, for the relief for the land bought of William Cynton

And the relief is   3¼d

And from Roger Chelisfeild, for the relief for the land bought of the aforesaid William   3¼d

And from William Bedyll, for the relief of the land bought of the aforesaid William   ¼d

And from Alice Cynton for a relief   2d

And assigned to distrain all for doing fealty, against the next court.

And to remedy defaults of suit of court

The beadle was ordered that he should raise from William Bette, for the relief of three roods of land bought of Alan Bette.

And the same was formerly of John Weneytt
And the two-fold relief is   2½d

And assigned to distrain for doing fealty against the next court.

And from John Bacheler and Alice his wife, for the relief for five roods of land
which fell due to the same Alice after the death of John Beneyt, her father   3¾d

And assigned to distrain for doing fealty against the next court, and for default of suit of court.

At this court, Robert Morell comes and puts himself in mercy for default of suit of court, as above.

The beadle was ordered that he should raise

From Hamo Maas	2d
James Moncke	2d
Roger Chelisfield	2d
Robert Arnold	2d
Alice Cynton	2d
William Beddell	2d
John Burbache	2d
And from John Meggyll for Richard Burbache	[blank]

For default of suit of court and assigned to distrain for the same, against the next court.

The beadle was ordered thus to distrain several people, Joan, otherwise the Lady of Northwode, John Clyve and William Bette, that they should be at the next court to answer the Lord for default of suit of court.

Total of this court   2s 11½d

(end of document)

The Court of Ware, held there
on the Thursday next before the Feast of Saint Dunstan
in the [blank] year of the reign of King Richard II

From Simon Cutever, for a relief	1½d
He ([the beadle] was ordered to raise from Thomas Whyce, for lands bought of John Burbache and of the heirs of Richard Robasar, for a relief	3d
From John Burbache, for default	3s 2d
From Roger Cyntoner for the same	2d
From William de Helles for the same	2d
From William de Helles for the same [entry repeated]	2d

Total   [Blank]

He was ordered [blank] William Dyche for lands bought of Roger Cutever, Hamo Mars, James Monek, Robert Arnolde, Roger de Chelisfeild and William Bedell, for proper reliefs and fealties.

He was ordered [blank] Lady Joan de Northwood and Thomas Whyce for proper reliefs and fealties.

Rental of Thorneham

From John Sharstede	2s 6d
From John Sprynge	20d
From Roger Burbache	[blank]
From Thomas Whyce	6d
Joan Chapman	4d
From Joan Donne	1 day
From Lady Joan de Northwoode for [blank] from the performance?	9d

(end of document)

A Court held there on the Wednesday next, after the Feast of Saint Mark the Evangelist, in the twenty second year of the reign of King Richard II

[blank] should not have been essoined twice

Robert Morell by Richard Carde

John Meggill by John Sharstede

John Spryng by Edmund Arnolde

Of common suit

(~~Was~~) The beadle was ordered thus, at another time, to distrain Lady Joan de Northwood, that she should be at the next court to answer the Lord for remedy many defaults of suit of court.

And Robert Arnald for remedying many defaults of common suit of the court.

And at this court Edmund Arnold came and he put himself in the Lord's mercy for many defaults of common suit of the court, done by the same Robert, etc.

The beadle was ordered to raise 2d to the Lord's use from the goods and chattels of Robert Morell, making default at this court.

And the beadle [blank] was ordered to distrain the same Robert against the next court, to answer the Lord of remedying many defaults of common suit of the court etc.

The beadle was ordered to distrain

John Carde

Robert Arnolde

and John Chelisfeild

that they should be at the next court to answer the Lord for remedying many defaults of common suit of the court.

(end of document)

Document Six - Court held 29 April 1399

Manor of Ware Rental 1610

Bearsted, Allington and Thurnham

The *** ***** **** for a rent in The Street

William Eaton***** for a ***** in Barsted

Edward Walter for *****

George Roper for **** and hall

(end of document)

Court Book entries for the Manor of Ware
1613 - 1637

(folio 13)

A Court Baron of the aforesaid Dean and Chapter [of Rochester Cathedral], held there on Thursday, namely, the twenty second day of September in the twelfth year of King James's reign of England, etc., and the 48th of his reign in Scotland by John Somer, the Steward,

The aforesaid Dean and the Sub-dean, Master Collins and Master Barnwell, being then present.

Essoins

Robert Barling
Joan Tilden
George Coulter

The Homage

John Crompe (gentleman, now mayor of Maidstone)[2]
Richard Wynter
William Snowe (in his wife's right)
Robert Coulter

(folio 14)

Who say upon their oaths that William Coulter, John Spice, [blank] Shernden, [blank] Vidgyn are tenants of this Manor and owe suit to the aforesaid court,

And they have not appeared at this court, but they are pardoned their absence because they have not been summoned.

Also, they present that since the last court, Richard Wynter bought of a certain George Page, one messuage with one a garden or orchard, and one rood of land lying and being in Ware aforesaid, in the said Parish of Thornham, the messuage being formerly of a certain William Coulter, abutting upon the king's highway there, towards the north, and upon the lands of John Crompe, towards east, west and south

[holding] by fealty, suit of court, and 1½d yearly rent,

And, being present here in court, he did fealty to the Lords and has paid them the full aforesaid rent in the name of a relief, namely 1½d.

And he was admitted as the tenant, and he was put into the homage.

Also, they present that William Snowe, in the right of Joan his wife (the daughter and heiress), the sister to Robert Shernden [(holds of the Lords which certain Robert by his Last Will) held of the Lords interlined] of this Manor, as of this Manor, three plots or parcels of land and woodland with the appurtenances, lying and being at Ware aforesaid, next to a certain lane there called Ferrys Lane, abutting upon the said lane, towards the east, upon the land of William Artridge, towards the south, upon the land of Robert Barling, towards the west, and upon the land of the heirs of John Spice, towards the north, [holding] by fealty, suit of court and 6½d yearly rent

And (~~now~~ which certain Robert by his Will in writing gave the same lands to the same Joan during her lifetime, and afterwards to William Eaton and Agnes Eaton, the daughter [interlined] (~~being present here in court, he did fealty to the Lords and has paid them in the name~~)

[in margin] of the same

Joan

And the aforesaid William, being now present at court, did fealty to the Lords and has paid

[in margin] them in the name

of a relief, the full rent, namely, 6d.

And (~~he did~~…) he was admitted as the tenant thereof, and he was put into the homage.

Also they present that Robert Coulter is a tenant of this Manor, but because they do not know for certain the lands which he claims (to hold of this Manor [interlined]), so a day was given to the same Robert, and to other tenants of this Manor, to put forward in writing (~~all~~), for certain, the lands and tenements which each one of them claims to hold of this Manor by the next court.

Memorandum that this Court has been kept for many years past by the Farmer of the Dean and Chapter and therefore I have hereunder written the rents now paid in Court:

Firstly, of Johane Tilden for 3 years rent due	9d
Of John Crompe, for the like	5s 6d
Of Robert Barling for the like and for his relief	9s
Of George Coulter, for the like, and being heretofore the land of John Cromp	2s 3d
Of Robert Coulter and Edward Coulter being the land of Robert Sawyers, for 3 years rent now behind	4s 2d
Of William Snowe for 3 years rent now behind	18d

(folio 24)

Manor of Ware in Thurnham

A Court Baron of the aforesaid venerable Dean and Chapter [document torn away] held there the day and year last mentioned before the aforesaid John Somer, the Steward.

Master Doctor Tillesley, the Archdeacon of Rochester and Receiver of the aforesaid Cathedral Church, being then present

Essoins

Edward Coulter
George Coulter

The Homage, sworn by

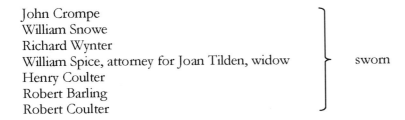

John Crompe
William Snowe
Richard Wynter
William Spice, attorney for Joan Tilden, widow   }   sworn
Henry Coulter
Robert Barling
Robert Coulter

Who say upon their oaths that to their knowledge there is nothing within this Manor presentable at this court.

An Entry of the Rents now paid in Court

Paid by Robert Barlyng for three years ending at Michaelmas next	6s 9d
Paid by William Spice for Johane Tilden for two years ending at Michaelmas next	6d
Paid by Richard Wynter for two years ending at Michaelmas next	2d
By George Coulter for three years ending at Michaelmas next	2s 3d
By Robert Coulter and Edward Coulter for three years ending at Michaelmas next	4s 1½d
By William Snowe for two years ending at Michaelmas next	12d
By Henry Coulter, for his part for three years next ending at Michaelmas next	2s 6d
By Robert Coulter, for his part for three years next ending at Michaelmas next being for lands late William Coulter their father	19½d
By master John Crompe, for two years ending at Michaelmas next	3s 8d

They chose William Snowe as the beadle of this Manor for the year following, who has taken the oath to carry out his office faithfully.

(end of document)

Document Eight - Manor of Ware Court Book 1614

Court Book entry for the Manor of Ware 1648

(folio 5-6)

[in margin] **Manor of Ware in Thurnham** see Book Five, 1630

A Court Baron of the Dean and Chapter of the Cathedral Church of Rochester, held there on the sixteenth day of January in the twenty fourth year of the reign of our Lord Charles, now King of England, etc., before Peter Buck, esquire, the Steward there, 1648.[2]

The Homage
Nicholas Muddle
Richard Hatch } They were sworn

Who say and present upon their oaths that Jane Coulter, widow, James Wood, Thomas Crump and Thomas Allen, in his wife's right, are free tenants of this Manor, and they owe suit to this court, and they have made default at this day.

Thus each one of them is in mercy 4d.

[margin] Transfer of property

Also, they present that Robert Coulter, who held of this Manor certain land for fealty, suit of court, and the service of a yearly rent of 1s 11d, has alienated[3] the aforesaid land since the last court to Jane Coulter, widow, from which there falls due to the Lords for the transfer of the property, the full rent, according to the custom of this Manor.

And the bailiff was ordered to distrain, etc.

Memorandum, that at this court, the aforesaid Jane Coulter is in arrears for six years' rent.

[margin] Transfer of property

Also, they present that Thomas Bills, who held of this manor land a certain parcel of land called Weltes, for fealty, suit of court, and the service of a yearly rent of 1s 10d, has alienated and sold the aforesaid parcel since the last court to James Wood, from which there falls due to the Lord for the transfer of the property, the full rent, according to the custom of this Manor, namely 1s 10d.

And the bailiff was ordered to distrain etc.

Transfer of property

Also, they present that William (Roades [interlined]) who held of this Manor three acres of land lying next to certain land called Braces, for fealty, suit of court and the service of a yearly rent of 9d, has alienated and sold the aforesaid three acres since the last court to Thomas Crump, from which there falls due to the Lords for the transfer of the property the full rent, according to the custom of this Manor, namely 9d.

And the Bailiff was ordered to distrain, etc.

Transfer of property

Also they present that Henry Muddle, Richard Hatch

[in margin] and

Elizabeth Bell, who held of this Manor one messuage and one rood of land, lying towards lands of James Wood, towards north, east and south, and towards the lane called Ferris Lane and towards the land of Thomas Brewer, to the west, for fealty, suit of court and the service of a yearly fee of 1d, has alienated the premises since the last court to Nicholas Muddle, from which there falls due to the Lords for (three [interlined]) transfers of the property the full rent, according to the custom of this Manor, namely 3d.

Which the aforesaid Nicholas has paid this into the court.

(folio 6)

Transfer of property

Also, they present that Henry Muddle, who held of this Manor one messuage, one acre of land called Ferris, lying towards the land of Daniel Godfrey, towards the north and east, towards the land of Anne Eaton, towards the south, and towards the lane called Ferris Lane, towards the east, for fealty, suit of court and service of a yearly rent of 3d, has alienated and sold the premises since the last court to Richard Hatch, from which there falls due to the Lords for the transfer of the property, the full rent, according to the custom of this Manor, namely 3d.

Which the aforesaid Richard has paid in court.

Also they present that (Richard) Thomas Allen, holds of the Manor in his wife's right, one messuage in which the court is held, for fealty, suit of court and the service of yearly rent 1d.

[in margin] Doing fealty

At this court, Nicholas Muddle and Richard Hatch did fealty and put into the homage.

Rents and other duties now paid in court to Henry Nichols

Paid by Nicholas Muddle *** 1d for six years rent *** behind at this court	6d
Paid then like wise by him for three alienations	3d
Paid then by Richard Hatch for six years then rent behind	1s 6d
Paid then by him for an alienation	3d
Paid then by Anne Eaton *** 6d for six years then behind	3s 6d

(folio 14)

[in margin] **Ware, Thurnham,** [book] 5

Also they present that William Shornden holds of this Manor three plots of land and woodland, lying and being at Ware aforesaid, next to a certain lane there called Ferriss Lane, for a yearly rent of 6d, which were once of Robert Shornden.[4]

The aforesaid William was admitted into the homage, he has paid a rent for transfer of the property of one shilling.

[in margin] Elsewhere

John (Bills interlined)] comes, and he acknowledged that he holds of this Manor, one messuage, one garden and one rood of land, lying and being in Ware aforesaid, for a yearly rent of 1d.

He has paid the rent and was admitted into the homage.

They chose the aforesaid John Bills as the beadle of this Manor for the year following, who has taken the oath to carry out his office faithfully.

Also they present the heir of Godden on account of the land once of William Coulter which he holds of the Manor for a yearly rent of 19½d.

Also they present the heir of Solhurst on account of the land lying and being at Four Wents[5], once the land of Robert Sawier, which he holds of this manor for a yearly rent of 16½d.

[written in margin] (Book Six?, *folios 32 ,59, 60)*

Rents paid in Court and the tenants Names

James Wood at 22*** and paid seven years quit rent	12s 10d
William Shornden at 11 *** and paid seven years	3s 6d
John Bills at 1d ***and paid seven years	7d

[written in margin] *(folios 11, 24, 54)*

Names of the Tenants

William Cage, knight, for two rents

James Wood

William Shornden

John Bills

(Thomas)

the heir of John Godden for two rents

(end of document)

A Copy of Customs and Quitrent of
ye Manor of Ware, Thurnham

Manor of Ware in Thurnham

It ii (6)

There is a Court Baron belonging to said Manor with fines and ameniaments of Courts, Issues, Post Fines upon descent or alienation being certain and according to Custom double or quit rents

Quit rents	£	s	d
Robert Bance for a Tenement in ye street			7½
William Carter			9½
Edward Walter			10½
George Roper		2	3
Sum Total		4	6½

The free holding of the said Court, whose lands lye in Thurnham, Barsted or Alington are to pursue their suite of service to ye Lord at ye place accustomed upon summons, ye place referred whereon to Keep the Court at Tile hoste in Bersted

(end of document)

Manor of Ware 1668 – 1669

A Notice of Quitrents 1668

<u>Ware in Thurnham   28 June</u>

James Wood for seven years

William Shornden for seven years

John Bills for seven years

<u>Bearsted, and also paid in court</u>

Richard Iden

Robert Brookes

Dorothy Deadrix

John Allen

Richard Spire

John Goslyn

John Esum***

Michaelmas of St Michael 1669

Ware and Thurnham rental

Sir William Cage Knt formerly East Barling for a messuage and barn and garden and six acres of land, wood and arable lying in Thurnham	2s 3d
More for lands formerly Con. Brird	5d
James Wood of ffaversham, farmer, formerly John Gumts for lands called Weltis Croft, Elnor Arnor by affirmation six acres, and a half, and six dayworks[2]	1s 10d
John Godden of Newington beyond Efyngton formerly Robert Jemmet for three acres of lands lying in Beriscombe under Galley Downe	1s 7d
William Shornden for three parcels of lands arable woods formerly Robert Shornden	6d
John Bills for a tenement garden and a rod of land	1d
The heirs of Solhurst, formerly Robert Sawyer for certain lands in Thurnham	1s 4½d
Luke Godden heirs, formerly William Coulter, and certain lands	1s 7½d
Robert Burr for a tenement in ye Streete	7½d
William Carter	9½d
Edward Walter	10½d

(end of document)

Rents to Dean and Chapter of Rochester
1682-1690

Ware and Thurnham

Sir William Cage Knt, formerly of Barlings for a messuage, barn and garden Six acres of land wood and arable in Thurnham	2s 3d
More for lands formerly Brirds	3d
James Wood of ffaversham, tanner, formerly Crumps for lands called Eft Croft, Elnor Arnor, six acres and a half and six dayworks	1s 10d
Jno Godden of Newington beyond Irlington formerly Robert Jommet for three Aces of land lying in Berifrombe under Gally downe	1s 7d
William Thornden for three parcels of land, arable and wood formerly Of Robert Shornden	6d
John Bills for a tenement garden and rod of land	1d
The heirs of Solhurst formerly Robert Sawyers for certain lands in Thurnham	1s 4d
Luke Goddens lands formerly William Coulter	1s 7d
Robert Bunne for a known land in ye Street	7d
William Carter	9s
Edward Walter	10d

(end of document)

A Closer Look at
the Early Manor of Ware

The Early Manor of Ware

Few people, as they travel through Ware Street in Thurnham today, are aware that in medieval times a manor called Le Ware in Thornham ever existed. It also has to be admitted that the records for the manor of Ware do not look very pre-possessing: contained in heavily bound, rather battered, quarto volumes of Victorian dark red leather. With the passage of time, the leather has become worn. Parts of its surface are now beginning to disintegrate into a dry powder which spreads easily over a search room desk. Although the bindings of the volumes have suffered, only one record is in a bad condition; the rental for 1610. As the parchment is very creased and worn, the ink and surface of the document is flaking in places. After thorough examination in January 2004, the Court Roll documents were deemed unfit for production. They are now stored away, awaiting conservation and a careful re-binding.

These volumes contain the records of Court Rolls and Courts Baron for all the properties and manors owned by Rochester cathedral. The details in the documents for Ware are recorded in clear handwriting using an ink that has become brown with age. The majority of them are written on sheets of cotton rag paper of superb quality, rather than a continuous, rolled, parchment membrane, from which usually arises the term 'roll' as the description of the document. The Court Book contains several manor courts held between 1380 and 1399, and a detailed rental. All of these were originally recorded during the reign of Richard II, but were later copied. It is curious that the earliest surviving records, from the fourteenth century, for the manor of Ware are found in a Court Book written between 1613 and 1637.

It was once thought that because a proportion of the manor of Thurnham was owned by Combwell Priory at Goudhurst, that the land holdings also included Ware Street.[1] The confusion seems to have originated in the close proximity of Ware to Thurnham, and of Thurnham to Bearsted. Sometimes this proximity led to a lack of distinction in descriptions of boundaries found in documents recording land transactions after the Middle Ages.

There have also been incorrect interpretations of some endowments made by the de Thornham family. The de Thornham connection with Combwell Priory began around 1160, when Robert de Thornham gave the priory the advowson of Thurnham and some other lands that he held.[2] Further confusion has been caused by the documents granting other lands to the priory by Mabel de Gatton. Charter V refers to lands next to Dun Strete and Charter XX mentions a street leading to Eynton. The spelling of the names varies but both of these places names are also mentioned in the early manor of Ware records.[3]

A preliminary reading of the charter documents can easily lead to the conclusion that Ware was also owned by the priory. However, it is only after careful examination of both sets of records that a subtle, but essential, difference can be found: the lands in the charters are recorded as 'lying towards' Dun Strete and 'leading towards Eynton' rather than the place itself as described in the Court Rolls. The descriptions of the boundaries are essential to perceiving the extent of the property: the Combwell Priory land holdings are in the vicinity of Ware rather than in the manor. Through the generosity of the extended de Thornham family, the priory gradually acquired other sections of Thurnham which abutted and adjoined Ware but not, it seems, the manor of Ware itself.

The earliest record that exists for Ware states that the tenements were owned in 1380 by the Chapel of St Mary the Virgin which was part of Rochester cathedral. This information indicates an earlier bequest made by Hugh de Thorneham to Rochester cathedral rather than Combwell Priory. Hence, in the record of the Court held on 17 May of that year, it is recorded: [4]

> These are the tenants mentioned before, who are holding the tenements, once of Hugh de Thorneham aforesaid, pertaining to the Chapel of St Mary at Rochester....

Below is shown the original entry:

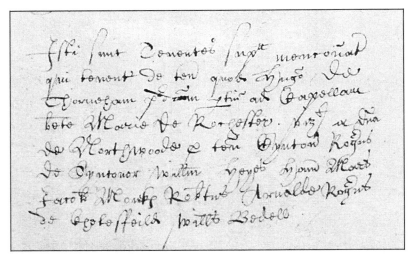

Reproduced by kind permission of the Dean and Chapter of Rochester Cathedral
and the Director of Community Services, Medway

The ownership of the landholdings is again emphasised in the rental document dated from 1390, as the compiler is described as from the chapel.[5] From the documents there is no indication that there was a Lord of the manor; this role seems to have been fulfilled by the representative of the cathedral. After the Dissolution, the administrative body of the cathedral became known as 'the Dean and Chapter of Rochester Cathedral'; later documents for Ware certainly include this phrase.

The land was described as 'the manor of Le Ware in Thornham' and estimated to measure thirty six acres. The income gained from the manor was very small and by the end of the fourteenth century, was recorded at below eleven shillings: around £280 today.[6]

The documents for the manor are held in a rather jumbled sequence in the Court Book. As mentioned previously, the earliest record concerns a court held on 17 May 1380. However, this record is placed third in a sequence of copied documents which actually commence with a rental covering 1390 to 1399.

The next document concerns a court described as: [7]

..held in the thirteenth year of the reign of Richard II…

and thus indicates that it was held sometime between 22 June 1389 and 21 June 1390. Only after these two documents were recorded, were the details of the court that had been held ten years earlier then copied in to the Court Book.

The details in the earliest document are sparse and part of the writing is not clear. However, it is possible to find details of tenants who held four acres of land in various parcels: [8]

The Names of the Suitors of the Court of Ware

John Sherstede
John Springe now John Meggys
Richard Burbache
Joan Dunne
Simon Sucener, now Robert Morrell
Thomas Whyce
Joan Chapman

These people owed the manor a total of 4s 3d; just over £85 today. For the same reason, the Lady of Northwood also owed 9d, or just over £15 today. Other names mentioned in the document included William Suconer, Hamo Mars, James Monk, Robert Arnold, Roger de Chelisfeilde, and William Bedell.

The most complete and detailed document is the copy of a rental originally compiled by Brother Roger, a monk and warden of Rochester cathedral in 1390. The details were renewed twice between 1390 and 1399. It often took many years to assemble this type of record as evidence was collected from tenants at the Manor Courts, which only sat once or twice a year. Felix Hull, the former County Archivist for Kent, was amongst the first to recognise the importance of the document, as it yielded information about Thurnham in medieval times.[9]

This shows part of an original Court Book page and the first section of the rental: [10]

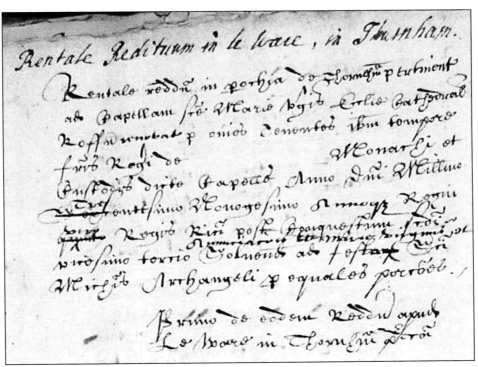

Reproduced by kind permission of the Dean and Chapter of Rochester Cathedral
and the Director of Community Services, Medway

Manors in Kent were rather different from elsewhere in Britain.[11] Although there are many interpretations of the written evidence, it is clear that by the later years of the Middle Ages, the manor usually operated as an administrative unit by which to collect rents. One aspect of Ware was typical of many other manors in different areas of England: it had a Court Baron attached to it which ensured that the payment of rents and other charges were levied when properties changed hands.[12]

The rental document for Ware officially recorded information about the land holdings and the finances of the manor. Manorial custom often required a 'relief'; usually a sum of money, which was paid when a holding was transferred.[13]

It is evident from details in the documents, that the manor was small. However, it did not just comprise the main street in Ware which is today called Ware Street, though it is probable that the main land holdings were located there. It is readily apparent that the manor was in three sections: Ware Street, and areas described as 'Thornham Street under the hill' and 'Upon the hill at Ainetone'. Thornham Street was the road leading up to Thurnham castle and Ainetone, Eyntone or Eyntone Crouche (the term and spelling greatly varies) was probably in the vicinity of where the present Castle Hill joins the A249 near the county show ground.[14]

Although it was a dispersed manor with several separate and scattered parcels of land, the records show that individual entries included the name of the tenant recorded, the area of the land holding and the rent paid. The holdings were pinpointed by a description of the adjacent land and holder. Occasionally, place names are sometimes given. However, the documents, like the Domesday survey, do not usually indicate if the land holders actually lived in the manor of Ware. It does not take into account the number of families in the manor, as sub-letting arrangements were not included. As a result, the poorer residents are not recorded. Neither is there any indication of the extent to which land and property lay waste and untenanted.[15] Unlike rentals for other manors in Kent, neither was the land valued by the fertility of the soil or hints of land management such as coppicing or pannage.[16]

One of the largest pieces of land in the manor recorded was that held by John Spring, described as, 'of Bearsted', so perhaps that is a hint to where John's major landholdings were located: [17]

> From John Spring of Berghestede for one plot of land called Welteghe Croftes, containing five acres of land, lying between the lands of John Sharsted and of the heirs of Richard Burbach towards the south and the king's highway towards the north and the land of the said heirs and of William Wrecok towards the east and towards Northrokesacrestrete.

From further information in the rental, it is evident that nearby was land called Ferrays. Four properties of less than an acre lay between Welteghe Croftes and Ferrays to the south of Ware Street. Felix Hull surmised from the information in the rental, that it was possible the holdings were located in the vicinity of what is now called Hog Hill; a route which leads into what became known as Roseacre Street, later Roseacre Lane, in the twentieth century. In this interpretation, Welteghe Croftes would then lie roughly in the same area as that which Sandy Mount in Ware Street largely occupies today.

From the description of the boundaries, and using some later maps as an indication of a possible road layout, Northrokesacrestrete evidently divided around a triangular piece of land, almost forming a crescent. Using this information, the following diagram is an interpretation of this section of Ware:

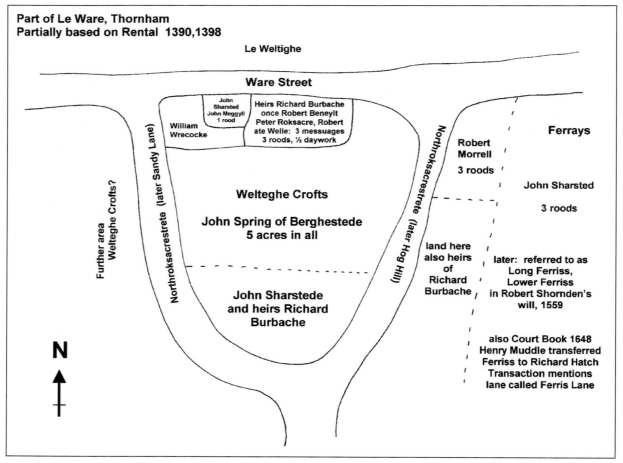

Reproduced courtesy of Malcolm Kersey

As can be seen in the diagram, the lane branched into two sections around and down past Welteghe Crofts to Ware Street, forming a roughly triangular shape. The two sections of the lane probably retained the same name, but later became known as Sandy Lane and Hog Hill. The triangular-shaped piece of land is persistently recorded in later maps. Another location for the Welteghe Crofts land holdings could be the land lying in a corresponding position to the west of Sandy Lane[18] but this fails to take into account the deliberate inclusion of the name Northrokesacrestrete in the rental. Intriguingly, a detail of Ware Street which was included in Hasted's map of 1798 may also yield a hint as to the location of John Spring's land holding.[19] Either one of these two plots in the middle and right hand side of the details (shown below as shaded), could have once been occupied by Welteghe Croftes.

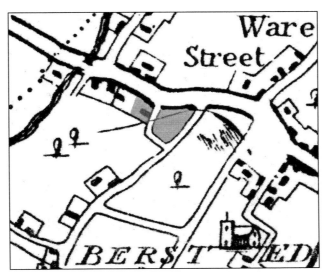

A house, of largely mid-Victorian construction, called Mount Pleasant now occupies the left hand shaded area, but there is every possibility that the land boundary predates the property.[20]

If Welteghe Croftes originally lay to the west of Sandy Lane, the boundaries mentioned in the rental make it clear that many of the plots lay to the north of the road now called the Pilgrims Way. This would suggest that at the time the rental was compiled, much of the land between the road and the scarp of the hill by Thurnham Lane was farmed. However, the plots would have been quite small as the total area of the land was estimated to be just over twenty two acres.[21] It is possible that the land holdings were remnants of ancient cultivated areas, established long before the construction of both Thurnham and Binbury castles.

It has been acknowledged that there are difficulties in using the information in rentals in an attempt to locate the land of the manor and in subsequent records.[22] At Ware, and in Thurnham, by 1581 only a few early field names survived to be recorded.[23] When new maps of the area were drawn in the eighteenth century, there were very few original names left.

Occasionally, there may be a derivative which can be found as recorded instead. One example of this is an area of land once called Eastcombe and recorded in the rental: [24]

> **From Roger Chelisfelde, for one acre of land lying in Le Eastcombe, the ends towards the land of William Bedyll towards the south and the land called Ganelatelond towards the north, and the land of the aforesaid Roger, towards the west and the land of William Bedyll towards the east.**

Although the name no longer exists, a partial remnant of the name may be found in a map dated of Thurnham compiled by John Watts in 1709,[25] which shows land called The Combe. However, it should also be noted that there were also areas called Kitcombe and Belcomb which lie to the west of Castle Hill in Thurnham.

Other snippets of information about previous times for the manor were written down in the rental, suggesting that the memories of tenants had been recalled as these two entries show: [26]

> From Alexander Dirland, for one plot of land where the barn of John de Aynetone had once been built, containing one rood of land, lying between the lands of the heirs of John Clyve, towards the south and west, and the land of William Bedyll, towards the north, and towards the king's highway, towards the east.

> From William Bedill, Edmund Arnolde and Margaret Maas, for twelve half day-works and the eighth part of one day-work of land, where the messuage of Hugh de Thorneham had once been built, lying at Thornehamstreete, towards the west and the land of John Broune, towards the east and the messuage of William Whytewonge, towards the north and towards the messuage of the aforesaid Margaret Maas towards the south.

The phrases 'where the barn of John de Aynetone had once been built' and 'where the messuage of Hugh de Thorneham had once been built' points to earlier information that had been carefully remembered but there was no formal deposition. It does, however, tantalisingly indicate that both John and Hugh had owned a substantial amount of property. The phrase 'twelve half day-works' is similarly interesting. Originally the term 'day-work' referred to the area of land which a man could work in a day. Later the measurement it became standardised. However, accurate land measurements did not become standard practice until the late sixteenth century and so earlier unmeasured areas became known as 'Customary' and were never altered.[27] This particular entry shows that by 1390 it had been realised that a sub-division of the measurement was required.

There is one rather curious section in the rental concerning a package of land which is separately listed: [28]

> ### Also concerning the same Rent, upon the hill at Ainetone
>
> From Lady Joan, the Lady of Northwoode, for one garden, where the messuage of Roger de Aintetone was once built, with one plot of land adjacent in the croft called Ayntonscroftes otherwise called Eastbynne, once of Roger and William de Aynetone, containing in all three acres and three roods of land, lying between the land of the aforesaid Lady in the aforesaid croft, towards the south and the way leading towards Aynetone Daue, towards the east and Ayntonstreate towards the west, and towards the croft called Northaytonescroftes and the wood called yppintonswoode towards the north.
>
> And for one plot of land called Aldiflonde, containing three and a half acres, once of the aforesaid Roger and William de Aynetone, lying towards the king's highway, towards the north and west and Le Brome and Skelkisdale, otherwise called Cokkisdaue towards the east and towards Eastdowne towards the south.
>
> And for one and half acres of land once of Robert and John de Aynetone, lying in Skelkisdale, otherwise called Cokkisdaue, next to the way, towards the north and towards the lands of the aforesaid Lady, towards the west, east and south.

Again, the rental income was minute: fifteen pence or just over £26 today.[29] From the description, Felix Hull estimated that the location of the property lay between the scarp of the Downs and the main road. 'Cokkisdaue' was probably to the south and east of the current A249 and the road which runs north west from the settlement at Eynton, leading to what is now called Cox Street.

Could it be possible that the land was part of the original land holdings for the Aineton family? In addition to the manor of Ware, other members of the Aineton family certainly held many lands in and around the manor of Thurnham.[30] Was it once included in the dowry of an important marriage into the Northwoode family, and so considered a little special? Hasted recorded that the Northwoode family had received Binbury castle and other lands around 1272.[31]

The circumstances of the separate listing may never be known, but it is feasible that the name Cox Street shows an example of a medieval place name becoming used for a wider area.[32]

Below is shown the start of the entry concerning the hill at Ainetone:

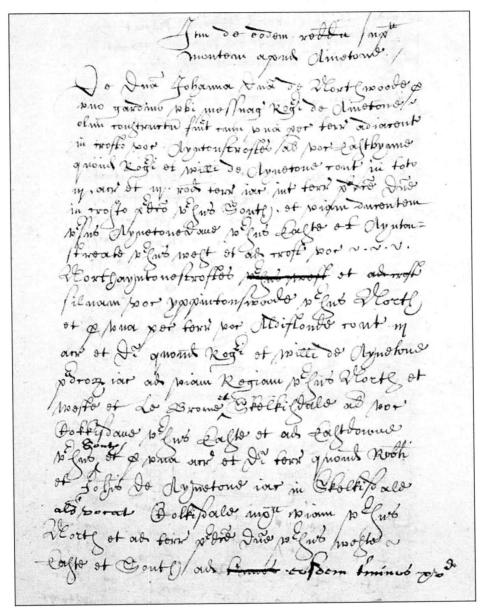

Reproduced by kind permission of the Dean and Chapter of Rochester Cathedral
and the Director of Community Services, Medway

Although the records are fragmentary, the details of all the properties and land held by the de Aineton family, Hugh de Thornham, and even the established settlement of Eynton, only cover a few years. So what happened to the holdings listed in the rental? Felix Hull suggested that the land became vacant through an outbreak of disease, or a local pestilence, which resulted in the families recorded in the rental perishing in a very short space of time.[33]

Whilst no evidence for a brief period of rapid mortality within the community exists,[34] amalgamation of some of the holdings may have eventually occurred. Perhaps this is why the outlying sections of Le Ware, particularly that of Eynton, became part of Thurnham. A re-organisation of the holdings on a rather more rational basis would have been sensible in these circumstances. Whatever the reason behind the land becoming untenanted, the Dean and Chapter of Rochester cathedral needed to address the situation. It is of enormous regret that the documents that would have given information upon subsequent land tenure do not exist.[35]

It is entirely probable that once the earlier pattern of land tenure was recorded, it would have been a relatively simple matter to amalgamate or absorb the untenanted holdings into the rest of the lands held at Thurnham.[36] The land was then passed onto the tenure of other families whose successive generations are recorded in the Court Books and Rolls. Some of these names include Coulter, Eaton, Godden, Muddle, Shornden and Spice.[37]

This illustration shows part of a later Court Roll and gives details of the rents that were paid in 1648: [38]

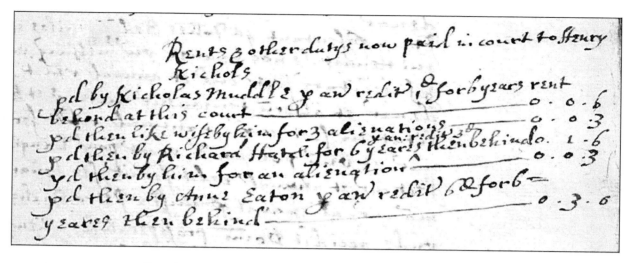

Reproduced by kind permission of the Dean and Chapter of Rochester Cathedral
and the Director of Community Services, Medway

One of the last documents to record the phrase 'the manor of Ware' is the Parliamentary Survey of 1649.[39] The lands held by Robert Bance, William Carter, George Roper and Ed Walter earned the Dean and Chapter of Rochester cathedral the annual sum of 4s 6½d in rent: just under £18 today. Rents continued to be paid from Ware as late as 1690, so at least part of the medieval manor persisted.

The rent from the manor of Ware was never lucrative. The size of the manor was not extensive. What is remarkable is that the Court records for 1380 for a tiny, otherwise obscure, manor survive at all. So, could there be a very simple reason which led to the copying of the early documents for the manor of Ware in the seventeenth century? Perhaps it was just because a clerk was blessed with sufficient foresight to realise that there was a chance that one day, the information about the manor might be considered important. It is a haunting thought.

The Court of the Manor of Ware at work

The main social and administrative structure of the manor of Ware was the Court Baron. As Sir Edward Coke wrote in the Compleat Copy Holder, 1641: [1]

> ...the court baron...is incident to, and inseparable from, a Manor...[and] is the chief Prop and Pillar of a Manor, for that no sooner faileth, but the Manor falleth to the Ground...

Although the term seems strange to a modern day reader, the name 'Court Baron' derives from the original granting of the manor. The right to hold a court could only granted by a king to a noble. This was to prevent individual land owners creating their own manors by setting up a court and making tenants subject to its jurisdiction. By 1500, one of the tests used to establish the legal existence of a manor was to determine whether it had a Court Baron. [2]

Although the custom and rule of the manor was often recorded in a manorial survey, this was no guarantee that those rules were respected. [3] However, a survey was rather more than a written description of an estate as it often included details of demesne lands and of tenants obligations, with a value set on every piece of property and every service. By 1242, it was recognised that the value of the land in a survey was not the price that could be obtained if it were permanently sold but its annual value; the price that would be paid if it were leased. [4]

The manor held courts in order to regulate its administration. The main business of the Court Baron concerned payments of debts, matters of trespass and minor disputes to the value of forty shillings, between tenants. It also dealt with matters concerning the tenure of land, recording the surrender and admission of tenants to holdings. It was this latter aspect of the court that led to its survival until relatively recent times. [5] All tenants of the manor owed 'suit to the court', this meant that they had to attend the manor court when it was held.

The earliest court roll entries for Ware are a relatively straightforward record of administration. A heading describes the jurisdiction of the court and when it was held but there were several distinct stages to holding a court. The first of these would be the steward issuing an order, or precept, to the bailiff of the manor. The precept gave notice to the tenants that a court was to be held and gave details of the time and place of the session.

There is no information in the manor of Ware records to clearly indicate the location where the court convened other than two late references. [6] The first of these was in 1648:

> ...Thomas Allen holds of the Manor in his wife's right, one messuage in which the court is held...

and this reference in 1649:

> ....at ye place accustomed upon summons, ye place referred whereon to Keep the Court at Tile hoste in Bersted...

There are no further references in other Thurnham records for Thomas Allen or the messuage which his wife had brought to the Allen family. [7] Ware was such a small manor, that there can not have been many venues which were large enough accommodate the court. It is possible that this entry reflects an arrangement to hold the court at a well known location, such as where tiles were made and dried, or at venue which was nearby, in Thurnham or Bearsted. In other villages in Kent, the names of properties such as 'Court Farm' provide an indication of the location. To this day, there remains a property known as Court Farm in Thurnham but there is no proven link to the manorial courts for Ware.

Once the court was assembled, the details of the name of the manor, the date, the name of the lord in whose name the court was being held and the name of the steward were recorded. As the early records of Ware are so fragmentary, this is a rather later example from 1614: [8]

> A Court Baron of the aforesaid Dean and Chapter [of Rochester Cathedral], held there on Thursday, namely, the 22nd day of September in the 12th year of King James's reign of England, etc., and the 48th of his reign in Scotland by John Somer, the Steward, the aforesaid Dean and the Sub-dean, Master Collins and Master Barnwell, being then present…

The tenants who did not attend the court were noted in an early form of 'apologies for absence' that are still minuted in formal committee meetings today. Payments called 'essoins' were then made by the tenant in his absence.

From the same court roll, several people made essoin payments:

> Robert Barling
> Joan Tilden
> George Coulter

The amount of the payment was normally a few pence and was agreed by the manor but there were times when it was subject to the steward's discretion. The majority of manors also ruled that tenants could not absent themselves for more than two or three successive courts.[9]

Absent tenants that had not sent their excuses could be subject to heavier penalties. The names of those tenants who were in default were also recorded. Thus in the court roll dated between 1389 and 1390, these tenants were liable to be fined, a process known as amercement: [10, 11]

> The beadle was ordered to distrain Hamo Maas, Roger Chelisfeild, Robert Arnold, Alice Cynton, William Bedell, Roger Cynton, against the next court, for many defaults of common suit of the court.

The next item in the manor court was a swearing-in of a jury. It is not known how these people were selected but it is possible that they were chosen on the day of the court.[12]

The court then turned to the process of making the presentments. As the word suggests, the jury were required to state or to present the various matters to be dealt with by the court. Sometimes the court rolls state that 'the homage' was present. This occurs when the jury made their presentments on behalf of all the tenants, collectively called 'the homage'.[13] Below is an example of this from the 1614 Court Roll: [14]

> **The Homage, sworn by**
>
> John Crompe
> William Snowe
> Richard Wynter
> William Spice, attorney for Joan Tilden, widow
> Henry Coulter
> Robert Barling
> Robert Coulter
>
> Who say upon their oaths that to their knowledge there is nothing within this Manor presentable at this court.

A copy of the original entry:

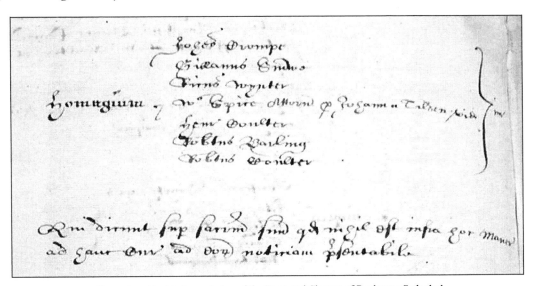

Reproduced by kind permission of the Dean and Chapter of Rochester Cathedral
and the Director of Community Services, Medway

Presentments were normally minor disputes or offences of a petty nature but it also included matters against the common good, such as the allegations of over-grazing, neglect of hedges, the blocking of watercourses or clearance of ditches.

For all offences against the custom of the manor, the steward acted as judge. Usually the tenant was amerced. The amount was left to the discretion of the steward. Occasionally, jurors, known as 'affeerors', were chosen to ensure that the level of the fine was reasonable. If the tenant could not pay an amercement the bailiff had the right to distrain, or impound, the goods or chattels of a tenant until it was paid. Sometimes payment was only achieved after several sessions of the court.[15] Distraint was used in the manor of Ware to enforce attendance at the court rather than to satisfy amercement.

The other main business of the Court Baron concerned the tenure of land. As discussed elsewhere, in the manor of Ware this was largely copyhold or customal. Freeholders of land were free to dispose of their land without involving the manorial lord. However, customary tenants held their land by the will of the lord. New tenants could only take possession of customary land through the process of surrender and admission by conducted at the manor court.[16]

At a Court Baron, the jury noted and presented the death of any tenant, so that a heriot, or payment, could be collected for the lord. If the late tenant had held the land through custom or copyhold, the heir then came forward to seek admittance to his holding. If the heir did not seek admittance within a specified period, or there was no heir, the holding became forfeit to the lord.[17]

In 1614, the court recorded that there was doubt over the right of Robert Coulter to inherit lands: [18]

..Also they present that Robert Coulter is a tenant of this Manor, but because they do not know for certain the lands which he claims to hold of this Manor, so a day was given to the same Robert, and to other tenants of this Manor, to put forward in writing, for certain, the lands and tenements which each one of them claims to hold of this Manor by the next court...

A copy of the original entry:

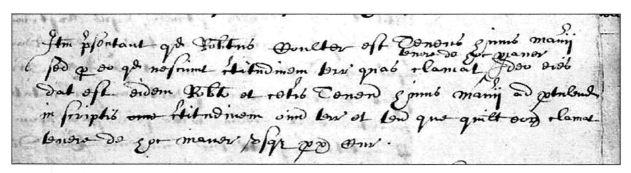

A subsequent court recorded a payment made by Robert and Henry Coulter for the lands described as late of William Coulter, their father, so the matter was evidently resolved.[19]

The new tenant was admitted through a small ceremony conducted by the steward. The ceremony varied according to the manor, but the majority of them seem to have involved a steward holding a stick or rod, sometimes known as a 'verge'. The new tenant would grasp the stick held by the steward in open court. This signalled admittance.[20]

At Ware, an act of fealty took place. From the court roll: [21]

> …Also, they present that since the last court, Richard Wynter bought of a certain George Page, one messuage with one a garden or orchard, and one rood of land lying and being in Ware aforesaid, in the said Parish of Thornham, the messuage being formerly of a certain William Coulter, abutting upon the king's highway there, towards the north, and upon the lands of John Crompe, towards east, west and south, holding by fealty, suit of court, and 1½d yearly rent,
>
> And, being present here in court, he did fealty to the Lords and has paid them the full aforesaid rent in the name of a relief, namely 1½d.
>
> And he was admitted as the tenant, and he was put into the homage.

An account of the transaction was recorded on the court roll and a copy was given to the tenant as his record of his land title. The tenant's record became known as 'a copy of court roll' and contains potentially valuable information: a single account of a surrender and admission may include information on three generations of tenants.[22] Customary tenants had the right to let their copyhold land but it was usual to obtain the permission of their lord. Permission was usually granted through a licence,[23] but there is no record in the manor of Ware documents for such licenses being granted.

The amount of business conducted in the manor courts declined over many centuries. By the eighteenth century, the business conducted was solely to record the surrender and admittance of copyhold land. Many manorial lords favoured converting customary land to leasehold. The amount of copyhold land was reduced and in some manors, dwindled to nothing.[24] Although the records are patchy, there are no court rolls for Ware dated later than 1690; perhaps there was no longer a reason for the manor court to meet.[25]

Land Tenure in the Manor of Ware and Ware Street: copyhold, freehold or gavelkind?

In 1579, William Lambarde indicated in his Perambulation of Kent, that the system of land tenure in the county known as 'copyhold' was not widespread.[1] However, from examination of the Court Rolls, the comment is not applicable to the manor of Ware, nor parts of the manor of Thurnham.

It is thought that copyhold is a form of land tenure with ancient roots; possibly originating though the legal systems practised in Viking settlements in Britain. It remains a matter of speculation as to whether copyhold and gavelkind were amongst the ancient customs believed to have been permitted to continue unaltered after the Norman invasion of 1066.[2]

The main difference between freehold and copyhold tenure of land is that a freehold tenure was not subject to the custom of the manor. After the person holding the land had died, it could pass to anyone named in the will of the land holder.

Copyhold land tenure is generally recognised as being derived from the holding of lands by unfree tenants of a village or settlement. By the fourteenth century, the idea had begun to be formally developed. The copyholder had liabilities for rent and other services for the Lord of the Manor. There were no rights under common law as rent and services were prescribed by custom and there were no other definitions. Eventually, after many centuries, copyhold and labour services became converted to a financial liability.[3]

Like freehold land, copyhold was held from a Manor and was subject to a quit rent payment. Quit rents were annual sums paid by manorial tenants in order to be released from services to the Lord of the Manor. The Steward of the Manor usually made a written copy of the land holding on a strip of parchment for the copyholder to retain. This document was the copyholder's proof of legal land ownership and was an accepted form of evidence.

There were advantages to copyhold land tenure. The title to the land was considered secure as the Court Rolls formed an early type of land registry. The rolls sometimes included rental documents giving valuable information about the land uses and customs should a dispute arise. Sometimes a copyhold was converted to a freehold through a process called enfranchisement but a fee was still payable for a quit rent. The process of enfranchisement will be discussed later in this chapter, but there are no records about enfranchisement for the manor of Ware.

The first seven documents in the Court Roll entries for the manor of Ware reproduced in this book do not specifically record that the courts were Courts Baron. The main business conducted at them concerned the recording of changes in copyhold tenancies. Occasionally, Courts Baron records also include details of the management and cultivation of open fields, meadows and common land but this is not found in the manor of Ware records.

The first Court Roll entry which specifically uses the term 'Court Baron' is document eight, dated 1614:[4]

> A Court Baron of the aforesaid Dean and Chapter...

Below is shown part of the original entry:

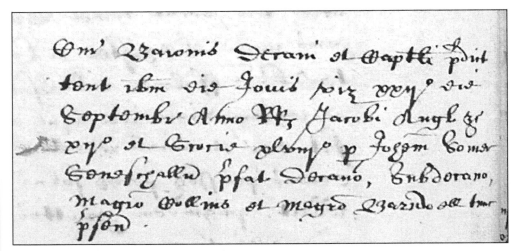

Reproduced by kind permission of the Dean and Chapter of Rochester Cathedral
and the Director of Community Services, Medway

Some of the earlier records do show that that the land was subject to copyhold tenure rather than freehold as they included the type of phrases which is normally accepted as being used to indicate copyhold such as 'doing fealty', or seeking admittance to tenure of the land. Thus in document two, dated between 1389 and 1390, can be found details of tenants precisely described as performing this action: [5]

Hamo Maas, Roger Chelisfield and William Bedell for doing fealty ...

Similarly, in document four, dated 19 October 1391, there are a number of named individuals to which the beadle is assigned to apply distraint for performing fealty. Document eight also uses these phrases and bears every indication that copyhold is a long-established system of land tenure within the manor.

Document nine also clearly states: [6]

..according to the custom of this Manor...

The same document indicates that there were free tenants of the Manor but they still owed suit to the court and were therefore regarded as tenants, rather than freeholders.

The manor of Thurnham which was adjacent to the manor of Ware, included copyhold tenure in the manor's system of land holdings. The last document which mentions the manor of Ware is dated 1668. Later documents concerning the sale of properties and land in the area indicate that at least part of the manor of Ware holdings had been assimilated into that of Thurnham. Thus it is found that in 1822, a Court Baron for the Manor of Thurnham specifically recorded that Bedingfield Wise was to be admitted to a copyhold premises, although it should be noted that the description of the document is particularly misleading as it includes 'freehold estates' in the title.[7]

A further example of a Court Baron from the Manor of Thurnham, but seemingly the only one to mention copyhold in Ware Street is that shown below: [8]

As To Copyhold
20 October 1828

At a Court Baron of Sir Edward Cholmely Dering, Lord of the Manor of Thurnham, holden at the Bell Inn in Thurnham for the Manor of Thurnham, Kent, this day

The Homage presented (inter alia) as follows:

Thomas Philpot applied to the said court on behalf of the heirs of Francis Armstrong for leave to enclose:

About twelve perches of ground in Ware Street in Thurnham aforesaid, part of the Lords Waste which the rest of the homage recommended the Lord grant accordingly on payment of the yearly fee of one shilling which was then paid with the entry fee…

Gavelkind is also believed to have pre-Conquest or Anglo-Saxon origins, although the precise date of its adoption in Kent as a recognised legal system is open to considerable debate. However, gavelkind operated as a system of inheritance rather then land tenure. The name is derived from: [9]

'Gavel': a sharing or holding where rent is paid
'Kind': from 'kinder' or children.

Although use of the term 'gavelkind 'was retained in Kent, elsewhere in Britain the same system was known as partible inheritance. All land held in Kent was subject to gavelkind. Gavelkind was a system of inheritance by which land was equally divided between the male heirs on the death of the father. This was intended to further equal inheritance. Under the gavelkind provisions in Kent, a widow was entitled to up to half of her late husband's estate rather than approximately one third of the estate elsewhere. To make land not subject to gavelkind required a Private Act of Parliament and a process called 'Dis-gavelling'.[10]

Under gavelkind, once a widow had adequate provision, all remaining land was equally divided between the male heirs on the death of the land holder. By the eighteenth and nineteenth centuries, the practice resulted in equal shares of inheritance being divided into smaller and smaller amounts with 'one share' being held by many people. It also led to many disputes concerning the right to inherit, particularly if people died intestate or were under the age of 21 and so were considered to be in their minority or an infant. It was not unusual for people to obtain credit and borrow money secured on their interest in land holdings.

There is no evidence for gavelkind in the Court Roll documents for the manor of Ware, reinforcing the impression that it did not control land tenure. However, the laws of gavelkind certainly were invoked in 1843 after Ann Armstrong had died intestate. At least nine people claimed an interest in her land holdings which included part of Weltighe Crofts, Sandy Mount, Ware Street.[11] The matter was resolved by the sale of the holdings and subsequent re-distribution of the proceeds.

It took many years to abolish copyhold tenure and gavelkind. Although part of the process was begun under the 1832 Great Reform Act there were immense political delays to the proceedings. In 1838 a Select Committee concerning copyhold tenure was set up under William Blamire. The Committee investigated the matter on a similar basis to the Tithe Commission. Blamire was confident that copyhold could be abolished in a few years but despite enactment of the legislation in 1841, widespread abolition was not achieved until 1922 [12]

The process of de-copyholding land was known as 'Enfranchisement' and was rather similar to the redeeming tithe payments under the Tithe Apportionment scheme. Land had to be registered before it could be enfranchised in order that the procedure could be controlled. Occasionally, enfranchisement could cost as little as the sum of three years rent payment but the main opposition came from large landowners fearful of losing control of their estates on a piecemeal basis. It was a highly contentious issue.

Before the First World War the process of enfranchisement was slow: before 1900, nine Amendment Acts concerning copyhold tenure were devised. The war seems to have acted as a catalyst on copyhold tenure as many members of aristocratic families that held manors with copyhold lands were killed in battle leaving few heirs. Perhaps it no longer seemed an appropriate form of land tenure in a changed world.

In 1922 new Laws of Property abolished liability for Quit Rents on freehold land. It did not take long after this for the abolition to become accepted, just as tithes had eventually been redeemed. By 1926 copyhold land, like tithes and the manor of Ware, had virtually ceased to exist.

A Yeoman's Tragedy:
The Bedell family in Ware and Thurnham

The Bedell family were Kentish yeomen. Their land holdings were the result of hard work by which they established themselves within the local society and communities of Ware and Thurnham. Ultimately, it was their yeoman status that was to prove to be their downfall.

Glimpses of the Bedell family are found in the early documents for the manor of Ware. They were sufficiently prosperous to be able to buy and sell areas of land. Entries for the family begin with the name of William Bedell. He is mentioned in 1380 as a tenant holding four acres of land.[1]

At a court held at an unspecified date, but between 22 June 1389 and 21 June 1390, William was ordered to be distrained. He also had to pay a separate sum of 2d although the specific reason for this second payment is not made clear.[2]

In the manor rental from 1390, lands held by John Bedill and William Bedyll are frequently mentioned as part of boundary descriptions for holdings by other tenants in Ware. William Bedill is also recorded as sharing in a 1d payment for twelve half day-works and an eight part of one day work of land.[3] Below is this entry; William's name is on the fifth line:

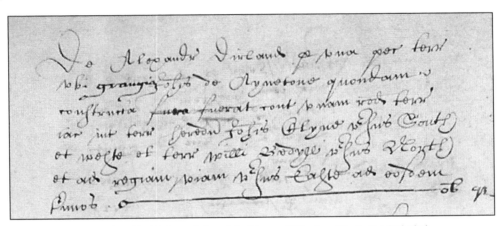

Reproduced by kind permission of the Dean and Chapter of Rochester Cathedral
and the Director of Community Services, Medway

Before the manor court was convened on 19 October 1391, William Bedyll had purchased land. This time it was from William Cynton and a payment of a farthing was due. William had to pay a further 2d as he had not attended the court.[4]

There is one further mention of William in the early manor of Ware documents: in Document Five it is noted that William Dyche had bought land from William Bedell. As a result of this transaction, further payments, reliefs and fealties, needed to be made.[5]

This is the last glimpse of the Bedell family in the manor of Ware documents. Despite this, it is relatively easy to complete some of the gaps in the story of the family after 1400 as they were mentioned in several records for the neighbouring Manor of Thurnham. The Bedells had, therefore, evidently continued to live in the locality during the first few decades of the fifteenth century and were able to expand their landholdings. In 1411, a Manor of Thurnham document noted the limits of a boundary had been testified by Bedell of Thurnham.[6]

In 1434, Henry Bedill, described as 'from the parish of Thurnham', confirmed all his rents and tenements to William Ayndon, John Pixe, Edmund Arnold of Thurnham and John Wilmot of Newenton. The reason for this confirmation is unclear but may have been connected with the appointment of John Massem as chaplain to the parish of Thurnham and chapel of Aldington.[7]

By 1450, the Bedell family had established themselves very firmly as prosperous yeomen. They were members of the solid, lower middle ranks of society around Ware and Thurnham. The Bedells might not necessarily have held official posts, but they were respected and notable people.[8] As such, they were just the sort of people to become involved in the unrest in Kent generated by the events surrounding and leading up to the Jack Cade rebellion of 1450. Unfortunately, and disastrously for the Bedill family, that is exactly what happened.

Between 18 and 20 May, an annual fair was usually held at Rochester. It attracted crowds from all over Kent and was an ideal means to distribute news and opinions concerning the state of both King and the county.[9] It is possible that Henry Bedell attended the fair and realised his concerns were shared by many others from his social class.

At the fair, Henry would certainly have learned about the other matters causing economic problems in Kent and the Weald. Henry VI's domestic and foreign policies were now widely perceived to be disastrous. There were the beginnings of financial hardship for yeomen caused by a ban on imported goods by the Dutch and Lowland countries. This ban on wool and woollen goods had been in place for some time and yet both King and government seemed paralysed to act. Kent was the main route to Europe and British territorial interests in France. Hostilities with France had simmered for many years but had been held in check by a truce. This truce was ruptured when Charles VII of France invaded Normandy in 1449. The ensuing warfare had led to further economic suffering in Kent as members of the army moved through the county, requisitioning provisions. There was little prospect of the suppliers being repaid by the Crown. The King pressured parliament for further funds which he hoped to secure by levying more taxes, but many thought that the money raised would not be spent on defence. The loss of Rouen, surrendered by the Duke of Somerset without a siege, further exacerbated matters.[10]

Then an incident involving the Duke of Suffolk gave cause for great concern for all land holders in Kent. The duke had been intercepted and then murdered whilst sailing across the Channel on 1 May 1450. There was a widespread rumour that the King intended to take retribution by turning the county into a wild forest.[11] As a result, Henry Bedill may have felt an urgent need to protect his family and property. The latter was subsequently estimated to be sixty acres.

Jack Cade's rebellion, then, was not an insurrection similar to that led by peasants earlier in 1381. It was led by the prosperous yeoman class of Kent: those that had much to lose.

Henry left his normal duties on his land holdings in the spring to join Jack Cade. This was a time of year in which the Kent countryside would have looked at its most attractive. As he moved closer to London, there were constant reminders in the countryside of the new season. Spring was always a busy time of year for yeomen, husbandmen and labourers. There were myriad activities to be undertaken which included undertaking the maintenance of meadows and grassland, watching the crops growing in the fields and the beginnings of the preparations for haymaking. Spring was also the time of year when animal husbandmen took advantage of the maximum milk yield given by their herds and flocks which had recently delivered their young.[12] It was this very way of life that was now under threat and which spurred Henry on.

The level of Henry's participation in the rebellion is not clear. Perhaps he camped with Jack Cade's followers at Blackheath in June. Did he then enter the city of London with Jack, clashing with the citizens in a series of night time skirmishes? Whatever the truth of the matter, Henry was sufficiently involved for his name to be included in the general and free pardon offered to Jack and his followers on 7 July 1450. This extended to all transgressions committed prior to 8 July and guaranteed that anyone holding such a pardon would go unmolested by the King's justices, sheriffs, coroners or bailiff.[13]

But this was not the end of the rebellion. The exchequer rapidly announced that Jack Cade was a false name, and so the pardon for him was invalid. It was spread abroad that Jack's real name was John Mortimer or John Aylmere. Jack countered this by publicly doubting the validity of his pardon as it had been issued without the authority of parliament.

On 12 July 1450, Cade was captured at Heathfield in Sussex, but died from injuries before he could be brought to trial. Nevertheless, the authorities were determined to set an example and so his corpse was taken back to London and ritually beheaded at Newgate.[14]

The main leader of the rebellion had perished but unrest in Kent continued into 1451. Jack Cade's followers had dispersed into the countryside and despite the pardon given in July 1450, were now living under the distinct possibility of county-wide reprisals and hangings.[15] If Henry returned to his home, it is likely that he was not there for long. Perhaps stepping outside the normal structure of society had changed Henry forever and he was now permanently armed. There is some evidence for this because on 15 April, 1451, he participated in a violent assault in Thurnham upon three men carrying baskets of fish to a fishmonger in London. Significantly, all the assailants were later described as being arrayed for war.[16]

A week later, on 21 April, men gathered at Eastry and Brenchley and there was further disturbance. The main ringleader was Henry Hasilden, a shingler from Rotherfield. It did not take long for the Sheriff of Kent to arrest the main agitators. At an inquest held in May, at Lewes, Hasilden was hanged.[17]

Henry was apprehended after Hasilden's arrest on an unspecified date, but probably in the first few days of June. He was taken before a group of justices at Tonbridge who had been commissioned to deal with the supporters and participants of the unrest. He was initially indicted with assault and a theft of fish, but he was the only man amongst those indicted as followers of Hasilden whose name had been included on the pardon roll of 7 July 1450. It is therefore possible that he was well known as a supporter of Cade and the authorities decided to finally deal with a trouble-maker.[18]

Below are some of the details of the indictment.[19]

It is to be inquired for the king whether Henry Bedell of Thornham, husbandman, William Batcheler of Detling, labourer, John Bux of the same, labourer and Thomas Cokke, late of the same, labourer, together with other evil-doers arrayed for war, on 15 April 1451, assaulted, beat and ill treated Richard Felde, Roger Stede and Richard Walwyn at Thornham, so that they despaired of their lives; and feloniously took away seven baskets filled with fish to the value of 20s belonging to a certain William Hampton, citizen and fishmonger of London, then in their keeping.

It is to be inquired whether Henry Bedell of Thornham, Stephen Heath, late of Rainham, 'smyth', and John Mathewe late of Wrotham, labourer, together with other unknown traitors, rebels and enemies of the king on 21 and 22 April 1451, assembled at Eastry and Brenchley, and there and elsewhere in the said county on diverse previous occasions imagined and compassed the death of the king and the destruction of his realm. And they finally agreed that they and other felons, traitors, lollards and heretics being their accomplices and of their association would depose the king from the government of his kingdom and take the government of the said king down upon themselves; and that they would take, kill and finally destroy the lords spiritual and temporal of the realm, especially those opposing them in their plans; and that they would institute twelve peers from among themselves to rule the said kingdom.

And these traitors on the aforesaid 21 and 22 April assembled to carry out these plans &c. at Eastry and Brenchley to the number of hundred men and more arrayed for war, and rose in insurrection and war against the king, saying that there would be forty thousand men with them in a short time; and believing and proposing as lollards and heretics that all things should be held in common; against the sacred law of the church and the laws and customs of the kingdom used and approved time out of mind.

Dorse: True bill   By John Payn and his fellows

Taken 29 June 1451 at Tonbridge before Edmund, Duke of Somerset, John, Earl of Shrewsbury, John, Earl of Worcester, Ralphe de Cromwell, knight, William Beauchamp de Saint Amand, knight, John Prisot and John Portyngton, justices of oyer and terminer to try all treasons and other offences specified in the king's letters patent of 24 January 1451 directed to them.

Reproduced courtesy of the Kent Archaeological Society

Henry was hanged at Tonbridge on 24 June 1451. Almost immediately afterwards, the King's justices declared that he was a man attainted of treason. As a result, Henry Bedill's family forfeited to the King his land holdings. These were noted as comprising a quarter of a tenement and sixty acres held of the manor of Thurnham, though the precise location was not described.[20]

Henry VI then made a gift of the forfeited property to a squire, named as John Roger.[21] The Bedill family were now completely disgraced and regarded as enemies to the Crown. They lost all the property in Thurnham that they had acquired over many years. For the remaining members of the family to survive without any land would have required a massive degree of adjustment. Undoubtedly they would have fallen back on the various skills that they possessed, hiring out their labour. Their skills in animal husbandry would have been a marketable commodity too, but they no longer belonged to the yeoman class.

The later records of both Ware and Thurnham are virtually silent concerning the Bedill family. There are a few exceptions to this: between 1553 and 1651, Henry's former package of sixty acres in Thurnham changed hands several times. Nearly every transaction records the lands as: [22]

> ...formerly of Henry Bedill, a convicted traitor...

By 1640 the land was referred to as merely 'Beadles'. In 1652 the land holding was estimated to be fifty two acres. The name of Beadles persisted until 1745 before dropping from common usage and land transactions. It took barely two centuries for the association with the turbulent times in which Henry Bedill had lived, struggled and vainly protested about to his King, to be forgotten.[23]

The Later Manor of Ware

The Later Manor of Ware

For many centuries, there were only a few, rather scattered dwellings in Ware Street. The main industries were farming, sand quarrying, tile and brick making. Mount Pleasant, the farm at Chapel Lane and Bell farmhouse were the main holdings. There were smaller farming businesses located at Sandy Mount, Winter Haw and Stocks. Sand quarrying exploited a wide deposit of fine white sand which was distributed relatively evenly across both the north and south side of Ware Street. However, the deepest deposits of sand were on the north side of Ware Street where the tile and brick field works operated for many years.

The majority of this section of the book examines the later manor of Ware and is arranged as a perambulation along the main area of Ware Street, reflecting its slow development. It commences with a discussion about the forge; the first property on the south side of Ware Street to be encountered whilst travelling from Bearsted green. The journey then continues along to Mount Pleasant before the route is slightly retraced on the north side by examining Church Cottages. Several other properties are then regarded before moving up to Chapel Lane. The journey ends by crossing once more to the other side of Ware Street to examine Bell Lane. The final part of the book looks at the area during the twentieth century and more recent times.

A diagram to show the principal properties in Ware Street before the twentieth century (not to scale):

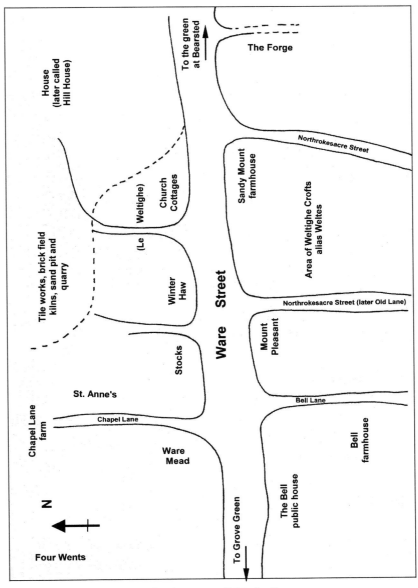

Reproduced courtesy of Malcolm Kersey

Before the middle of the nineteenth century, the main road through Bearsted was Ware Street, from a junction with the Sittingbourne Road as it progresses out of Maidstone. The traffic that passed through Ware Street was either on foot or riding a horse. Today, the name of the road changes from Bearsted Road to Ware Street, before changing once again to The Street.

Ware Street and Thurnham, together, could not be regarded as a large community before the twentieth century, but there was a great variety of occupations. The population expanded as people moved into the area, drawn by the need for employment and the demands of agriculture. Some of the industries and properties evolved and changed; part of the forge premises in Ware Street later became a shop. Even the farms did not solely concentrate on one area, their interests ranged from cattle, pigs and chickens to market gardening with fruit and vegetables. The owners of the tile kiln and sand quarry also adapted to changes in building techniques, making and supplying bricks. Other trades and professions; the railway and its staff, the professional at the golf course, were deliberate introductions.

The manor of Ware and Ware Street was never large, but it bears witness and evidence to an astonishingly rich history of property, people and social change.

The Forge in Ware Street

Today, many people as they pass by 1 Ware Street are unaware that the property was once a forge. Until the twentieth century, it was the first industrial premise on the south side of Ware Street to be encountered whilst journeying from Bearsted green.

As a forge, it was probably in existence for many years before it was part of package of property and surrounding land that was used between 1710 and 1724 as security for mortgages and leases. It was eventually inherited, via John Gosling, by the family of Henry Stoakes. In 1735, it was purchased from Mary Stoakes by Edward Watts. Mary was Henry's widow and acted as executrix of his will.[1]

By 1742, the forge was part of the estate holdings of Edward Watts. Edward's property also included a small area of woodland called Marks Beech. Evidently, he was not living there as part of the forge was occupied by Widow Clifford. Both the forge and wood were left in Edward's will to his nephew, Richard Barton, a victualler from Staplehurst, as this extract shows: [2]

> All estate of wood and woodland called Marks Beach situate in Thurnham...late in the tenure of Catherine Allman, widow, and all that...other messuage &c., and Smith's forge and appurtenances etc., lying and being in Bearsted late in the occupation of Widow Clifford....

Unfortunately, other documents about the tenure of the wood and forge are burned in places, so the written records concerning this area of land are particularly incomplete. However, a recital attached to a later deed which is rather blackened, but undamaged, yields some further information about the history of the forge. In 1762, Marks Beech Wood was mentioned in a lease. Although the forge is not specifically named, it is probable that it was included in the general description of other lands that were leased. The attached recital indicates that both Marks Beech and the forge comprised part of a settlement on the occasion of the marriage on 7 June 1765 of Thomas Gosling to Bennett Frosfield. Thomas was the son of John and Anne Gosling.[3]

Some of the land later passed to the Green family, via a bequest made by Daniel Jones in his will dated 24 May 1807.[4] Two of Daniel's nephews, Samuel Green of Sevenoaks, a surveyor, and John Green of Penshurst were the recipients.[5] Following the death of Samuel in 1853, the land holdings were sold at an auction held at the Bell Inn, Gabriels Hill, in Maidstone on 7 June 1854. James Whatman bought it for £2000.[6]

It is curious that the forge was not specifically mentioned when the tithe apportionment map and schedule was drawn up for Thurnham in 1843. The land was recorded as leased to Samuel and Elizabeth Murton. who were sub-leasing it to Thomas Bridgland, but there are no further details about this arrangement.[7]

The location of the premises certainly seems to have caused some confusion in the census returns. In 1851, a blacksmith and his family was recorded as living in the vicinity of the forge, but it is not clear exactly where they were living as the description is merely 'Bearsted Street'. If the blacksmith's family were resident at the forge in Ware Street, the enumerator's schedule involved a route which included a terraced row of cottages called Fancy Row in Thurnham Lane, the School House at Bearsted School, and then a very sharp right hand turn into Ware Street. This route is not unfeasible as the next enumeration area for Ware Street commences at Sandy Mount.

If this interpretation is correct: William Groombridge, born in West Farleigh, was trading from the forge. He is described as a blacksmith, but living on his own means. William was 46 and his wife, Harriet, was 47. Harriet came from Wateringbury. They had two children: Sarah, aged 10, born in Boxley, and William, aged 8, who had been born in East Farleigh. They were sufficiently prosperous to employ Thomas Rose, from Thurnham, aged 22, as a blacksmith's journeyman.[8]

Before 1861, the forge was taken over by Charles Burbridge. He was a widower and came from Lenham. The census return shows that he shared the accommodation with James and Rachel Randle who were born in Frinstead and Chart, respectively. James Randle was an agricultural labourer.[9] Also resident there was their daughter, Amy, who was aged 14 and had been born in Ulcombe. Charles was recorded as employing one man and one boy, but neither of these was apparently living on the premises.

This photograph of the forge is undated, but gives a clear indication of the farrier at work:

Reproduced courtesy of Chris and Sue Hunt

For the purposes of the 1861 census, the property was regarded as situated in Bearsted, but by the time of the 1871 census, the enumeration areas had changed slightly. The property was now regarded as part of Thurnham and was empty on census night.[10] However, in 1881, Edwin Smith, who was born in Aylesford, aged 38, was occupying the forge, together with his wife, Caroline, who was aged 32. The Smith family had four children, but only the youngest child, Edith, aged one, was born in Thurnham.[11]

When the 1891 census was undertaken, Edwin was evidently away on business, but Caroline and their children were resident at the forge.[12] It is possible that by this time, Edwin had an assistant, as further down Ware Street, another blacksmith; Albert Bensted, was living in a cottage with his wife and family.[13]

In 1882 a plot of building land between the forge and the White Horse was put up for sale by Richard Webb. The surviving details about the matter are sketchy. Once again, it seems that the boundaries of Bearsted and Thurnham were relatively flexible, at least to the vendor, as the land was noted as located in Bearsted. On the next page is shown the map that was produced for the proposed auction, to be held by Mr Day on 23 May 1882. It can be seen that it was intended to sell the land in plots, presumably for housing, although the location on the side of a hill would have made this purpose unrealistic. Although it is not clear whether the land was sold through this means, it was all bought by Mr Tasker and became part of the Snowfield estate.[14]

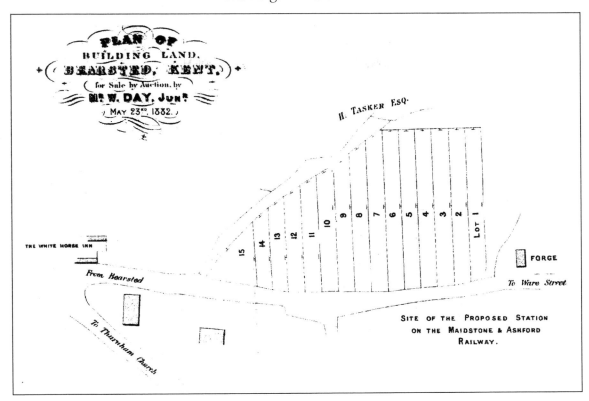

Reproduced courtesy of the Centre for Kentish Studies

By the second decade of the twentieth century, the property had become known as 1 Ware Street but the forge was no longer used. It has become part of the Milgate estate and was owned by Walter Fremlin. Henry and Ellen Hodges lived there and part of the premises was run by Ellen as a small shop called Old Forge Stores. In 1923, the Hodges family moved to a new house in Ware Street that they had built and which became Rosemount Dairy Farm. The full story of Ellen and Henry is told in a later chapter.

Mr and Mrs Stemp then took over the running of the shop. Nurse Beeton Pull also lodged there and was summoned by a separate bell by the front door. This photograph was taken in 1929 of Nurse Pull standing by her official transport, which was known as 'Bongo, the District car', in front of the shop.

Reproduced courtesy of Jean Jones and Martin Moss

Following Water Fremlin's death, the premises were included in a sale of some of the Milgate estate which was held 3 December 1925 at the Royal Star Hotel in Maidstone. Other properties in Ware Street were also sold: Sandy Mount Cottages and Station View Villas.

Below is shown details of lot fifteen from the sale particulars: [15]

Lot 15

THOSE TWO FREEHOLD

SHOPS AND DWELLING HOUSES

SITUATE AT

Ware Street, Thurnham

They are brick built and slated.
Each contains Three Bedrooms and an Attic,
Shop, Living Room and Scullery,
W.C. Water and Gas.

THERE IS A

Considerable Building Site

at the side with the disused

FORGE BUILDINGS & STABLING,
and Gardens at the rear of the Shops

The Grocer's Shop and Land at the side are let to Mr. Stemp
at 15/9 per week, or £40 19s 0d. per annum.

The Cobbler's Shop is let to Mr. Watkins at 7/4 per week
or £19 1s 4d. per annum
Owner paying rates

Reproduced courtesy of the Kent Messenger group

Many residents of Bearsted and Thurnham will recall that for the great majority of the twentieth century, the shop was run by the Black and Vidler families. Roger Vidler has many memories of living at 1 Ware Street whilst his parents traded from the premises. These are some of his recollections:

Whilst I was growing up at 1 Ware Street, I knew that the property had not always been a shop. In 1926 it had been bought by my uncle, Malcolm Marshall, along with 3 Ware Street, 3 Mote Hall Villas and four other properties around Bearsted green for nearly £2,000: around £285 per property![16]

The Marshall family came from seven generations of farmers who in the eighteenth century were based at Hastingleigh. In the late nineteenth century they moved to Detling, and just over a century ago, Malcolm's father Fred, moved to Bearsted with his wife, following the purchase of a seed merchants business in The Street. Fred and his wife lived next door to the premises in a house then called John's Villa, but which is now known as Caldicot.

Malcolm married Phyllis Black, my mother's middle sister, and they lived at 3 Mote Hall Villas until buying Beaux Aires farm in Binbury Lane, Stockbury in the 1930s. Following the break up of the Whatman Estate in the mid 1950s they acquired Newnham Court farm. The farm holdings extended from Gidds Pond to the Chiltern Hundreds public house. It also included a large area of land to the south of the Bearsted Road which in the 1970s was developed as the Vinters Park housing estate.

Whilst my mother, Joyce Black, was growing up, her family lived at Gidds Pond Cottages at Grove Green. My mother would recall that her parents would occasionally apply to the Mistress at Grove Green school for permission for their daughter to leave school early. This was to enable Joyce to help her father drive sheep from Vinters Park either to a field near the golf course, or to the sheep pen in the railway station yard in Ware Street. She was rewarded with either a halfpenny or a penny. If the sheep were taken to the station, she would spend the money in the little sweet shop-come-dairy opposite. The sweets were put into a paper cone made out of newspaper. The majority of the cheaper sweets were not wrapped and to prevent any danger of becoming stuck to the paper, would be eaten fairly quickly. If the sheep were driven to the field next to the golf course, the money would be spent at Mr Hunt's off-licence-come-sweet-shop lower down Ware Street. Little did my mother realise that the sweet-shop-come-dairy was later to become the family business and a much-loved family home.

In the 1930s, my maternal grandparents, John (usually called Jack) and Grace Black, moved to 1 Ware Street as the new tenants. They needed the entire property and so Nurse Pull moved to a flat in a house opposite The Yeoman public house. By this time my grandfather was in his late fifties and had worked on the land all his life, most recently as a shepherd and wood reeve on the Whatman Estate at Vinters Park. But he had always hankered after running a small shop and was now to have his chance. This undated photograph below shows Jack by the shop door:

Reproduced courtesy of Roger Vidler

The shop was very small in the 1930s and comprised a space no larger than fifteen feet square. It supplied general groceries, greengrocery and sundry other items: sweets, cigarettes, candles and a host of other items then in use in most homes, but long since disappeared, such as gas mantles (7s 7d per dozen) and blakies. Blakies were small metal studs that people hammered into the heels of their shoes and boots to take the wear and prolong the life of their footwear. The shop also sold boots and shoes thereby complementing the cobblers business run next door from 3 Ware Street by Bert Watkins.

The sloping roof extension at the side of the shop was used as a tea room during the spring and summer months. As the shop was located half way between London and the coast, and at a time long before the Maidstone bypass was constructed, the tea room was a favourite stopping off point for cyclists. My cousin remembers groups of sweaty cyclists crowding round the large, plain wooden table being served tea or cold drinks by our grandmother. Out of season, the room reverted to part of the family's accommodation with a special role at Christmas when the wider family arrived for tea. The large table was pushed to one side of the room and loaded with cakes and sandwiches as relations gathered round the open grate which held the Yule log.

On 27 July 1939, my mother, Joyce Black, married my father, Edward Vidler, (usually called Ted), at Holy Cross church. Even then, the boundaries of Bearsted and Thurnham were causing confusion and I still have the letter from the vicar of Bearsted advising my father that Station View, as he referred to the shop and house, was not in Bearsted. The vicar then advised that either my mother or father had to arrange to live in Bearsted during the three weeks when the banns were called in order to be married at Holy Cross church, as my mother wished! I am still not sure how this was resolved, but they were married at Holy Cross. As these photographs below show, the tea room and grounds were the venue for the reception. Note both the goods shed for the railway station and the golf club house in the background.

Left to right: Frederick and Edith Vidler, Ted and Joyce Vidler (née Black), Grace and Jack Black

Both reproduced courtesy of Roger Vidler

66

The Forge in Ware Street

My father was a fully trained carpenter, having served a seven year apprenticeship at Tilling Stevens in Maidstone. During the Second World War, he worked there assembling gear boxes for tanks, but in the evenings and weekends, he was part of the Home Guard. My parents took over the shop towards the end of the Second World War, when my grandparents moved to Mote Hall Villas. They were to run it for another twenty five years.

This photograph below was taken around 1949, and shows Joyce and Roger as a small boy, by the front door of the shop. Note the posters which Roger recalls listed the details of peoples' allowances under rationing. Before rationing was finally discontinued in the early 1950s, it was a constant feature of everyday life.

Reproduced courtesy of Roger Vidler

During the 1950s, small retail businesses were still very much the backbone of the community. There were usually a great number of small shops in villages and this reflected the fact that people did the majority of their day to day shopping close to where they lived. I can recall that in Bearsted as I grew up, there were four grocers, two butchers, two newsagents, a cobbler, a watch repairer, two garages, a blacksmiths and, of course, a post office, all within 400 yards of one another in Ware Street and The Street.

Grocers' shops relied for their income on those who worked locally, passing trade and regular deliveries to long-standing customers. Access to the shop was open to the road. There was no wall, no path and no parking restrictions, so it was easy for passing motorists to pull up outside. The men who worked in the coal yard and the railway opposite were regular customers - especially in the summer, when hot weather and coal dust combined to build up a thirst that did wonders for the sale of lemonade and other soft drinks supplied largely by Lyle's in King Street, Maidstone.

As the most westerly of the four grocers' shops, my father's deliveries were mainly in the area of Ware Street, Hockers Lane and Weavering Street, though his delivery round extended into other parts of the village as well. Wednesdays, Thursdays and Fridays were delivery days and close contacts were built up with many of the customers, especially the elderly and infirm.

Not many women worked in those days, and there were few cars about. Someone was invariably at home when the groceries were delivered, but it was not uncommon to find the back door unlocked with a message on the kitchen table indicating where the groceries should be left. Today that arrangement would be unthinkable.

The area west of the station was then quite different. Allotments were on the land later developed as Sharsted Way, and at Sandy Mount there was still a working dairy farm operated by Eric Foster and his family. Along with other local boys I would sometimes help to drive the cows from their pasture to the milking shed behind the farm house off Hog Hill.

Beyond the Bell public house, the area had a far more rural feel about it. The fruit store owned by Mr Stokes stood where Edelin Road has now been built. Bearsted Park was, in part, scrubby orchard land. Only a narrow, unmade road gave access to two houses and a bungalow that stood on land now occupied by Port Close. One of these properties was a smallholding where Mr and Mrs Ely raised goats. Farms and woodland filled the area between Hockers Lane and the Sittingbourne Road.

The railway was also a great source of fascination to the local lads and we used to spend time on the bridge to the golf course watching the shunting of coal wagons into the coal yard. A favourite pastime was dashing from side to side of the parapet to get enveloped by the steam that billowed up from the engines as they emerged beneath the bridge.

Occasionally, horses or cattle would be delivered to the station and held in the animal pen. The regular sheep droves which my grandfather and mother had undertaken from Vinters Park in the 1920s had now diminished, and so by the 1950s, animal movements were relatively rare. Today, only the engineering bricks that made up the floor of the pen now remain.

One particular treat was to be had on a Sunday morning as The Golden Arrow with its baggage car and fleet of Pullman carriages sped through the station en route for Dover. This was sometimes pulled by a Britannia class locomotive, but the ones we always looked out for were the iconic West Country class 4-6-2 (Weymouth and City of Wells) resplendent in their green livery with a large forward pointing golden arrow on their side and another angled arrow across the front of the locos. They always attracted admiring looks and there were often photographers present to record the passage of these great trains.

One of these photographers was Arthur Maxted, a founder member of the Rifle Club. Arthur would come to the shop for sweets before going to the station. Week in, week out, Arthur never seemed to change: always on a bicycle, always wearing a flat cap with a mackintosh strapped over his shoulder and the obligatory cycle clips round his ankles. He was quite one of the nicest men you could hope to meet and he was an excellent photographer who always used black and white film which he, in common with many others, considered more atmospheric.

Sometimes on a Sunday morning, as a special treat, I was allowed into the signal box to help the signal man change the signals and points. This 'help' comprised of nothing more than me placing my hands on the large heavy levers that operated them and pulling when the signal man said so. It was, of course, all his efforts that moved the levers but to a young boy it was enough to believe that I had given valued assistance in making the railway work.

My parents shop was open from 8am to 6pm, Tuesdays to Saturdays, from 8am to 1pm on Mondays, and 9am to 1pm on Sundays. There was work to be done before opening and after closing; a working week of between 60 and 70 hours was quite normal. Traditional family holidays were unheard of; snatched long weekends being the best that could be managed, as and when a relative might be available to stand in. For someone brought up in this environment it did not seem the least bit unusual, and, of course, it was not because there were many people in similar circumstances.

Holidays for me were invariably spent with my aunts and uncles, often on their farm. Beaux Aires farm at Stockbury, was by modern standards very basic, though it did not appear so at the time. In the late 1950s, my aunt and uncle moved from Stockbury to Newnham Court farm near New Cut Road, Maidstone. While the outside of the house remains largely intact the interior was gutted when it was turned into a restaurant many years later. Only the old entrance hall and what was my aunt and uncle's lounge remains. What was later to become a snug with an inglenook fireplace was, fifty years ago, their dining room; the inglenook containing an Aga range. This was very much the heart of the home and the place where a ritual was performed which appeared to me, at the time, to border on the magical. The post would arrive at the time my aunt served breakfast. It was handed to my uncle who, having looked through it, divided it into two piles. One pile was opened; the other was taken unopened to the Aga and dropped into it to be consumed by the fire. I used to watch this process with amazement, believing he must possess x-ray vision. In practice he was, of course, able to judge the important from the unimportant in the same way as we sort junk mail today. Though less easy to spot in those days, canny farmer that he was, he had an unerring instinct for which envelopes contained cheques!

Our shop was run along very different methods to those used by retailers today. Far fewer goods came pre-packaged. Sugar, currants, sultanas and other fruit all came in large paper bags, sacks or wooden boxes that had to be levered open with a crow bar. The fruits inside were so tightly packed that, at first, they were a sticky nightmare to extract. They were then weighed up to the customer's order and placed in blue or brown bags made out of waxed paper.

Cheese was also cut to customers' requirements; often in small amounts of four ounces and less. Even this modest amount may have seemed a luxury to some people though, after the one and a half ounces of cheese a week allowed under rationing. Likewise, small amounts of other fats and butter were cut and sold. Bacon was sold by the rasher if necessary, and cut on a machine that would never pass today's health and safety requirements. A large circular steel blade which was lethally sharp, and only partially protected, formed the business end of the machine. Sides of bacon were placed on the feeder plate and the thickness of rasher to suit individual customer requirements was set using a dial to one side. Despite having to clean the thing by hand, I do not remember any member of the family having a single accident with the machine.

For pensioners and many others, life in the early 1950s was hard as the country emerged from post-war austerity. Owners of small shops had to respond by offering credit 'putting it on the slate' but, unlike today, repaying debts was a matter of honour. Sunday trading laws forbade the sale of a whole range of goods and were enforced by a small army of inspectors. These laws were often honoured in the breach - at least to people we knew. But strangers had to be treated with care and many sales were declined to those who might be from the dreaded enforcers!

Rising prosperity brought with it changes in the range of goods available and the way they were packaged. Tea was still the most popular drink. Tea bags made their first appearance in 1952. One of the biggest revolutions came with the introduction of frozen food. Frozen peas were the first product to be made widely available and fish fingers appeared in 1955. Within two years, the sales of frozen food had doubled and by the early 1960s, a wide range of goods were available. From a small fridge mainly used for ice cream we soon had to invest in two large open top chest freezers to accommodate the increasing range of products. This move to pre-packaged goods was the precursor of another change: self service stores and the emergence of the supermarket. In the middle of the 1950s there were around 3,000 self-service stores. Twelve years later, the number had expanded by 800%.

Another difference came in the way goods were obtained. Many came from wholesalers; those essential links between manufacturers and the grocers. Several companies however, dealt directly with small shops. One of these was Fyffe's Bananas, whose weekly deliveries came in wooden crates four feet long and fifteen inches square with a sliding top which, when removed, revealed the hands of bananas packed in straw. On one occasion the box contained an unwelcome surprise: a tarantula spider! For months afterwards the boxes were opened with extra special care.

The rationing of sweets ceased in 1953 so these and other confectioneries were largely supplied direct to shops by the manufacturers. The local factories of Sharps and Trebor, sent representatives to take orders, but national companies such as Cadbury and Rowntree also had salesmen who were keen to promote new products. In the autumn, and early in the new year, these and other manufacturers would organise evening events to which shop keepers were invited to see and learn about the range of goods they were about to launch for Christmas and Easter. Christmas was always associated with special presentation packs of chocolates with attractive pictures printed on the boxes which were tied at the corner with ribbon; the whole being wrapped in cellophane. In those days when smoking was commonplace, the cigarette manufacturers produced special presentation packs of 100 or 200 cigarettes which always sold well.

But the invitation that was particularly prized was to tour Cadbury's factory at Bourneville in the West Midlands. A special Pullman express train was pulled by a Merchant Navy steam engine and made its way from the coast, picking up passengers at given stopping points in Kent and through London. The journey was then fast and direct to Bourneville. The day was spent looking round the factory and the town of Bourneville, group photographs were taken and, as I remember, a very good meal provided on the train coming home. This was one 'jolly' no small shop keeper reckoned to miss.

We received regular calls from representatives of many other firms. There were three big wholesalers in Maidstone at the time: Charles Arkcoll, Hammonds and William Laurence. My parents largely dealt with the latter two companies. Spears bacon at Lenham was represented by a Mr Tucker. He and his wife lived at Barty Cottage on the corner of Roundwell and the road leading to Barty Farm. Mr Tucker was a small, dapper man always immaculately turned out: brown slacks, a sports jacket, yellow waistcoat, well pressed shirt and tie and trilby hat which he doffed every time he greeted customers. I remember the only paper currency he ever used comprised ten shilling notes and preferably new ones. He never carried £1 or £5 notes: all this to ensure that he knew the denomination of the paper money he had used to buy some purchases, just in case there was any argument about the change.

Our shop's other supplier of bacon was the Danish Bacon Company based at Aylesford. Their representative was George Newton who was a chum of my father's since their days as members of the San Fairy Ann cycling club. A jolly, amiable man with a plentiful supply of good stories which were always essential to the job, he called every Wednesday morning at around half past nine to take our order.

On one occasion my father decided to test out a tape recorder he had just bought by recording George as he came in the shop. That particular morning the recorder was carefully set up with the microphone lead threaded through the tube of a toilet roll with the working end of the instrument protruding at the top. This rather Heath Robinson, but nevertheless effective construction, was carefully hidden behind a display of other goods and the microphone lead was trailed through to the recorder which was positioned in the dining room behind the shop.

My father's desire to catch George unawares, and therefore at his natural best, worked beyond his wildest expectations because that morning as George got out of his car he managed to pinch his fingers very painfully in the door. His arrival in the shop was greeted with an outpouring of pain and profanities that, unknown to him, were being captured for posterity on the recorder's tape.

After the weekly order was placed George was, as usual, invited into the dining room for a cup of coffee. As he sat down my father told him that he had something to show him. As my father started the tape and George listened to his own voice, he sat utterly transfixed and, most unusually for him, speechless, as the tape was replayed. Like most other people at that time he had never heard his own voice played back to him and, fortunately, he took it all in good part.

Perhaps it is a question of viewing the past through rose-tinted glasses, but there seemed far more characters about fifty years ago then than there are today. I was always pleased to see Iris Foster. Iris worked for Brooks, opposite the White Horse, but lived just over the brow of the hill in Ware Street. She always travelled by bicycle and on her way home for lunch she would often call in for cigarettes and other goods. Iris's conversation was always colourful and by carefully listening to her lively, animated and uninhibited exchanges, I learnt much about the more interesting aspects of the English language!

As well as the representatives from the companies with whom we regularly did business, there were those traders who called at the shop from time to time with all manner of goods for sale: many of them with decidedly dubious origins. One afternoon a van drew up loaded, so the driver and his mate claimed, with Indian carpets of incomparable quality at incredible prices. Despite my parents refusal of this amazing offer, they declined to take no for an answer and insisted on bringing one of the carpets up the drive and into the house where only then would we appreciate its quality. This, they added, was a special favour since the carpet was so heavy that the two of them could barely carry it. And so amidst much straining and groaning the carpet was slowly extracted from the back of the van and carried under bending knees and straining backs up the drive.

At the top of the drive they came face to face with our dog, a fierce-some looking chow called Ching-Ching. The dog dashed across from the back door to the fence that divided the back yard from the drive and, hackles rising, began snarling and barking at the intruders. The first of the con men promptly dropped his end of the carpet and hot-footed it back to the safety of the van. His mate then picked up the carpet that seconds earlier had been so heavy the pair of them could barely manage it, tucked it under his arm, ran down the drive, threw it into the back of the van and drove off. The excellent Ching-Ching was rewarded with a particularly juicy bone that evening.

Animals played a significant part in our lives in the 1950s. Apart from the dog and a pair of cats, we kept rabbits. My father bred fan-tail pigeons for a while and my mother kept chickens for their eggs. From time one of the chickens would find its way into the pot. One chicken, however, was immune from danger, an amazing leghorn that my mother had christened Mary. She was incredibly tame, would regularly peck corn from one's hand and generally enjoyed the pampered life of a household pet. While the other hens were confined to a hen house and large pen, Mary had free run of the garden yet somehow managed to escape the depredations of the foxes from the adjoining wood.

During 1956 to 1957, one particular animal became very much the centre of our lives, a pig which, for reasons that now escape me, we christened Fred. Fred was part of a litter born to a landrace sow on my uncle's pig farm at Beaux Aires. Each Sunday we delivered groceries to my aunt and uncle and stayed to tea. Sometimes, the highlight of the meal would be a wonderful Fullers iced walnut cake bought for the occasion. On arrival, it was not uncommon to be roped into some form of farm work. The pigs managed to break through the farm fences with monotonous regularity and had to be rounded up with the help of corrugated tins to steer them back to their pens and a bucket of food to tempt them. If there were no pigs to be rounded up there were new litters to be admired.

Fred was the runt of one of these litters with the added disadvantage of having no trotters on his front legs. In this state he would have stood little chance against the competition from his siblings. So my aunt and uncle offered me the chance of rearing him. No doubt they and my parents had decided that it would do me no end of good to take on a bit of responsibility. The deal was that my uncle would provide all the materials needed to build a pig pound and run in the garden. The feed would, however, be provided at full cost; the idea being that when Fred eventually went to market the whole exercise should show a profit.

Some days later my uncle arrived with a trailer of straw bales that were to form Fred's home. These were turned into the walls of a hut and surrounded by chicken wire. The wire was supported and kept in place by stout stakes to stop Fred from tearing at the straw. The roof was made from sheets of corrugated tin supported by timbers. The run was made out of stout pig wire. There Fred was fed and watered and, freed from competition and given one to one attention, prospered mightily. My grandfather, in particular, although now rather elderly, could not resist the lure of feeding Fred from time to time.

Nine months later he was in his prime, and the time had arrived for him to be taken to slaughter. Eric Foster arrived one morning to take him to the bacon factory at Lenham. Fred's sty was at the end of the garden on top of the steep bank that rises behind the house. In order not to lose control of Fred as he made his way down the slope from the sty to the trailer a rope was attached to one of his back legs which acted as a kind of brake. Amidst much squealing and under considerable protest (do animals have a sixth sense of their impending doom?) Fred was eventually loaded into the trailer and made his final journey as a live animal.

We often wondered, however, whether Fred made a return to 1 Ware Street. After slaughter, the carcasses of pigs were graded and Fred achieved triple A status - the highest he could achieve. A week later Spears delivered to my father one of the best sides of bacon we had received for a very long time.

Below is shown the certificate which was issued to Roger's uncle, Malcolm Marshall, for Fred. Note the highest grade of carcase indicated by three A's:

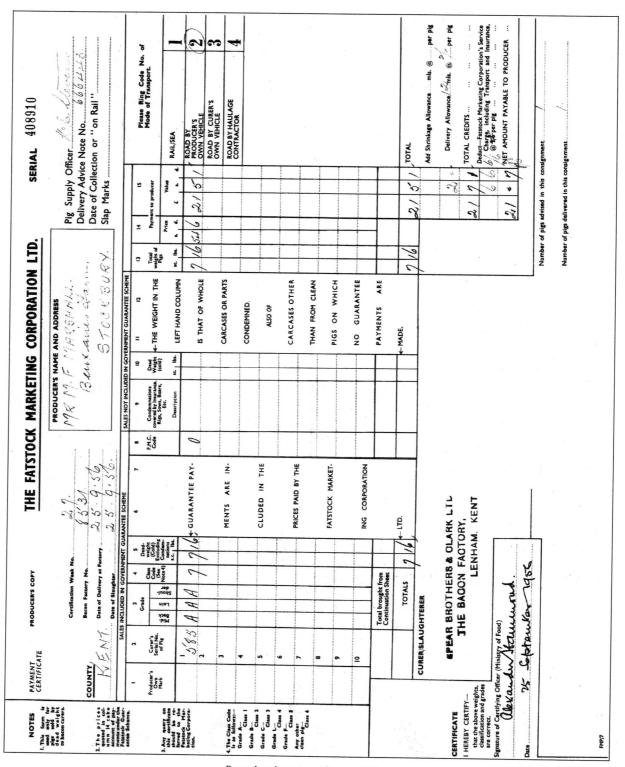

Reproduced courtesy of Roger Vidler

72

Small shops prospered during the 1950s and were sought after by people of British descent returning to this country from overseas as British colonies were granted independence. But in the early 1960s, things began to change. Supermarkets were spreading and were making their buying power felt even then. It was not long before they were selling sugar and other goods as loss leaders more cheaply than any small grocer could hope to buy them.

Increasing competition forced small grocers to seek out the cheapest source of supply and this frequently meant so-called 'cash and carry' wholesalers which emerged as a result of the competition from supermarkets. They were effectively giant shops where, instead of buying individual products, goods were bought by the case. To cut down on costs, buyers had to load and push their large trolleys around these giant warehouses. It was no easy task trying to control a trolley when it was piled high with boxes. Once clear of the checkout the goods still had to be loaded into vans and then unloaded at the shop. All of these arrangements added still more hours to an already very long day.

The abolition of retail price maintenance in 1964 dealt a further blow to the small trader's viability. By the late 1960s, facing increased competition, the prospect of Sainsbury's building a supermarket at what is now The Spurway on the new Landway housing estate,[17] and the need for new investment to meet decimalisation, my parents decided to close the business. Over the next few years, the shop front was replaced by a large picture window, the shop fittings were gradually removed and the space converted to living accommodation.

One by one many of the other traditional businesses in the heart of the village closed. One era of retailing was coming to an end. The future would lay with the big battalions and the specialist niche retailer.

Today, no traces of the building's past existences are readily evident. The property remains a much-cherished home with a lovely garden full of spring and summer flowers. Few people would guess as they pass by, that 1 Ware Street did not start life as a private house, nor of its rich and detailed history.

Weltighe Crofts and Weltes landholdings

The names of Weltighe Crofts and the land holding called Weltes in Ware Street have many and varied spellings in the documents about them. It is possible, but not proven, that the derivation of the names may come from the Old English words, 'welt', which meant 'turned over', and 'croft', which was used to indicate a piece of ground used for cultivation or pasture near a dwelling. Perhaps, then, this was an area containing a substantial amount of land, near a property, which had been dug or excavated.

The Court Roll documents do not include any reference to a house at Weltighe Crofts but if there was a dwelling in the vicinity, where was located, and does anything remain? One candidate is the house which is today called Mount Pleasant, but there is no mention in the Court Roll documents to associate it with Weltighe Crofts. It is also curious that Sandy Lane effectively cuts across the land by the side of Mount Pleasant: the lane's origins may lie as a sunken, or green lane, once used for the ease of moving animals around pastures. Could the property known as Stocks farmhouse once been the main dwelling for Weltighe Crofts? Again, there are few details for the medieval manor to confirm or reject this suggestion. However, when considering the areas which comprised the holdings, perhaps it is significant that Stocks is sited on the north side of Ware Street and that the property is believed to have been built between 1475 to 1500; too late for the early entries in some of the Court Rolls.[1]

In the absence of any firm indication about a dwelling in the Mount Pleasant area, the records for the land should be considered instead. The written records for a parcel of land in the early manor of Ware, referred to as Welteghe Crofts, lapse around 1398. Thereafter, there is a gap until the Reformation. Ownership of Weltighe was caught up in the religious reforms introduced by Edward VI. In 1483, the will of John Pokyll left money raised from part of his lands named as Weltye to fund a light in Holy Cross church. Much of John's estate was evidently located in and around Bearsted and were described as 'of Bearsted' but, in reality, lay in and around Thornham and Otham too.[2]

If it is significant that Weltye is not specifically described here as 'of the manor of Thornham', it should also be recognised that Weltye is not described as part of the manor of Ware either. Boundaries were fundamental to the legality of property holdings; but were there occasions when the written evidence became secondary to a shared common knowledge. Was the common belief regarded as more relevant if several, but separate, holdings of land in an area had similar names in a largely illiterate community? Over five centuries later, the exact truth will probably never be known. From a modern viewpoint, descriptions of boundaries in contemporary medieval records leave the extent of land holdings in Bearsted and Thornham open to a degree of interpretation.

Although land in Ware Street evidently continued to be held in the Pokyll family, there is only one other reference to it, found in the will of Thomas Pokyll dated 1508, but there are no specific details as it says: [3]

> ...William my son shall have my piece of land lying at Ware paying to my daughter Elizabeth ten marks of lawful money of England...

There are several later wills for the Pokyll family but neither Weltes nor Ware is specifically mentioned, so there is no record of subsequent members of the family as owners of the land.

By 1538, Weltes was in the tenure of Thomas Hendley, who had bought a ninety-nine year lease from William Godden at the price of 6s 8d, (around £127 today) but there are no further details.[4]

John Pokyll's bequest from 1483 was recorded in a certificate filed in 1548 in compliance with the Chantries Act which had been passed the previous year.[5] The Act was part of religious reforms introduced by Edward VI. The main aim was to address the question of the purpose of chantries and religious gilds that financially supported them but the king's urgent need for money also lay behind the legislation. The foremost religious and political advisors influencing the king believed that the chantries were not being run properly. Chantries were usually financed through bequests in wills which left money for prayers and masses for the dead, for candles or lights in the building, and other expenses.

The measures in the Chantries Act were little short of a disaster for lay religious life. It dissolved all the religious gilds and they were stripped of any remaining property and funds. The act justified the dissolutions on the basis of religious principle but the Crown simultaneously confiscated immense resources. Commissions were issued for a survey of all the possessions of the chantries prior to confiscation. Inventories which listed all church plate, vestments and lights as well as lands had to be drawn up and certified.[6] How many Kent parishes attempted concealment, or only a partial declaration, of their possessions cannot now be ascertained. The chantries were swept away in further legislation pursued by Edward VI and Archbishop Cranmer. As a result, there was an abundance of confiscated and dissolved land holdings which became available for sale by the Crown. In 1548, George Harper, knight, and Richard Frye, of Penshurst, bought a package that included a great deal of the lands mentioned in John Pokyll's will and:

> ...at Sandepitte in the tenure of John Atwood...in a field called Weltes in the tenure of Thomas Hendley, gentleman...

The sale was entered into the Patent Rolls for 2 September 1548.[7] Subsequently, Thomas Hendley recorded in his Memoranda Book, that he had bought Weltes in 1549-1550[8] but there is no further information about this land holding.

There is then a gap in the records for the manor of Ware, until a lease was signed between the Dean and Chapter of Rochester and Robert Banse, 12 October 1561. It is not entirely clear what Robert had agreed to lease, but it was specifically noted that he was a tile maker. It is not unreasonable therefore to suggest that there is a faint hint here that the land or property was of use to him in his business. Perhaps this is the earliest record of a tile and brick field in Ware Street, although the exact location of the kiln and workings within the holdings varied in later years. Robert was to pay fifteen shillings at Midsummer and twenty six shillings at Michaelmas.[9] The lease was for twenty one years. Robert evidently held other property in Ware Street, as in 1576 he signed a bond with William Taylor. This bond will be discussed later.

When the lease was renewed in 1578, the negotiations beforehand had not progressed smoothly. It was now stipulated that in addition to the sums payable at Midsummer and Michaelmas, Robert had to supply a load of lime three times a year: [10]

> 1 April, 1 May and 1 June... of good new lime in the stone, well turned and made, and not slaked or run, each load to contain thirty two bushels, every bushel heaped...

There was also an endorsement on the document:

> Memorandum that I Martyn Cotys perswadyd with the withinamyd Roberte Banse that thys lease which he woold take in this order was not good in Lawe and give him a note of yt to aske counsell of by whome he assuryd that yt was good etc. but for more certentye at Mr Rockreyes 24 November 1579. I dyd, perswade to have these wordes (st michaell tharch next) stroken out before he Sealed or ere yt was delivered. But seinge Banse avowed yt good and that he wolde have yt as yt was; by Mr Wybarnes perswasyon yt thus passed for that Banse sayde he was contente to take yt as yt was etc
>
> [Translated into modern English:]
>
> Memorandum that I, Martin Cotes, persuaded the within named Robert Banse that this lease which he would take in this order was not good in Law and gave him a note of it to ask Counsel, of whom he assured that it was good.
>
> But for more certainity, at Mr Rockyeres, 24 November 1579, I did persuade him to have these words 'Feast of St Michael the Archangel' struck out before he sealed it or it was delivered. But seeing that Banse avowed it was good, and that he would have it as it was, by Mr Wybarnes persuasion, it passed, for that Banse said he was content to take it as it was etc

Robert Banse continued to hold the lease until 1589, when Henry Brockill of Thurnham took it over.[11]

The bond between William Taylor and Robert Banse previously mentioned is an important document. It enables the location of a holding repeatedly referred to in a bundle of later records to be pinpointed. The bond bears the date 14 June 1576, and is one of two papers grouped together concerning a messuage at Ware Street although the land described is called Argall. It was agreed to sell it to William Godfrey of Barsted.[12] The second document is a counterpart to a marriage settlement dated 1635.[13] Although on the face of it, the two papers do not appear to relate to each other, they formed part of the written evidence to support a legal title to land and so were kept together. James Wood, of Maidstone, carpenter and widower, obtained a licence to marry Barbara Wood. The licence describes Barbara as a virgin, of around thirty-three years of age. The marriage took place at All Saints parish church, Hollingbourne on 2 February 1635, the day after the licence had been obtained..[14] James was a widower and Barbara's parents had died. It is possible that they were cousins but this cannot be confirmed. Thomas Wood of Hollingbourne stood as bondsman.[15]

Barbara's marriage settlement acknowledged that James Wood now lawfully owned the demesne, messuage and tenement where Edward Cloke and William Cawman were now residing, and included: [16]

> ...of all and singular, the closes, garden, and ....to the rest belonging, containing and lying and being in the parish of Thurnham in the above county of Kent at a place there called Ware...

James agreed that after his death, the lands would pass to Henry Coulter. James also agreed that if Barbara outlived him, she was to receive twenty shillings from the land in quarterly payments for the rest of her life. Although the Coulters were a long-established family in the Thurnham area, Henry's exact relationship to Barbara cannot be ascertained but he was able to make arrangements for her welfare.

Through subsequent documents concerning other property in the area, it is evident that this marriage settlement gave James the opportunity to establish himself owning land in Ware Street. In 1642, Thomas Bills and John, his son, formally released their right and interest in their messuage and lands in Thornham to James Wood.[17]

By 1648 James was able to purchase land called Weltes from Thomas Bills, as the Court Roll records: [18]

> ...Thomas Bills, who held of this manor land a certain parcel of land called Weltes, for fealty, suit of court, and the service of a yearly rent of 1s 10d, has alienated and sold the aforesaid parcel since the last court to James Wood, from which there falls due to the Lord for the transfer of the property, the full rent, according to the custom of this Manor, namely 1s 10d.

By Michaelmas the following year, James paid a further rental sum for land that he had also acquired in 1648. This included a piece called Weltis Croft but which was described as previously owned by John Gumts, so was considered separate from Weltes.[19]

The records now become patchy, but a further bundle of documents indicate that James Wood purchased other land holdings in Ware Street.[20] He used these to finance a series of mortgages and leases between 1642 and 1675.

During this time, the Godfrey and Watts families of Boxley and Thurnham owned interests in Ware Street. Although the records are sparse, subsequent documents support an interpretation that at sometime between 1642 and 1657, James Woods disposed of some of his holdings. These included the section of Weltes on the north side of Ware Street which passed to the Godfrey family. As later records prove, he had separated some of the land from his principal dwelling on the south side of Ware Street.

In 1657, William Godfrey died and his estate had to be settled. In the deed of arrangement, it was recorded that his package of lands in Thurnham was partly bounded by the lands of James Woods.[21] This information enables part of the Godfrey estate to be located in the vicinity of the land once known as Weltes. However, this specific name had probably fallen into disuse as it is not mentioned.

On 14 June 1691, William Godfrey, the younger, of Boxley drew up his will. He directed that his nephew, Edward Godfrey, was to receive a messuage and land described as once occupied by William Hendley, gentleman. However, any temptation to connect this holding with the land called Weltes bought by Thomas Hendley, should be slightly curbed as the location was described as being in Bearsted.[22] Nevertheless, details from a lease that was signed between Edward Godfrey of Thurnham and John Watts of Boxley in 1709, gives information concerning part of the land holdings. These enable a section of the estate to be identified: [23]

> ...and all that other messuage or tenement barn stable and tile kiln and other edifices and buildings with the gardens, orchards, and the kiln yard and two other pieces of land called The Wood and Childrens Field abutting south to the said road leading from Maidstone to Ashford...lands and premises are situated lying and being together, all or near Ware Street in Thurnham aforesaid and containing in the whole, sixteen acres and now or late in the occupation of Edward Godfrey and Elizabeth Watts, widow ...

The exact site of The Wood and Childrens Field have now been lost, but it is the specific mention of the tile kiln and kiln yard which enable the land to be located in Ware Street. This is corroborated by the 1709 map drawn up by John Watts for William Cage of Milgate. This shows land owned by Edward Godfrey on the north side of Ware Street. An interpretation of the relevant section of the map is shown below: [24]

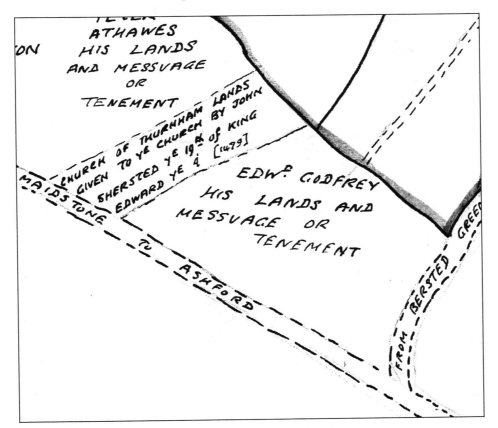

Reproduced courtesy of Michael Perring

Further documents kept in the Centre for Kentish Studies enable the later history of Weltes to be pieced together. Although some of the papers date from around 1750, it is a lease dated 1762 that actually names part of the land as 'Old Orchard' [25], thus enabling some of the holdings to be located. By this time, the land had passed from the Godfreys to the Watts family of Thurnham.

Around 1750, Catherine Watts, a widow, made her will.[26] Before marriage to Edward Watts, Catherine was a member of the Clifford family. Edward and Catherine had at least three children: Edward, John and Ann. One of the land holdings is described: [27]

> ....and all other messuage, tenement and farm together with barns, stables, lying and being in Thurnham late in occupation of Richard Pett and Thomas Packham...also a piece of hop ground with appurtenances lying and being in Thurnham and part of the last mentioned farm containing by estimation two acres more or less and now in my own possession....And all messuages or tenements where I now dwell with stables, outhouses, yards, gardens, orchards, kilns, sandbanks and appurtenances being and lying in Thurnham to be given to John Watts then to Edward Watts or if no heirs then to Ann Watts and if...no heirs then unto my own right heirs forever...

By 1762, John Watts had died and Edward Watts had inherited his share of the estate from his father. Edward arranged to lease some of his land holdings to William Twopeny. This included: [28]

> ...one messuage or tenement now in two dwellings and land in barn, stables...and two pieces of land (formerly one piece) called The Old Orchard, estimated at five acres and a half, lately orchard and hop ground in occupation of Catherine Watts and the other of the same two pieces or parcels of land late in the occupation of Richard Pett and Thomas Packham, now [blank] Brigg, situate lying and being in Thurnham...
>
> ...also several parcels of land called Kiln Yard, three acres and other parcel known as Sand Banks part whereof now a messuage and plantation of young ashen trees estimated two acres or more... now occupied by John Brenchley...

The messuage occupied by John Brenchley and included in the parcel called Sand Banks is today known as Hill House. The current property is believed to have been constructed during the middle of the eighteenth century from red bricks. If the materials for the house were made at the nearby brickfield, the house would have made an excellent advertisement for the products.

By 19 November 1800, the land had passed to Ann Armstrong through her connections to the Watts family. One of the tenants was known only by the surname of Brigg but Elizabeth Russell was the next occupier of Sand Banks and the kiln yard. She was succeeded by Thomas Wise.[29] Ann owned the land until her death in 1843. She did not make a will and so, under gavelkind,[30] there were many people that could claim an interest in her land holdings.[31]

During Ann's ownership some of the land holdings evidently became sub-divided but there are no records about it. However, through recitations of previous owners and their holdings in later leases, it is possible to determine that the Old Orchard had become separated from Sand Bank. The house and land at Sand Bank were occupied by John Brenchley, who was succeeded by Bidingfield Wise, and later, Thomas Philpot.[32]

Development continued on the north side of Ware Street in the first two decades of the nineteenth century. There were two separate holdings: the kiln, brick and tile works together with a brickyard, and a plot of pasture. Bidingfield Wise had been admitted to the copyhold of the adjacent premises, which had become part of the manor Thurnham, on 30 October 1822: [33]

Court Baron

Court Baron of Sir Edward Chomeley Dering, baronet, Lord of the Manor of Thurnham, Kent, holder in the said manor this day…

…The homage presented that Bedingfield Wise begged to be admitted tenant…

Of a small piece or parcel of the Lords Waste ground containing altogether about 20 rods more or less adjoining the garden of the house and which the said Bidingfield Wise lately purchased of and from Edward Filmer of Thurnham aforesaid and also adjoining the premises of Francis Armstrong, deceased, which he had permission to enclose upon paying an annual quit rent of sixpence which had been done of the period of five years last past, together with the entry fees the same appearing to have been omitted to be entered at the last court there held.

After Bidingfield's death, his heirs, William Gascoin and Lewis Wise, were admitted in 1840. The holding then passed to Alfred Wise.

The plot of pasture had been enclosed in 1828. A transcript of the request to undertake this work is given below and shows that the tenant, Thomas Philpot, applied to a Court Baron on behalf of the heirs of Francis Armstrong: [34]

As To Copyhold
20 October 1828

At a Court Baron of Sir Edward Cholmely Dering, Lord of the Manor of Thurnham, holden at the Bell Inn in Thurnham for the Manor of Thurnham, Kent, this day

The Homage presented (inter alia) as follows:

Thomas Philpot applied to the said court on behalf of the heirs of Francis Armstrong for have to enclosed:

About twelve perches of ground in Ware Street in Thurnham aforesaid, part of the Lords Waste which the rest of the homage recommended the Lord grant accordingly on payment of the yearly fee of one shilling which was then paid with the entry fee…

The details of both of these Courts Baron indicate that at some stage between 1668 (the latest date which specifically, and separately, record rents from Ware) and 1828, this area had also become assimilated into the Manor of Thurnham.

By 1858, another sand pit in the vicinity of the kiln yard had been developed and was considered to be a separate part of the holding. James Ellis, occupied the kiln, brick and tile works and sand pit. A meadow was rented by Mrs Wayth. The latest sand pit was rented by Mrs Hobson. [35]

The first official record to use the name Sandy Mount is the 1841 census when Elizabeth Philpott, a sand dealer, was recorded as living there. [36] It is not clear if she was related to Thomas Philpot. It is possible that the phrase 'sandy mount' had first been used on an informal local basis to differentiate from Sand Bank on the north side of Ware Street before the name passed into everyday acceptance. John Apps, an agricultural labourer, was also living at Sandy Mount, as were Eliza and John Apps. Due to the lack of information in the census return, it is not apparent if they were members of the same family and if they all resided in the two dwellings mentioned in the 1762 lease. Other households recorded as living in the Sandy Mount area included George Allman, Robert and Emily Bridgland, James and Hannah Waters. Two years later, Thomas Bridgland was noted on the tithe apportionment for Thurnham, as living at Sandy Mount.[37]

By 1851, different families were living in the Sandy Mount area.[38] These included Edward Habgood and his family; Hannah Hodges, a widow, and her children; Edward and Emily; Edward and Louisa Hobson and their family; Ann Bolton, a widow, and her family; and the family of Luke Hepton. Edward Habgood was described as a 'Proprietor of houses' but he did not own the cottage in which he lived.

It is not clear whether all the interested parties to Ann Armstrong's estate agreed that the simplest way to achieve an inheritance of substance was to sell the holdings, but this is what happened. Sale particulars were prepared. Lot eight comprised the house once inhabited by Thomas Philpot but now rented by Samuel Sapsworth. Lot nine was the kiln, brick and tile works, meadow and sand pits. Lot ten comprised the Old Orchard, described as an enclosure of meadow leased by James Gibson, together with two dwelling cottages called Sandy Mount; occupied by Messrs Habgood and Bridgland.[39]

Part of the sale particulars are reproduced below together with the associated maps:

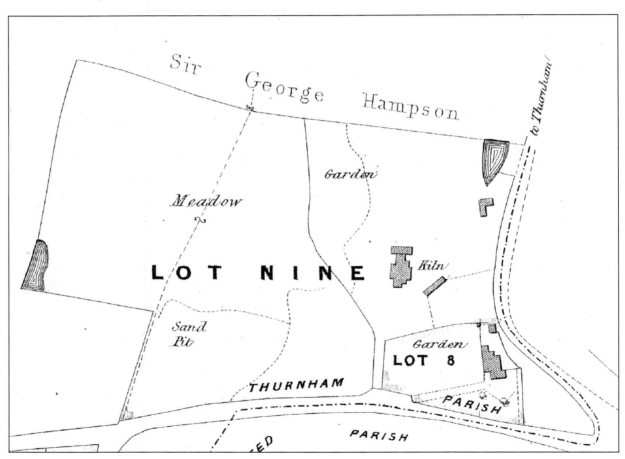

Reproduced courtesy of the Centre for Kentish Studies

LOT 8. THAT

FREEHOLD RESPECTABLE PRIVATE RESIDENCE,

WITH GRASS PLOT, SHRUBS, & GARDENS,

SITUATE AT WARE STREET, IN THE PARISH OF THURNHAM,

In a cheerful and healthy situation, near to Bearsted Green.

THE HOUSE IS BUILT OF BRICK, WITH A TILED ROOF,

And is arranged internally as follows:—

In the Basement—There are 2 good Cellars.

On the Ground Floor—A Hall (15 ft. 10 in. by 8 ft. 10 in., 9 ft. 6 in. high) with a Window looking toward the Garden, a Dining Room, (20 ft. 3 in. by 15 ft. 9 in.,) well papered, the ceiling corniced, fitted with a marble chimney piece, and having 3 windows; a Breakfast Parlor, (14 ft. by 11 ft. 6 in.,) neatly and newly papered, and having 2 windows; a Kitchen, (14 ft. 2 in. by 13 ft.,) with 2 closets, 2 good Pantries, a Wash-house, with oven, sink, and copper, and a Coal-house adjoining the house at the back.

On the First Floor—A Drawing Room, (17 ft. 5 in. by 16 ft. 6 in., 8 ft. 6 in. high,) with 2 windows, and fitted with a marble chimney piece; a Front Bed Room and 4 other Bed Rooms, a large Store Room, Servant's Bed Room and Water Closet. There is a

DETACHED TIMBER & TILED BUILDING IN THE BACK YARD, 17ft. by 12ft.

There is a Garden and Grass Plot in Front, enclosed by a Dwarf Wall, with a
Carriage Drive to the Front Door, also a

LARGE KITCHEN GARDEN, PLANTED WITH SOME EXCELLENT FRUIT TREES,

And at the end of one of the paths is

A SUMMER HOUSE BUILT OF BRICK AND TILED.

These Premises occupy an area of 0A. 2R. 38P. more or less,

And are occupied by SAMUEL SAPSWORTH, ESQ., a Yearly Tenant from Michaelmas, at the very inadequate

RENTAL OF £27 6s. PER ANNUM.

LOT 9. THE

FREEHOLD BRICK AND TILE MANUFACTORY,

WITH KILN, SHEDS, AND PREMISES, MEADOW LAND, GARDEN GROUND, AND A

VALUABLE SAND PIT, &c.,

Situate at Ware Street, in the Parish of Thurnham, adjoining to Lot 8.

In the Brick Yard, is a BRICK and TILE KILN, chiefly used for burning Tiles, 18 ft. 6 in. by 14 ft., with Sheds adjoining, covered in with a Tiled Roof; the Kiln contains

12 BENCHES FOR 38,000 TILES, OR 16,000 BRICKS,

A newly built Timber and Tiled MOULDING SHED, 41 ft. by 14 ft.; 6 ft. high to the Eaves, one other Shed, a newly built PUG MILL SHED, 21 ft. by 31 ft., and 21 ft. by 12 ft., built of Brick and Stone, with a Tiled Roof, A DRYING SHED, 51 ft by 9 ft., together with

ABOUT 2A. 2R. 18P. OF LAND SURROUNDING THE BUILDINGS,

From which Brick and Tile Earth is obtained. Also

AN ENCLOSURE OF MEADOW LAND,

Adjoining the Brick Yard, and a

VALUABLE PIT, CONTAINING SEVERAL VARIETIES OF SHARP, WHITE, RED, & YELLOW SAND,

Used for Building and other purposes.

The Meadow and Sand Pit containing about 5a. 2r. 39p.

Summary of Lot 9.

	Annual value or rental per annum.			Tenants.
	£.	s.	d.	
Tile Manufactory and Buildings, Pits and Garden	25	0	0	Mr. Jas. Ellis
Meadow	5	10	0	Mrs. Wayth
Sand Pit	11	14	0	Mrs. Hobson
Garden Ground	1	10	0	In hand
	£43	14	0	

TOTAL QUANTITY OF THIS LOT, 8A. 1R. 17P.

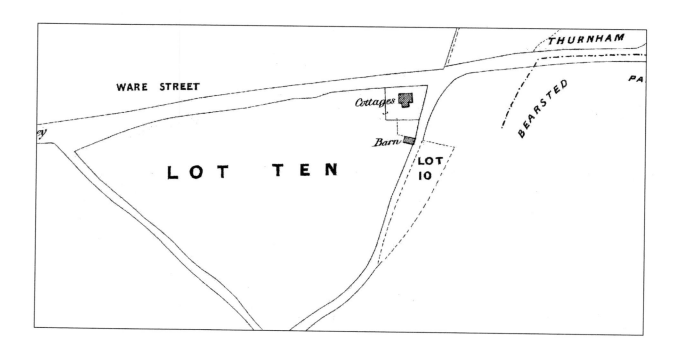

All the lots were sold at the Bell Inn in Maidstone on 29 July 1858. Lots eight and nine were purchased by Sir George Hampson who paid £420 and £430, respectively, for them. James Whatman expressed an interest in lot ten prior to the sale and the parish rate book for 1862 confirms that he did subsequently buy the property.[40]

It took some time for the paperwork concerning the sale of the lots in the auction to be drawn up and concluded but on 18 December 1858, Sir George conveyed the holding to his mother, Dame Mary Foreman Hampson: [41]

...also all that the messuage or tenement situate in Thurnham wherein Catherine Watts and Francis Armstrong formerly dwelt [the lengthy description here includes Kiln Yard] called or known by the name of Sand Bank, formerly in occupation of Bedingfield Wise now [severally] occupied by Samuel Sapsworth, James Ellis and Mrs Wayth and Mrs Hobson...

Schedule:
Parish of Thurnham
Messuage, garden and grass plot   0 acres   2 rods   38 perches

Tile manufactory
Meadow
Sand pit   } together   8 acres   1 rod   17 perches
Garden ground

Lady Hampson later consolidated her holding by purchasing the remaining piece of land occupied by Alfred Wise, but the date of the sale is not recorded. [42]

Three years after the sale, different families were living in the Sandy Mount area: Thomas and Elizabeth Curtis; Edward and Jane Budden; John and Margaret Flood; Henry and Elizabeth Slender. [43, 44]

In 1862 Thomas Bridgeland, senior, was liable for a £9 parish rate on the property and land at Sandy Mount although it is not clear if he was living there. [45]

However, by the 1871 census, members of the Bridgeland family were living at Sandy Mount as the return records Emily Bridgeland, a widow, aged 56, farming the land. She was assisted by her nephew Walter Turley. [46] Walter was aged 18, and unmarried.

Later census returns show Walter had married Harriet and they were running the farm together with their children. [47] The precise dates when this family lived at Sandy Mount and ran the farm are not recorded, but by 1901 the farm had changed hands once more. [48] After five hundred years, a new chapter for Sandy Mount began just before the twentieth century arrived.

Sandy Mount in the twentieth century

By 1900, the medieval name of Weltes and Welteighe Crofts in Ware Street had long been forgotten: it was now known by the name of Sandy Mount. For much of the twentieth century, Sandy Mount was run as a dairy and arable farm holding by the Tolhurst and Foster families. The exact date when they took over the farm is not recorded but the 1901 census return certainly shows William and Amy Tolhurst at the farm.[1] They had two daughters: Rose and Ellen. Rose Tolhurst then ran the farm following her marriage to Charles Foster.

At an unknown date, but after the 1858 sale, the two cottages mentioned in the sale particulars became one dwelling and with the landholding, became consolidated into a small farm. The house retained the small rooms with low ceilings and very uneven floors. This photograph of the farmhouse is undated but was taken in the early 1900s. Rose Foster is standing by the front door with one of her children. The stone above the doorway says 'Sandy Mount' and the date of 1812 in roman numerals, but there are no further details available which would shed light on its significance.

Reproduced courtesy of Barbara Foster

The dairy room was attached to the farmhouse and faced what was locally known as Fosters Lane but was later formally called Hog Hill.[2] The origins of the name Hog Hill are now unclear, but may have originally come from the practice of moving animals around the area for pasture. To meet hygiene standards, the dairy room was only used for milk processing and cleaning the equipment. A small amount of cheese and butter was made but only for family consumption.

The main entrance to the farm was round the back of the house where vegetables were sold. Many of the cow sheds were at the side of the house by Fosters Lane, as was the heap of manure. A small pig yard with sties, and a chicken shed for the large white cockerels reared for Christmas was located in this area too. There was also a substantial land holding at Chapel Lane farm which was used for arable purposes.

The Fosters rented small pockets of land throughout Bearsted and Thurnham for pasture, especially when the cows were regarded as 'dry' or not producing milk. They maintained the land in return for the hay crop, with which to feed the cattle during the winter.

This undated photograph shows Charles and two of his men, paused in collecting a hay crop from the Green:

Left to right: Ambrose Croucher, Charles Foster, Neddy Chawner

Some of the usual routes for taking the cows to pasture and to milking involved travelling between Sandy Mount and the rear of Holy Cross church. This photograph from 1925 shows cows in Yeoman Lane walking by the area of land that was part of the walled kitchen garden for Snowfield:

Both reproduced courtesy of Chris and Sue Hunt

Charles and Rose were thorough and careful people in their business transactions and running the farm. An example of this is the paper-bound, small notebook of receipts that Charles compiled to assist in his animal husbandry. Although it is undated, he probably began it before the First World War. The contents, which include cattle, sheep and horse cures, treatments and other useful information, were carefully copied from other sources. It remains as an example of the sort of knowledge that was needed by a farmer to treat animals before the advent of effective veterinary medicine.

These are two pages from the note book:

Reproduced courtesy of Barbara Foster

This advertisement, from 1929, appeared in the parish magazine:

Reproduced courtesy of Jenni Hudson

By the time Ella Cardwell (née Foster) was born, her Tolhurst grandparents shared the accommodation in order to assist her parents in the running of the business. The dairy and cattle stock section was the largest part of the farm. All the Foster children; William, Eric, Dolly, Ivy, Iris and Ella, like many others in the village, began to help their parents as soon as they could walk. They undertook milk deliveries and odd jobs around the farm so they never really had the chance to go hop-picking in the summer holidays. However, there were hop-pickers huts built in Lilk Meadow by the Ashford Road that they used to see as they walked around that area.

This photograph, taken around 1913 shows William and Dolly at the front of Sandy Mount:

Reproduced courtesy of Tony and Sheila Foster

The children began work by accompanying their father with the horse and cart on milk deliveries. When they were older, the children went on their own rounds with milk cans, measures and bicycles. Each milk can had a capacity of four to five gallons. They were balanced by hanging two of them, one on each handlebar of a bicycle. Both cans had to be put down on the ground, though, whilst the milk was being measured for sale and dispensed. The weight of the milk cans was distributed by drawing equally on both cans. The milk was poured directly into whatever vessel the house-holder had available - this was usually a jug or a basin.

This undated photograph below shows Charles by his bicycle at Holy Cross Church. Note the milk can he is holding on the left hand side of the picture:

Reproduced courtesy of Barbara Foster

This next photograph shows Charles with some of his children delivering milk around Bearsted and Thurnham using a horse and cart. Note the milk bottles that he is holding.

Two vans were also used for delivery purposes and this photograph shows one of them parked outside the houses opposite Holy Cross church:

Both reproduced courtesy of Barbara Foster

When they first left school, the Foster children earned half a crown a week, with 'everything found'.[3] After a year, the wages were increased. However, Wellington boots, shoes and overalls then had to be bought. When Ella was growing up, the people that lived in Bearsted and Thurnham were extremely good at looking after each other. Clothes and other items were always passed on to someone else if a use could be found for them. At the time of the Depression in the 1920s and 1930s many families in the villages suffered hardship as jobs were particularly difficult to find and wages were low.

Milk deliveries were undertaken twice a day but the Fosters also undertook work for other local farmers and smallholders. Charles Foster had a regular trade in carting sieves of fruit to the railway station during the summer and early autumn. 'A sieve' is an old Kent measure for forty eight pounds of fruit. The farm records show that one regular client was Mr Hodges of Rosemount Dairy, who also grew some fruit. This was not an unusual arrangement as many of the small dairy farmers in the area grew, delivered and sold fruit and vegetables. Some of the land around the Mission Hut and in Chapel Lane was cultivated as a market garden by the Foster family. Rhubarb was regularly sold to the army barracks in Maidstone.

Ella recalled that work on the farm was always physically demanding but it seemed worse in bad weather. Picking sprouts and harvesting swedes just before Christmas in very heavy frost aggravated chilblains. Scratches and nicks to hands and arms were not helped by trimming the very cold vegetables after they were harvested and before they were delivered.

Sandy Mount farm also had a large flock of chickens. Ella quite liked collecting the eggs to sell. On cold mornings the chickens were warm from their roost in the hen house so she ran her hands through their feathers to warm her fingers.

Sometimes bullocks were sent from the farm to market in Maidstone. They went on cattle trucks that were housed in the goods yard at Bearsted station. It was always a treat to see the stationmaster greeting the trains looking smartly turned out. He wore a suit and tie, a white shirt, a hat and carried a rolled umbrella. There were two porters at the station that worked alternate duties. The porters were in charge of the goods yard. The goods train was known as 'the shunter' and moved freight trucks back to the yard.

On some of the land at Sandy Mount, a Mission Hut had been erected by the Vicar of Thurnham before the First World War. This was in order for the people in Ware Street to attend a local church service rather than make a much longer journey to St Mary's in Thurnham Lane. It was heated by an old farrier's stove. The stove had a gap in the top of it to heat the iron tools used in horse shoeing.

Winifred Harris (née Guest) could recall as a child that part of their Sunday routine involved attending Sunday School in the afternoon. This was either held in Thurnham vicarage or the Mission Hut. If it was the latter venue, the vicar's daughter, Miss Wigan, took some of the children there from Thurnham Lane in her car. The children called the vehicle 'the Crystal Palace' as it seemed to have large windows.

This undated photograph of Ware Street shows the Mission Hut on the left hand side:

Reproduced courtesy of Michael Perring

The Mission Hut was used during the Second World War as shared accommodation between Thurnham School, Bearsted School and Purrett Road School, Plumstead. The latter had been evacuated and was billeted in Bearsted and Thurnham There was no air raid shelter nearby, but all the staff at the schools had to use whatever accommodation was available. In the war, the Mission Hut was also used as a venue for the Fruit Preservation Centre. The centre had been set up by members of Bearsted and Thurnham Women's Institute, under the direction of Mrs Derrick. Initially, a room of the former Thurnham vicarage was used but the property was then used to billet service personnel. Among many astonishing statistics for the centre was that in six days, over 800lb of jam was once produced.[4]

The building continued to be used for services until just after the Second World War when it was closed due to the amalgamation of Bearsted and Thurnham ecclesiastical parishes. The Foster family then used it as a convenient barn in which to store hay for the farm. Cows were also kept in it upon occasion. Some of the land around the Mission Hut was cultivated as a market garden.

During the Second World War, the government was faced with a severe food shortage. The Ministry of Agriculture and Fisheries undertook a survey, via the County War Agricultural Executive Committee, to ascertain the amount of land that could be ploughed up or planted to increase food production. Although there was no census during the war, these records provide a snap shot of all but the smallest farms between 1940 and 1941.[5]

In August 1941, Sandy Mount farm holding comprised: [6]

> 67 acres at Howe Court and Water Lane in Thurnham and Hollingbourne
>
> Hockers Meadow, Detling
>
> Chapel Lane Farm, Ware Street
>
> Gidds Pond, Grove Green
>
> Old Lands in Bearsted and Thurnham
>
> Sandy Mount, Bearsted and Thurnham
>
> Snowfield Meadow, Bearsted
>
> Nether Milgate, Thurnham
>
> Mote House Meadows, Bearsted
>
> Cross Keys Meadow, Bearsted
>
> Gore Meadow, Bearsted and Thurnham

The dispersed nature of the holdings merited a comment by the inspector. Below is a transcript of the general comments section where the following was noted (phrases in square brackets added for clarity): [7]

> A holding made up of eleven separate pieces of land in eight ownerships and very awkward to work. There is only one cottage [within the farm area] at Chapel Lane [on a service tenancy] and none elsewhere. There are a few buildings at Chapel Lane and at Sandy Mount only. The pastures at Hockers Lane, Water Lane and Howe Court are poor and wet. Mr Foster says he intends improving them this winter...Probably the drainage staff would do good work for and with Mr Foster. There are rabbits in places which are partly the landlords' or shooting tenants responsibilities. The arable is in satisfactory condition and Mr Foster is improving the pasture.

Despite the scattered holdings and pasture, only ten percent of the pasture for the livestock was noted as being in a bad condition with a crop of thistles. However, this problem was noted as being addressed. The arable land was rated as either good or fair. In 1940, oats were harvested at Chapel Lane Farm. Wheat and oats were grown on part of Hockers Meadow.[8]

Barely three years after this assessment, Charles and Rose Foster decided to reduce some of their holdings. The reasons for this are not entirely clear; although a wartime shortage of labour together with uncertainty concerning the question as to whether other members of the family would continue to run the holding, may have played a part. A section of the farm was sold on 24 January 1944. It is probable that it was around this time that the tenancy of Chapel Lane Farm was relinquished.

The front page of the 1944 sale catalogue is shown below:

SANDY MOUNT. BEARSTED

NEAR MAIDSTONE, CLOSE TO RAILWAY STATION.

CATALOGUE OF THE WHOLE OF THE
ALIVE AND DEAD

Dairy Farming Stock

INCLUDING

67 Head of Horned Stock

comprising Valuable Home bred Dairy Herd of 38 Young Cows, 10 In-calf Heifers, 12 Yearling Heifers, 5 Weanyer Calves, and 2 Pedigree Shorthorn Dairy Bulls,

THREE UPSTANDING CART GELDINGS AND A PONY

THE DEAD STOCK includes

Two Motor Delivery Vans, Ton Lorry, Fordson Tractor (October, 1942),

Paraffin and other Tanks and Troughs, Two Waggons, Bavin Tugs, 3 Dung Carts, 3 Spring Vans, Governess Car, TROLLEY ON PNEUMATICS, 6 Quoiler, Chain and Plough Harnesses, Pair Balloon-tyred Wheels for Fordson, Plain & Cambridge Rolls, MASSEY HARRIS 13-SHARE DRILL, a 7-share Drill, 3 Mowing Machines, 2 Horse Rakes, Swathe Turner, 3 Hay Sweeps, Hay Grab, Martin's Cultivator, Harrows, Ploughs, Brakes, Stack and Waggon Cloths, Chaff Cutter, 2 Root Mills, Ladders, Wheelbarrows, Fruit Scales, 55 Cow Chains, STERILISING CHEST, VERTICAL STEAM BOILER, Galvanized Wash-up Bins, the usual Small Tools and Effects ;

WHICH

Messrs

E. J. PARKER & SONS

Are instructed by Mr. Chas. Foster (who is relinquishing business) to Sell by Auction,

On Monday, 24th January, 1944

Commencing at 11 o'clock.

Catalogues Price 2d. each (proceeds to the R.A.F. Pilots' and Crews' Fund)
Auctioneers' Offices : **8 Pudding Lane, Maidstone** *Tel.* 2264/5

Reproduced courtesy of Barbara Foster

After Charles' death, Rose stayed on at the farm, assisted by Eric and his wife, Barbara. They decided to build the farm and stock up once more from what was left after the 1944 sale. They began with a few house cows and a smallholding and after a great deal of very hard work, expanded the holdings.

By 1959 Rose Foster had acquired other properties in Ware Street: these included Rose Cottages and Neatherton Cottages. She had also bought one of a terraced row of properties called Southview Cottages which was close to the Women's Institute Hall in The Street, Bearsted.

Bryan and Malcolm Salvage recalled that Harry and Gladys Rumble lived at Neatherton Cottages until the 1960s. They were good friends of the Salvage family. They recalled regularly going over to the farm with Harry in the late afternoon at milking time during visits from London to see Harry and Gladys.

Harry worked as a cow or herdsman for the Foster family for many years. His youngest daughter, Maureen Homewood (née Rumble) recalled that Harry had begun to work at Sandy Mount farm directly after leaving school. Although he was not born in Bearsted, his parents had worked for Baroness Orczy when she moved into Bearsted.

Although Harry never delivered the milk, there were times when Maureen lent a hand. She used to enjoy sitting on the pony and trap alongside either Charles or Eric Foster. There was always a background noise to the journeys: as they moved up through Church Lane, the tin milk measures of a pint and quart used to rattle in the churn.

Harry adored looking after the cows but milking them twice a day whilst coping with bad weather on dark winter days was hard at times. On one occasion there was a bad accident when a cow turned her head unexpectedly and caught Harry in the eye with one of her horns. Charles Foster became aware that Harry was taking longer at his duties than normal and went to investigate. He discovered Harry pinned to the wall in the cow shed. Despite permanently impaired sight, Harry continued working on the farm for many years, becoming a much valued and greatly appreciated member of the work force.

In the mid 1960s Barbara and Eric Foster made the difficult decision to sell the farm and the land for development as housing. There were many factors to be considered. There were diminishing financial returns from the farm but an equally big factor was that Bearsted and Thurnham were beginning to change. None of the changes had made dairy farming on a small scale any easier. Many of the small pockets of pasture around the village were sold for housing and other housing developments were planned. An increasing volume of traffic around the villages made it difficult to walk the cows to milking twice a day. Many commuters were not pleased with manure on the road and delays due to cattle sharing part of their route to the railway station.

As the village changed, it rapidly became uneconomic for a small farm to continue. The land and farmhouse were sold. During the sale negotiations, it was understood that the farmhouse would be demolished and all of the land used for housing. However, once the sale had been completed, the developers decided to retain the farmhouse and this was bought and renovated by the site foreman. His family added the porch at the front of the house that can be seen today. The rest of the land was used for a housing development called Sandy Mount.

This photograph of Ware Street and Sandy Mount was taken around 1967. Construction of the housing development was about to commence: the white marker posts used by the building company to indicate levels are visible towards the middle of the picture, right hand side:

Reproduced courtesy of Norah Giles

This photograph, taken in 2006, shows some of the houses that were built on the site:

Reproduced courtesy of Malcolm Kersey

Mount Pleasant

James and Barbara Wood occupied the messuage and land which was eventually called Mount Pleasant for many years. Between 1642 and 1675, James used his property in Ware Street to finance a series of mortgages and leases.[1] During this time, evidently, he relinquished some holdings which included the tile kiln and sand pit on the south side of Ware Street, as these passed into the ownership of the Godfrey and Watts families.

An indenture concerning Mount Pleasant dated 7 November 1675, includes an excellent description of it. A partial transcript is shown below: [2]

> All that messuage or tenement, one barn with outhouses, edifices, buildings, court yards, and gardens, orchards, one hemp plot, two hop gardens, eight pieces or parcels of lands, arable or pasture and meadow to the said messuage and tenement belonging containing the while by estimation twenty-seven acres more or less with all and singular, their appurtenances together situate, lying and being in the parish of Thurnham in the said County of Kent at a place there commonly called Ware…

By 1716 the same land package of twenty-seven acres in Thurnham had left the Wood family but there are no documents about this change in ownership. The tenants changed too, as the land was described as occupied by John Ffaulkener. The holding was now owned by Anne French, a spinster, of Maidstone. It is likely that it was around this time, that the existing property was re-built in a Queen Anne style.

On 30 March 1736, Anne sold the holding to Francis Cornhill for £450.[3] Barely nine months later, Francis used the land to raise two mortgages for a total £336 14s 6d.[4] Francis continued to use the property to obtain further mortgages and lease payments from 1742 to 1785. By 1785, the interest of the estate had passed to Arthur Harris. Thomas Harris inherited the interest, but he left it to John Mumford of Sutton at Hone and the estate now started to break up into smaller pieces. In 1785 Samuel Jones paid for a yearly lease of a land package described as containing twenty-seven acres, but which was the land previously held by James Wood. The current occupier of the land was given as Thomas Lee.[5] Samuel Jones already held land in the area as in 1760 he had bought some land called Mark Beech.[6]

The land was included in the same bequest as the forge at 1 Ware Street, which had been made by Daniel Jones in 1807. Ownership of the land passed to the Green family; Louisa and Elizabeth Green then passed their share to their uncle, Samuel Green, for £16 on 4 February 1840.[7] In 1843 the tithe apportionment map and schedule for Thurnham was drawn up. The twenty-seven acres of land is shown on the map as plot thirty one, owned by Samuel Green and occupied by John Budds.[8]

By 1841, the area around the house, which had acquired the name of Mount Pleasant, had begun to be developed and may have been regarded as almost a hamlet in itself. The name was specifically recorded in the census: Richard Kemp and his wife, Rosemary, both aged 50, were living there. Elizabeth Reach, Elizabeth Goldsmith, Sarah Richards and George Bills are also listed. They were servants but there is no indication that they were employed by Richard and Rosemary Kemp. Charles, Douglas and Perry Redgrave were also resident. However, details recorded in the census return are sparse so any relationships remain as a matter of conjecture.[9]

Ten years later, Benjamin Lobley, aged 26, was living there together with his wife, Emily, aged 20, and their daughter, Elizabeth, who was a year old. Benjamin was described as a landed proprietor and had been born in Liverpool. His wife came from Bonnington, but their daughter had been born in Birkenhead, Cheshire. Benjamin and Emily employed one servant; Sarah Cromp, who was unmarried, aged 18. Sarah came from Ashford.[10]

Samuel Green died in 1853 and Mount Pleasant was sold at a subsequent auction held at the Bell Inn in Maidstone on 7 June 1854. It was included in the same lot as Mark Beech Wood and was purchased by James Whatman for £2000.[11]

The 1861 census merely recorded 'Ware Street' for all the properties in the area, rather than more specific property names. However, at some unrecorded point between 1851 and 1861, the family of the famous cricketer, Alfred Mynn had moved into Mount Pleasant from a property at Friningham, Thurnham. It was rented from the Whatman family. In 1851, two of Alfred and Sarah's daughters, Mary and Eliza died and were buried in Thurnham churchyard.[12] It may have been due to their double bereavement that Alfred and Sarah decided to leave Friningham, with its sad associations, and move to a new house.

Alfred, however, was absent on census night as the return gives Sarah as head of the household. She was aged 49 and is described as a 'landholder's wife'. Sarah had been born in Lenham. Also recorded are some of Sarah and Alfred's unmarried daughters: Sarah aged 39, and Laura aged 22, both born in Harrietsham. Two nieces: Jane Norton and Charlotte Mynn, aged 24 and 25 respectively were also resident. The Mynn family had one servant, Jane Whitehead, aged 15, who came from Thurnham.[13]

Alfred's supreme talent was for cricket but this was not matched by a sound grasp of personal matters and finance which sometimes led to problems. On at least one occasion, Alfred narrowly escaped being prosecuted for debt.

Alfred stood over six feet tall and weighed over eighteen stones, so it is not surprising that he quickly received the nickname of the 'mighty Mynn' as at the height of his career. However, in August 1836 an untreated injury almost resulted in the end of Alfred's cricketing activities. Although some of the details are unclear, his leg was hurt during a match in Leicester, but he managed to complete the fixture, achieving 'Not Out'. However, his leg injury had been aggravated by the innings and a doctor advised him to go home and seek medical attention straightaway. A stage coach was leaving Leicester for London, but Alfred was so large that he could not get into the coach. Instead, he was hoisted up and laid flat on the roof of the coach where the luggage was normally stored. Upon arrival in London, Alfred was laid up at the Angels Tavern in St Martin's Lane and stayed there for some considerable time whilst doctors debated treatment. For a time it seemed possible that he might lose the leg. However, they reviewed their consultations and decided against the course of amputation. Unsurprisingly, Alfred's recovery from the injury problem was very slow indeed.[14]

At the end of October in 1861, Alfred suddenly died whilst away from home. He was staying at his brother Walter's house at Merrick Square, Southwark, London. It is thought that he developed diabetes which struck with alarming rapidity. This was many years before the nature of the condition was properly understood and insulin treatment developed so the condition was nearly always fatal. Alfred's funeral was held on 6 November, in atrocious weather. He was laid to rest in Thurnham churchyard alongside his daughters Mary and Eliza.[15,16] Below is a slightly-edited transcript of the report about Alfred's funeral which appeared in Maidstone Telegraph, Malling Chronicle and West Kent Messenger, 9 November 1861:

DEATH OF MR ALFRED MYNN

Mr Mynn helped to place his county in the very foremost ranks of the cricket counties of England...The last time we saw him match playing was on Mr John Walker's beautiful ground at Southgate, Mr Mynn then batting on behalf of his county, Kent...He has, now, alas! played in his last match. May the green grassy turf he loved so much to sport on lie lightly o'er his remains.

The funeral obsequies of the gallant cricketer took place on Wednesday. The funeral cortege started from his late residence at about 3 pm and was met at Bearsted by the members of the Leeds Castle and Hollingbourne Rifle Volunteer Corps (of which he was a member), under the command of Major Charles Wykeham Martin. The mournful procession, preceded by the Band, playing the 'Dead March in Saul'. then wended its way slowly up Thurnham Hill to the church where the funeral ceremony was impressively performed by the Rev E K Burney, vicar of Thurnham. At its conclusion, the corps took up a position round the grave and fired the usual volleys. There were a great number of villagers and others to witness the sad ceremony, and but for the rain which kept incessantly falling, there would have been a much larger assemblage....

Reproduced courtesy of Kent Messenger group

Below is a photograph of Alfred's grave:

Reproduced courtesy of Malcolm Kersey

In 1951, this plaque was placed on the wall of Mount Pleasant:

Reproduced courtesy of Ian Lambert and Bearsted Cricket Club

It is not known when the remaining Mynn family moved from Mount Pleasant, but it is probable that they were cared for by some of Alfred's brothers.

After Alfred's death but before the 1871 census, the curate of St Mary's church, Thurnham, Rev Edward Twopeny, lived at the house. He is known to have been a keen supporter of Kent cricket and probably appreciated the association with Alfred Mynn. Unfortunately, there is no record of Edward's tenancy, but in 1954, this card was found at the back of the sitting room chimney:

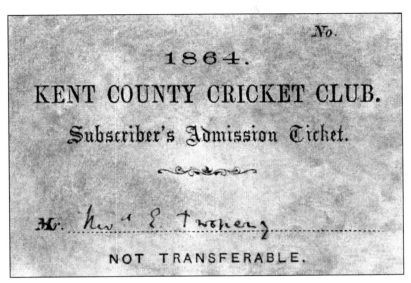

Reproduced courtesy of James Moore

The name of the house, is not included in the 1871 census, but the head of household, Edward Smith, was described as a 'general dealer' who had been born in Thornham. Edward was aged thirty, and lived there with his wife, Eliza. Thomas Winchester, an agricultural labourer, was boarding with them and he, too, had been born in Thornham. Also living nearby were William Pound, John Davis and Robert Attwood with their families.[17]

The 1881 census once more specifically refers to the area as:

> **Ware Street (Mount Pleasant)**

But it is not immediately apparent who was living at the property as the house is not clearly listed and the name seems to have also extended to the immediate area. Hannah Bedingfield, a widowed housekeeper, born in Norfolk, was living in the area but so were several other large families - by the name of Tilby, Pawley, Pound and Barney. Only John Barney, was not an agricultural labourer. He was listed as a farmer's son but still assisting on a farm.[18] After the census was taken, Mr Wykeham Martin moved to Mount Pleasant house[19] but his residence there was short-lived as although he is listed in an 1882 trade directory, he is not listed in any later editions.

For the next census, in 1891, again a difference between Mount Pleasant house and the use of the name to indicate a larger area occurs as it is once more under the overall description of Ware Street. Families listed include the Pawley; Pound, Golding and Parks and also Ann Creasey, a widow aged 81, who was described as living on parish pay.[20] In 1901 Frederick and Emma Boucher were living at Mount Pleasant house. Frederick was a retired farmer with three sons; Oswald, Archibald and Hubert. Subsequent owners included the Misses Furber.[21]

In 1914, Grace Dibble's family moved to Mount Pleasant. A year later, Frederick Bradley bought the property from the Whatman family. Grace recalled that the Saville family had lived there immediately before them and had now moved to Boxley. Despite the information found in previous records and title deeds, the memories that Grace wrote, and which were published, are the only source to convey what it was like to live in Mount Pleasant in the twentieth century.[22]

Part of Grace's memories are reproduced below:

After Poplar Villas in Roseacre Lane, this large old brick and Kentish Ragstone building, with its while wooden pillars above the steps to the front porch, seemed most palatial. We were proud to live in this home, because the great cricketer Alfred Mynn, the 'Lion of Kent' had lived there until his death in 1861.

To celebrate the Festival of Britain in 1951, a plaque was fixed to the north wall - 'Alfred Mynn lived here', by the Thurnham parish council. Though Mount Pleasant was in the ecclesiastical and civil parish of Thurnham, our postal address was Bearsted. We had a Victorian pillar-box in our ragstone garden wall so it was easy to post letters.

The front of the house was attractive because one side was covered with Virginia Creeper and the other by ivy until this had to be torn down, when it became too invasive round the windows. To the right of the massive front door, with its iron lion head knocker, was the long dining room, with a unique type of French window facing west across a lawn to a weeping ash tree. The upper sash window could be pushed up, and the two heavy wooden doors below opened outwards, so that we could go over a cement slab to the lawn.

In the dining room the large main sash window faced north, and was fitted inside with folding wood shutters, which were most useful for black-out in wartime. The very wide sills were ideal for plants. As the house was old, the windows rattled in strong winds and cords often had to be renewed - not an easy job! A carpet had to be especially made as the room was unusually long and narrow. The lower parts of the walls were covered with dark brown embossed paper, with a speckled beige paper above. A wide board, with a pelmet above the fireplace, was full of family photographs, flanking the large clock. The wide grate had a brass fender in front, and a fire-guard, when no one was in the room in winter. As the fireplace was at one end of the room, which had been extended at an earlier date, it was never warm, except in front of the fire. The smaller sitting-room opposite, also faced north.

Further down the long hall was the breakfast room or kitchen, with a large built-in sideboard, which held on the shelves, our blue dinner-service, and had three drawers. There was a large range, which we never used. This was flanked by two wall cupboards, with very deep shelves, annually filled with jams on one shelf. An oak beam was visible in the ceiling. This was a cheerful room because it faced east. On the wide window-sill there were always geraniums. This was the room where we did our ironing with a gas iron, and later with electricity, after it had been installed.

The farm house was built into a slope, and so the scullery was partly below ground level. Though it faced south, it was always cold, because the floor was of stone slabs! Under the space below the very wide chimney was a gas stove. On one side, the huge bread oven, and on the other was the brass copper for heating water.

Under the window was a long cemented sink, flanked by two hand pumps; the one to the left was connected to a rain-water underground tank in the yard, while the other pumped up cool, hard water from a well. This we used for drinking; it was most refreshing. There was a long wooden shelf down the side opposite the stove, and above, a wooden rack for plates to dry. The rough stone walls were always distempered in pink.

Next door was a small pantry with a brick floor and shelves, also half-below yard level. At right angles was the back door, from which stone steps led up to the yard. The hall widened to the door of the dairy, with its red flagstones and rough stone walls, which were whitewashed. Two sides were provided with wide shelves. The small window with leaded panes faced west, but was shaded by a high brick wall and tall shrubs, so that it was always cool. A steep step led up into a small wine pantry bit it was never used as such. Apples and pears were stored on the shelves in autumn and winter. At right angles was the door down into the cellar; entirely below ground level and very damp. In the wall by the steep stone steps, were alcoves, where we put our foods in the hot weather, because fridges were not available.

All the woodwork downstairs and up the banisters was stained brown, like the colour of the hall linoleum. Upstairs the five bedrooms were all painted white. My bedroom faced north, over the front garden, the road, the farm buildings, the railway, the brickworks, and the field with the elm trees, where the rooks roosted. High up beyond were the North Downs and Detling Aerodrome. To the right of the little fire grate in my room was a built-in wall cupboard, with shelves and hanging space for coats and dresses. The sash-window had to be wedged with a piece of wood to keep it from rattling; there was always a draught. The room opposite was rightly known as the 'Box Room', with trunks, portmanteaux and boxes galore. The other two bedrooms were used by our parents and as a guest-room. Although there was already a toilet upstairs, in later years one room was converted into a bathroom.

As the house was large, it was cool in summer, but so cold in winter! Seating was by fires in open grates, generally burning apple logs from prunings in the orchards, and some coal. There was an iron hob fixed on to the bar of the grate to support the big iron kettle, which provided hot water in winter for tea, for hot water-bottles, for baths, and for washing-up in the scullery. Sometimes in very cold weather, a Valor Perfection Oil Stove was lit and placed at the bottom of the stairs. At first the rooms were lit by paraffin lamps, with the hanging one in the dining-room. Upstairs candles were used but later, gas was installed, and finally, electricity.

A high brick wall linked the house to the stable and the oast house. We used the two parts of the former for storing coal the large wooden wheelbarrow, potatoes and later our bicycles. In the inner part with the two mangers, were the garden tools and lawn mower and more mounds of potatoes. Once some calves which had been allowed to graze in the orchard managed to enter the stable and somehow the double doors closed behind them, so that they were terrified and caused havoc. After that incident, a wooden fence was erected to separate the backyard from the road and the orchard.

The oast house was unique in that it had lost the upper part, leaving a flat roof above the ragstone roundel. It was in this building that the Methodists used to meet after the closure of their chapel in Chapel Lane and before the new one was built in Ware Street. We used the floor of the roundel as a house for poultry and turkeys, with boxes for nesting and poles erected for perching at night.

The main brick building of the oast house facing west, had a large bench for tools under the small window. Open wooden steps led upstairs, where apples were stored. Even then as a schoolgirl, I longed to convert the oast into a dwelling. In the angle between the roundel of the oast and the stable, a wall had been constructed. In this space all our broken china, glass, tins, saucepans etc. were thrown, because in our early days there were no dustmen to collect rubbish. Vegetable peelings were used to make compost, together with the chicken manure collected from the oast.

Beyond the new yard fence, was a stony road, and above this a steep, grassy bank, with one set of brick steps leading up to an orchard, with Derby, Beauty of Bath, and Bramley apple trees. The other orchard beyond the road had damsons, Victoria plums and more Bramley apples. Both orchards were grassed and cut with a scythe, unless grazed by a farmer's sheep or calves. The poultry enjoyed scratching in the orchards. We sometimes found that they were laying eggs in secluded corners. In springtime, the various tints of the blossoms made a beautiful Kentish picture. We planted dozens of primrose roots in the bank, where they seeded each year.

In autumn, peck and bushel baskets were used to convey the apples from the orchard to the oast for storing. The plums and damsons were made into jam or used for pies. On the south wall of the house was an old greengage tree with delicious fruits, but unfortunately always besieged by swarms of wasps. We used to catch a great many by hanging medicine bottles, partially filled with a solution of jam and water, on the tree. In the cherry orchards beyond ours, the farmer used to hire men to shoot the birds and to bang tins incessantly. There were many birds in the orchards, including cuckoos and woodpeckers.

The garden area was very large. The vegetable section was bounded by the orchard brick wall, and a wooden fence between us and the row of Mays Cottages, and at the bottom, by a steep slope. Shrubs cut the vegetable garden off from the lawns. The paths were grassed. There was a William pear tree against the wall to the west. A long area was planted with raspberry canes, which usually gave us much fruit for jam and tarts. Beyond was an extensive patch of red rhubarb. The rest of the vegetable garden was taken up with endless rows of potatoes and also brassicas and runner beans at different seasons.

Syringas, mauve lilacs, holly, laurels and laurustinus, surrounded the lawn to the west of the house. Around the huge weeping ash tree, there were naturalized celandines, white violets, single and double snowdrops, and double daffodils. There was a swing which was hung on a branch of the ash. In winter, half coconuts and pieces of fat were hung on a trailing branch for the birds. By the little east lawn there was a small copse of hazel nuts which we enjoyed. By the holly hedge were clumps of ferns. Over the path was a wire arch for an American Pillar rambler rose, which needed annual pruning. The steps from the lane were under an ancient yew tree.

Between Ware Street and the front of the house, was a steeply sloping lawn, bordered by herbaceous plants, and a very tall hedge of alternating holly and yew, so that we were quite secluded. The hedge was a lovely picture after a heavy fall of snow. The lawn was often spoiled by mole hills. For years we were horrified at the thought that we should lose the wonderful hedge and part of the garden, because there was one plan, whereby the proposed bypass would be a widened Ware Street! It was not until 1962 that a motorway was built at the foot of the North Downs.

Grace's parents were thoroughly involved in local activities: her mother taught at Bearsted School for a time. Her father, George, was Chairman of Thurnham parish council between 1943 and 1948. He was also a secretary and scorer for Bearsted Cricket Club for over twenty years and Treasurer of the Bearsted and Thurnham Conservative Association. This cartoon of George Dibble shown below, is from a press cutting, but is undated and unsourced. It appeared in a local publication:

Reproduced courtesy of James Moore

After renting the property for many years, George Dibble was able to purchase it, although the precise date of the sale remains unclear. In 1963, the property changed hands once more as Grace and her sister, Doris, sold it to the Moore family.[23] Eileen and James Moore lived at Mount Pleasant until 2000.

This photograph of Mount Pleasant was taken around 1999:

Reproduced courtesy of James Moore

Whilst living there, James investigated some of the history of the property. Through his researches, he was able to produce some notes about the house. Intriguingly, he included a memory from Thomas Gilbert (usually called Tom) about Mount Pleasant. He commented that whilst he was a child in the early years of the twentieth century, few people living in Ware Street actually called the property 'Mount Pleasant', but everyone living in the vicinity referred to it as 'The Manor' or 'The Old Manor'.[24]

If Tom's information is the last remnant of a community memory, what evidence is there to support this idea of a manor house at Mount Pleasant? James was already aware that his house stood on a greatly excavated platform, but could this be considered the remains of an earlier property on the same site? No one can be entirely sure. Further remnants of old ragstone foundations have now been found in the same area; hinting that it is entirely possible that a more extensive building once occupied the site.[25]

Although only a partial history can be established for the area which became known as Mount Pleasant, it would be good to think that it was the site for the original manor house, once known as Weltighe Crofts, and at the heart of the manor of Ware.

Church Cottages and Sharsted Way

In 1709, a map was drawn up by John Watts which was designed to show the lands in and around Bearsted and Thurnham held by William Cage of Milgate. The area upon which Church Cottages now stand in Ware Street is noted as: [1]

...Church of Thurnham lands given to ye church by John Sharsted in ye nineteenth year of King Edward ye Fourth...

Below is shown an interpretation of the relevant section of the map:

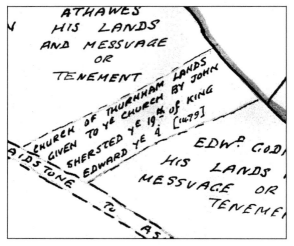

Reproduced courtesy of Michael Perring

John Watts recorded the gift of the lands as made during 1479. However the historian and researcher, Lambert Larking, noted the following: [2]

...Shrested John, Prior of Rochester, is shown as owning land in Thurnham parish from 1410 to 1421. He appears to have been succeeded by Thomas Sherested in the ownership of the land...

Larking felt that the discrepancy of dates was explained by the authorities at Rochester considering the land to be already part of church estate, but under the deed of gift, the transfer was delayed until the death of Thomas Sherested. The truth behind this suggested explanation cannot now be established as the documents which would shed light upon this matter have not survived.

The Sherstede family evidently had long connections with the area. The earliest remaining document for the manor of Ware records John Shersted as attending the manor court 17 May 1380. Below is shown the entry for his name on the court roll; it is the first name on the left hand side: [3,4]

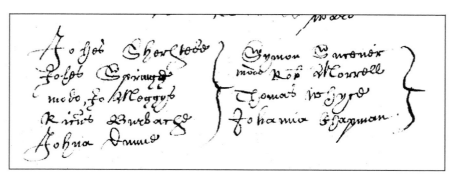

Reproduced by kind permission of the Dean and Chapter of Rochester Cathedral
and the Director of Community services, Medway

It was through the gift made by John Sherested to Rochester cathedral in 1410 that the lands were regarded as separate from those comprising the manor of Ware, even though they came to be part of the overall land holdings of the cathedral. The Sharsted family continued to be prominent landowners in and around Bearsted and Thurnham for several centuries.[5]

When Edward Hasted undertook the research for his survey, he specifically noted: [6]

> ...four houses known by the name of church houses, now let to the Overseers of the Poor for forty shillings per annum and four acres of land called Church Lands let at three guineas per annum....

When the Sharsted charity was set up in 1497, it was a generous bequest. However, there was no provision for the repair of any cottages built upon the land. This may have been because the charity stipulated that money gained as income from the land was to be equally divided between maintaining the services at St Mary's and maintaining the fabric of the church. It was not until the 1970s that the arrangements were reviewed and an accommodation made in the church accounts that was used to pay for the maintenance of the cottages.[7]

By 1846, it was noted that the church estate comprised two acres of land let as allotments and four cottages with gardens. At this time the houses were regarded as dilapidated. They were later described as utterly uninhabitable and incapable of being repaired, so they were re-built at a cost of £270. It would be good to think that bricks from the nearby brickfield were used, but there is no evidence to confirm this suggestion. The amount was advanced by Richard Thomas and to secure the payment, the Rev John McMahon Wilder, vicar of St Mary's, and the church wardens, John Ellis and Thomas Bridgland leased the estate for ninety nine years to Charles Noakes, Benjamin Ware, William Amos and Thomas Fillmer. They became responsible for clearing the debt.[8] The lease was surrendered on 30 November 1876 when it was noted with some satisfaction the debt had been repaid. Today, the properties bear a Grade II listing.[9]

This photograph shows Church Cottages today:

Reproduced courtesy of Images of England

One of the earliest accounts for the cottages is dated 3 September 1866. It concerns work undertaken at the property but nothing further is known about the matter or who was living there.

Below is shown this early account: [10]

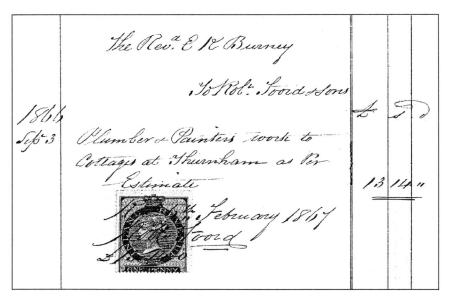

Reproduced courtesy of the churchwardens and Parochial Church Council of St Mary's church

The majority of the Sharsted estate remained intact until the middle of the nineteenth century when the arrival of new methods of travel marked the start of a gradual disposal of some areas. In 1877, the Charity Commissioners Scheme examined the church estate for Thurnham. The schedule submitted by Rev Burney, vicar of Thurnham described the Sharsted bequest. Below is shown a slightly edited transcript: [11]

First schedule:
A close of land containing four acres, three roods and seven perches together with four cottages in Ware Street known as Church Land and Houses. These are comprise numbers 40 and 41 on the Tithe Map and are now occupied by Robert Attwood, William Stanford, Thomas Lurcock and Thomas Sage...

Reproduced courtesy of the Gordon Ward Collection, Kent Archaeological Society

A Thurnham parish rate book for 1875 shows that part of the land was rented by Mr Tolhurst of Sandy Mount[12] but at an unknown date after this, part of the land around the cottages began to be rented as allotments. Some parishes clearly regarded renting out allotments as a means to reduce their poor rates but it is not clear whether this was the case in Thurnham; the provision for the poor in the parish already included the workhouse at Hollingbourne.

There certainly was a precedent for the provision of allotments found in neighbouring Bearsted. In 1844 the Maidstone Journal, Kentish Advertiser and South Eastern Intelligencer newspaper reported the benefits of a scheme established in 1834 by Charles Wayth. The plots ranged in size from thirty rods to half an acre, rented at forty shillings an acre. On the evening of rent day, 23 October, the tenants were provided with ale and a hot supper at the Royal Oak public house. The supper was financed by local subscriptions and became a regular event. Mr Streatfield, the Allotment Committee Treasurer, noted that not one farthing was lost through non-payment of the rent.[13]

The fruit and vegetables which were produced from the allotments were valued supplements to the limited diet of many people. The fullest sequence of records about the cottages and allotments cover 1891 to 1929. In 1891 there were twenty allotments which earned St Mary's an income of £6.[14]

The first full list of the allotment holders was recorded in 1892 and is shown below.[15]

Allotment Holder	Amount paid
R Attwood	5s
W Wilkins	2s 6d
Mrs Cheeseman	7s
F White	2s 6d
Mrs G Hodges	2s 6d
C Webb	10s
H Hodges	7s 6d
Grant	6s
Walklin	5s
N or W Tolhurst	5s
Mrs Tolhurst	10s
Kirby	5s
Pawley	5s
H Medhurst	5s
R Bolton	2s 6d
J Medhurst	7s
J Lurcock	2s 6d
Kitney	15s
Baker	5s

Reproduced courtesy of the Churchwardens and
Parochial Church Council of St Mary's church

All allotment holders had to agree to rules and regulations which governed the use of the land. Below is shown an undated, but typical, list of regulations: [16]

Regulations & allotments applied to Thurnham.

REGULATIONS

FOR THE TENANTS OF

FIELD AND COTTAGE GARDENS.

N.B. The Tenant must distinctly understand, that the Garden being intended for his own benefit, the continuance of his tenancy must depend on his industry in cultivation, sobriety, and general good conduct, as well as on his observance of these Regulations.

1.—The Rent   to be payable Quarterly.

2.—A Quarter's notice to quit on either side shall determine the tenancy at any period of the year ; and the Tenant on quitting, shall, after payment of all rent due by him, receive a fair remuneration for any crops then growing ; and for any manure, the effect of which may be fairly considered as not worn out, unless he be ejected under the provision of Rule 7.

3.—The Garden shall be cultivated by hand work only : and no horse shall be allowed to enter the ground, except for the purpose of carrying on manure, or taking away the produce.

4.—No Garden shall be underlet, or exchanged without permission.

5.—No Tenant shall take two crops of Wheat, or of Potatoes in succession from the same ground.

6. No work shall be done on Sunday, on Good Friday, or on Christmas Day, nor any Vegetables removed from the Gardens after nine o'clock in the morning of those days.

7.—Any Tenant convicted of any offence against the Laws of his Country, shall forfeit his Garden immediately, without claim to compensation of any kind.

We the undersigned hereby agree with The Vicar and Churchwardens to take of them   *of*
Land, situate in the parish of   *subject to the above Regulations and Conditions.*

As witness our hands this   *day of*   18

Witness.

Reproduced courtesy of the Gordon Ward Collection, Kent Archaeological Society

Although there were one or two persistent late payers for the allotments, the running of the land seems to have been relatively trouble-free between 1891 and 1929. There is only one instance, in 1900, where a summons had to be issued to an allotment holder to ensure that payment was made.[17]

Just as records were kept for the allotments, the names of the tenants renting the cottages and payments for work undertaken at the properties were carefully noted in the church records and some accounts have been preserved. It is fortunate that these details were retained as only one census return specifically records the properties as Church Cottages.

In December 1871, Robert Attwood began a tenancy at one of the cottages. The record of Robert's undertaking to pay a weekly rent of 2s 6d is the only rent agreement to be preserved in the church records. Below is shown the agreement: [18]

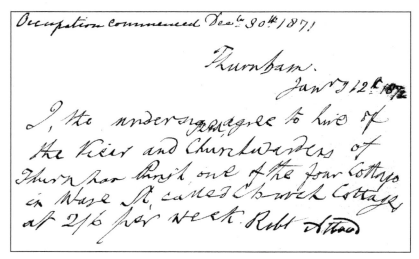

Reproduced courtesy of the Churchwardens and Parochial Church Council of St Mary's church

The records for the cottages during this time are partial, but in 1875, the parish rate book recorded that each cottage occupied twenty four perches of land and that three were occupied by Thomas Sage, William Sage and Robert Attwood.[19] In 1881 Thomas Sage, Thomas Lurcock, William Stanford and Robert Attwood were all listed in the census as the heads of their respective households. All but William Stanford were born in Thurnham. William came from Detling.[20]

By June 1883, Mr Sage was no longer occupying one of the cottages. From the details in the receipt shown below, Mr Sandland, one of the churchwardens, paid £2 for crops that Mr Sage had left in the garden of the cottage: [21]

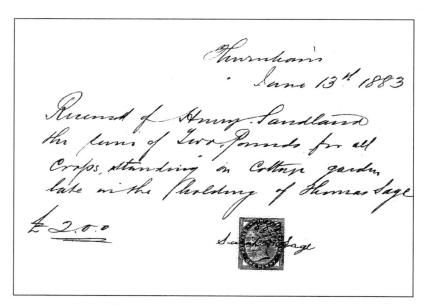

Reproduced courtesy of the Churchwardens and Parochial Church Council of St Mary's church

During 1882, the London, Chatham and Dover railway extended their line from Maidstone to Ashford. Part of the Sharsted land was sold to the railway at a cost of £191 13s 4d. The proceeds were invested by the Charity Commissioners and the interest in the capital was paid yearly to the Trustees. The railway line divided the estate so during the construction in 1884, a bridge was built in order that access to the land owned by both the church estate, and some land owned by Sir George Hampson which was also behind the line, could be achieved. Sir George secured permanent access to the land over the bridge through an agreement with the railway company in 1886.[22]

The amounts paid by allotment holders and tenants amounted to an income of £32 5s 6d for the church in 1892.[23] It is not clear whether the rent payments included a contribution towards the rates and a water rate, although payments for these services were certainly made by the churchwardens at St Mary's. Nevertheless, the tenants enjoyed a reasonable standard of accommodation and, from the details in the accounts, repair work was regularly undertaken. The names of local contractors that undertook work at the cottages are included in the accounts.[24]

Below are shown some typical entries for the church accounts; Mr Wilkinson lived in Bearsted and Mr White was located a short distance from the cottages.[25]

1897			
5 April	C Wilkinson for work at cottages		3s
	F White repairing copper for Mrs Hodges		5s 8d
14 June	F White for work at cottages per estimate	£2	10s
1901			
January	C Wilkinson for repairs to Mrs Attwood's cottage		5s 11d
1 June	Mr C Wilkinson for new fire place at Ware Street Cottage	£11	0s 0d
1927			
5 May	H Delves: emptying cesspool		15s
18 June	Mrs Weller Tool shed (moved to Mrs Summers)	£1	10s
8 August	Repairs:		
	Messrs Wallis and account		
	New earth closet to cottage no. 4, work at no. 1	£16	17s 9d
	Wilkinson account painting four cottages etc	£11	13s 3d
10 August	Sergeant and Parks: wallpaper for 4 cottages		10s 4d

Reproduced courtesy of the Churchwardens and Parochial Church Council of St Mary's church

A typical example, from 1885, of some of the accounts and bills for the cottages that were submitted to the church wardens, is shown below: [26]

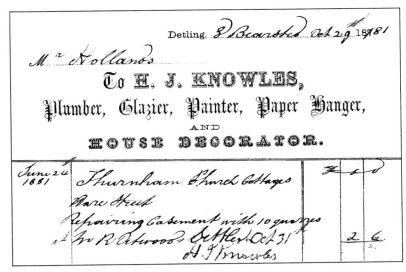

Reproduced courtesy of the Churchwardens and Parochial Church Council of St Mary's church

A list of tenants was compiled in 1894: Mrs Hodges, Mrs Tree, Mrs Stanford and Mrs Attwood all paid a weekly rental sum of 2s 6d.[27] It is curious to note that all the payments made by the tenants were women, but there does not seem to have been any rule governing the sex of the occupant.

In 1905 the insurance cover for the cottages was reviewed. The property attracted a premium of nine shillings for a policy to the value of £600. Ten years later, the premium was increased to twelve shillings for a policy to the value of £800.[28]

It is possible to trace the inhabitants of the cottages through the tenancy payments. Thus, the inhabitants remained the same between 1892 and 1910. In 1911 Mrs Hodges and Mrs Tree were no longer renting but had been replaced by Mrs Cooper and Mrs Sole. The following year, Mrs Stanford was succeeded by Mrs Coomber.[29]

Towards the end of 1915, Mrs Cooper moved out and was replaced by Mrs Rose. It would be good to think that the arrival of the widowed Mrs Sarah Rose and her daughters was a practical application of charity by the vicar and churchwardens of St Mary's, as Sarah's two sons were serving in the armed forces. The following year, Robert, her youngest son, was killed on 30 September whilst serving with the Queen's Own Royal West Kent Regiment during action at the Somme. The Rose family stayed at Church Cottages until 1919.[30]

A transcript of the report from the Kent Messenger, 18 November 1916: [31]

Photograph courtesy of Kent Messenger group

Pte. R. R. Rose (Bearsted)
Royal West Kent Regiment

KILLED IN ACTION

Pte. Robert R. Rose, Royal West Kent Regiment, was killed in action, September 30th, 1916, aged 19. He joined up February 23rd 1916 and went to the Front July last. Before enlisting, he worked for Mr Bradley, Rose Acre Farm, Bearsted. His widowed mother and sisters live at Church Cottages, Ware Street, Thurnham and he has an elder brother serving in the Army Veterinary Corps.

During 1928 to 1929, the list for the tenants at the cottages includes Mrs Cleggett, Mrs Simmons, Mrs Weller and Mrs Attwood. Mrs Attwood was later succeeded by Mrs Cole.[32]

In World War Two, the cottages were insured against aircraft fire and bomb damage. There was certainly some action around the cottages during the war but the properties seemed to lead a charmed life unaffected by wartime activities nearby. These included a section of the army camping upon part of the golf course behind them, a Messerschmitt 109 and another aeroplane crashing nearby. Due to the close proximity of Detling airfield, the explosions during the extensive air raids in August and September at Detling in 1940 were certainly felt by the residents. There were several near misses with bombs: one embedded itself in the railway embankment close to Rosemount Dairy Farm which was near to the cottages, and a stick of bombs dropped near to the Methodist chapel in 1943. Despite this, no damage was sustained to the cottages as a result of enemy action during the war, so an insurance claim was never submitted.[33]

On 7 October 1966 an application was made to build six bungalows on the site of the allotment gardens. The application was refused on 1 February 1967 on the grounds that the main drainage facilities were inadequate.[34] However, the application had evidently highlighted the lack of provision of housing for senior citizens. The Hollingbourne Rural District Council re-considered the matter and after main drainage was introduced in Ware Street, compulsorily purchased some of the land. It was then used to build maisonettes and bungalows for senior citizens. The development was called Sharsted Way.

Below is a photograph of Sharsted Way taken in 2006:

Reproduced courtesy of Malcolm Kersey

In 1985 a further section of the land owned by St Mary's church was sold. It was a small paddock area at the end of the allotment gardens. Although the land has been greatly reduced in area, the allotments continue to be cultivated. Patrick Finnis is in charge of them and although he has no official title, the allotment holders are collectively known as the Thurnham Allotment Association.

It took Patrick many years to gain his allotment. His first plot largely contained weeds such as mares tail and thistles that were over four feet high and seeding! The rent cost £3 a year. It did not take him long to begin to clear it and barely a year later, he was approached to take over the running of the allotments. At the time when Patrick started work on his patch, there were just six allotments in cultivation. Today there are around thirty five to forty different sized plots.

Patrick is a highly respected figure in the Association: in 2003, 2005, and 2006 he has won the allotment section of Maidstone in Bloom and was runner-up in 2004. The allotments are expected to be kept to a certain standard and if they are neglected or weeds allowed to flourish, the holder will be asked to tidy it up or vacate. The allotment holders are generous in sharing produce, time and gardening knowledge with people but this is reciprocated within the organisation: co-operation and communal spirit are abiding principles of the Association.

Today the allotment site is largely peaceful. Although close to the railway line and golf club, the noise of the trains and cars travelling to the club house do not intrude. The soil of the allotments is an excellent mixture of clay and sand in which plants do well. The site is warm and as a result it does not take long for seeds to germinate. A fantastic variety of fruit, flowers and vegetables are grown on the land ranging from asparagus and brassicas through to melons, grapes and nectarines.

The majority of the allotments are clean, tidy and with an impressive array of landscaping and equipment to gladden the heart of any eco-centred observer. As there is no water on site, most allotment holders have a phalanx of water butts but there is a good rainfall and drainage so many people have no recourse to use them even in warm dry summers.

Gardening is pursued on an organic basis: there are no insecticides. Most allotment holders use a mixture of soap and water to control such pests that are present. A small amount of Weedol is used to maintain the paths and a degree of controlled burning is allowed for persistent weeds. However, wherever and whenever possible, biological controls are used. As a result of this eco-friendly policy the area is rich in wildlife. There are nesting boxes all over the land.

Most allotment holders buy seed at reasonable prices from a supplier based at a small farm in Essex that offers 2,700 varieties of flowers, fruit and vegetables. The excellent range and personal service means that a supply of old fashioned varieties which are not often considered by national seed growers for retail can be maintained.

In 2005 a further section of wrought iron gate was added to the existing one on the left hand side at the entrance. Patrick and two other allotment holders, Michael Patterson (usually called Mick) and Barry Smith helped to erect it. The gate is not only substantial, but very beautiful, and blends superbly with its predecessor. It is fitting that it was made by Mick Patterson, who not only lives in Ware Street, but took over the allotment once cultivated by his father. Mick is one of the last generation of blacksmiths to work at Bearsted forge.[35] Below is a photograph of the gate taken in 2006:

Photograph courtesy of Malcolm Kersey

If one is closer to God in a garden than anywhere else, then for Patrick and the other allotment holders, there must be times when a day spent working there, when the sun is shining and the air filled with birdsong, must indeed seem like a fragment of heaven.

Winter Haw

Today, 62-64 Ware Street stands on the site of a dwelling once known as Winter Haw. The current property bears a Grade II listing and the construction date is believed to be between 1667-1699.[1] The name Winter Haw is an intriguing one: it partially derives from an Old English usage of the word 'haw': denoting a hedge, and may indicate that the land may once have been an enclosure for winter pasture.

Although it cannot be ascertained that Walter Chrisfield of Thurnham actually built a dwelling at Winter Haw, he was certainly occupying the land by October 1685. The land had once belonged to John Godden, described as 'late of London', when he conveyed it to Walter Chrisfield. Walter was a carpenter and is recorded as an Overseer of the Poor for St Mary's Church, Thurnham in 1628, before being appointed as Churchwarden 1630-1631. He became Overseer again in 1637.[2]

It is possible that Walter was related to John Chrisfield. An impression of the income and lifestyle the Chrisfield family enjoyed can be gained from the inventory that was compiled after John's death on 2 April 1684. John had occupied a property that included a hall chamber, a parlour chamber, a hall, a buttery, a brew house, a stable and a barn. His goods and chattels included twenty acres of wheat and twenty eight acres of ploughed ground and the seed for it. Evidently, John was a man of considerable substance as the listing for livestock included six horses, a score of sheep with lambs, two milk cows, six heifers of two years old and three yearling heifers, one colt and seven pigs.[3]

Below is shown some of the inventory:

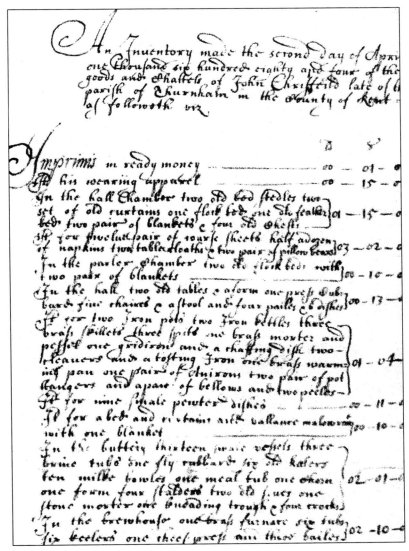

Reproduced courtesy of the Centre for Kentish Studies

111

In 1685, an elderly Walter and his wife, Sarah, together with Mary his daughter, agreed to lease their property to Henry Greene of Maidstone. Henry was described as a husbandman and he paid five shillings for the agreement.[4]

Thomas Chrisfield and John Sharpe were evidently later owners of the land as their names are included in a list of previous owners in a leasing agreement from 1705. Whether Thomas was related to Walter Chrisfield remains unclear. By this date, Henry Greene had married. He and his wife, Elizabeth, agreed to lease the land to John Pollard. John was to pay five shillings and a peppercorn was also required to be paid at the end of the lease. John was a bricklayer from Maidstone.[5] Perhaps John was interested in the close proximity of the tile and brick works in Ware Street.

Although subsequent records are fragmentary, some of the later history can be pieced together. On 30 October 1767 Hodsall Sale of Bearsted, yeoman, and James Price of Hollingbourne, farmer, leased a parcel of land to Thomas Southerden of Weavering, butcher. For five shillings, Thomas was able to occupy: [6]

> ...all seven several pieces or parcels, arable meadow and pasture known by the name of Winter Haw, Barnfield, Northfield, Two Twittens and the Two Meads...

Helpfully, some former occupiers of the land are also named in the leasing agreement and it is this information that links the documents together because Walter Chrisfield is included as a former occupier. Former occupiers were nearly always recited in this sort of property document. Although the aim was to prove the legal title to the holding, it also preserved its history. Thus, it can be learnt that subsequent occupiers were Christopher Forrester, Samuel Wilkins, Edmund Peachey and lately Mary Duckesbury, the younger, a widow.

Thomas Southerden also leased: [7]

> ...messuage, with yard, garden, and appurtenances, lately erected and built by Samuel Athawes upon parcel of the yard and ground...

Former occupiers were recorded as Samuel Neale, Thomas Peckham, Samuel Sale, Richard Peale and Hodsall Sale.[8] It is feasible that the property now known as 62-64 Ware Street was actually built by Samuel Athawes and replaced an earlier building.

The date of the leasing agreement is significant because of the next document in the sequence which is dated the following day; 31 October 1767. This is a copy of marriage settlement between Mary Duckesbury, the younger of Bearsted, a widow, and Hodsall Sale of Bearsted, yeoman. Mary's late husband was John Duckesbury, who was described as a gentleman of Bearsted.[9]

Mary and Hodsall married on 5 November 1767 at St Clement Danes parish church, London, by licence.[10] Perhaps Mary had already received her marriage settlement in writing. It confirmed that amongst her land holdings would be Hodsall's lands of Winter Haw and the same package of land outlined in the earlier document.

Hodsall made his will on 24 May 1768 and the same day, he and his wife leased the land package to Thomas Punnett.[11] Between 1770 and 1789 Hodsall and Mary used the land to assist the financing of a mortgage for £1800 (around £166,470 today)[12] from Mary Drewery of East Farleigh, widow, and Thomas Crispe of Loose Court of Loose, gentleman.[13] This was an enormous sum of money but whatever the reason for the loan, no further details survive.

However, whatever the reason for the loan, there was some difficulty in repayment as the property continued to be leased and re-leased to raise funds. The names of the tenants to take leases include Christopher Hull, the younger, of Inner Temple, Lincoln's Inn, gentleman, and Richard Webb, of Bearsted, yeoman. Occupiers of the property included Thomas Mills, John Jury and Hodsall Sale.[14] The money was eventually repaid following the marriage of Hodsall and Mary's daughter, Mary Duckesbery Sale to Richard Webb on 12 November 1790.[15]

Nine years later, Richard and Mary leased the property to Jesse Webb, who is believed to be Richard's brother, together with John Budds.[16] Hodsall Sale died in 1803 and under the terms of his will, his daughter Mary, inherited his estate, although she was a substitute executrix, as her mother had died after the will had been drawn up.[17] Mary Webb died in 1818, aged fifty. Five years later, Richard also died, aged fifty-two. Although Richard died intestate, under the laws of gavelkind, the land holdings passed to their sons; also called Richard and Jesse. They obtained administration of the estate on 14 November 1823.[18]

A map for the late Richard Webb's estate was prepared in 1824, the sale of which took place on 26 August at the Bull Inn, Maidstone.[19] This detail below is taken from the map and shows Winter Haw. The area marked C was the house facing Ware Street:

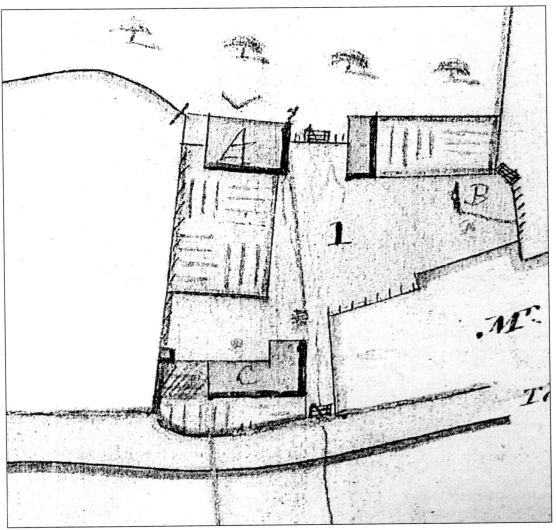

Reproduced courtesy of the Centre for Kentish Studies

Although it is not known who bought the property, a subsequent indenture, recorded that the premises listed in 1767 were now occupied by Bidingfield Wise together with Joseph Nealby and Edward Briggs. The leasing agreement was confirmed in 1826.[20]

Again, the records about the land become fragmentary until 1842, when an indenture of sale and re-lease was signed. The parties were Thomas Taylor, of Wormshill, farmer, William Brice also of Wormshill, a yeoman, and Joseph Nealby. The current occupier was recorded as Josiah Dawes.[21]

Josiah continued to occupy the premises despite the new owner, Thomas Taylor using the land to secure a loan from Henry Robert Coulter for £500 on 15 December 1842.[22] The schedule which accompanies the tithe map for Thurnham confirms Josiah's tenancy, listing him as occupying plots forty-three to forty-six, forty-eight and forty-nine. The total landholding amounted to fifteen acres and nine perches.[23]

In 1848 some of the holdings were sold by Thomas Taylor to Sir George Hampson, who is described in the sale document as Lord of the Manor of Thurnham. However, Thomas did not sell all of the holdings: two cottages, a garden and an associated right of way to them remained. Although it is not certain whether this was Winter Haw, there is a distinct hint about this in a later document because by 20 October 1848, Thomas and Henry agreed to separately convey Winter Haw to Lady Hampson.[24]

By 1866, Winter Haw was included on an estate map drawn for the Hampson family. Plot 83 included a barn, oast house and road recorded as occupied by William Streatfield.[25] The barn and oast house were still in good repair in the 1920s when the land became the site of Rosemount Dairy.

It is difficult to shed any more light upon subsequent occupiers of Winter Haw during the later half of the nineteenth century, as the census returns are not sufficiently detailed for Ware Street. The name Winter Haw appears to have fallen into disuse and the census returns do not give house numbers for Ware Street. In addition, the area now contained more houses, which were subsequently re-built or sub-divided, making specific identification of properties on records difficult. However, local people remembered that around 1900, a property in the vicinity of Winter Haw was occupied by a member of the White family.

Amelia and Horace White are certainly listed in the census returns for Ware Street although it is by no means certain at which property they resided. They had married in October 1864 at St Mary's church. Between 1873 and 1878, the parish rate books shows Horace as occupying a cottage and garden with seven perches of land which was owed by Mrs Tolhurst. Although names of properties in Ware Street regularly changed to reflect their owners, it is possible that this is one of the cottages included in what is now known as either Nos. 6-8 Ware Street, or Neatherton Cottages.[26]

Horace was a builder. One of their sons, Frederick, married Emma Jane Coomber 7 April 1890.[27] He followed his father in the same trade. Tom could remember that they lived at what is now referred to as Nos. 62-64 Ware Street. Below is shown an account issued by Frederick for work undertaken on the school house at Thurnham School:

Reproduced courtesy of the Gordon Ward collection, Kent Archaeological Society

In 1890 Frederick was commissioned to build a parish room next door to St Mary's church. However, it only functioned as a parish room for a short time because many people in Ware Street still preferred to attend services and other meetings at the Mission Hut. The building was later converted to a residence.

Emma and Frederick had five children. Their eldest child was named Ernest. He was married to Agnes and they lived at 2 Chapel Lane. He was tragically killed in action during August 1918 [28] whilst his wife was expecting their second child. The rest of the White family looked after his widow and children who became known as Little Agnes and Little Ernest.

Another of Emma and Frederick's sons was named Walter Victor to reflect his birth on Queen Victoria's birthday. Their youngest son was called Stanley. His niece, Evelyn Fridd (née White) could recall him telling her that at the time of his birth in 1907, his parents home had sufficient space for a stable with a couple of ponies, a workshop and a builder's yard.

Between 1891 and 1929 Frederick undertook a number of repairs to Church Cottages. There are many entries in the Thurnham parish accounts for payments made to him for work undertaken.[29] Walter carried on the building trade but it seems that he did not stay in Ware Street as in the 1930s, he moved to Sutton Street and then to Thurnham.

Although there are photographs and postcards of Ware Street, the Winter Haw area does not seem to feature in many of them. This undated photograph below is a detail from an overall view of Ware Street. Part of what is now known as No. 64 is on the right hand side of the picture. Note the dormer window and spacious garden at the side of the property:

Reproduced courtesy of Malcolm Kersey

However, this photograph does not make it clear that the property was rather more extensive than it appears today. By the twentieth century it was subdivided into several dwellings and they were known as Oak Cottages. Members of the Watkins and Martin families occupied two of them.

The photograph below shows Jessie Martin standing by the front door of what is today called 62 Ware Street. It is probably the only remaining visual record which indicates that there was once an adjoining cottage on the right hand side:

Reproduced courtesy of Ann Lampard and Lynda Copsey (née Martin)

In 1939 one of the cottages was occupied by George and Laura Bonner. Their nearest neighbour was Mary Bodiam, who was living there with her son Frank, a widower, and his daughter, Ellen.[30] Mary's great grand daughter, Audrey Fermor recalled that Mary's husband, Frederick had died in 1936.

Mary and Frank's cottage was badly damaged by a fire on 12 April 1940. A beam located by the chimney had smouldered all night before igniting. It was well known in the family that Mary, Frank and Ellen were only rescued by being pulled from an upstairs window. The family lost virtually all their possessions except the nightclothes they were wearing. Two pets; a dog and a budgerigar, died in the fire. A careful, but fruitless search was made for a wedding ring which had been kept in a piece of furniture in the bedroom over the front door.

After the fire, Audrey's great-aunt offered accommodation to the family at Tovil in Maidstone. Frank later re-married and returned to Bearsted, setting up home at 1 Triangle Cottages.

The property was subsequently found to be structurally unsound. It took some time to demolish the fire-shattered remains and a wall was later built over the site of the destroyed property. The area then became part of the garden and surroundings of 62 Ware Street.

These photographs, taken a few years after the fire, show part of the front garden of 62 Ware Street. The remains of the adjoining property are clearly visible in the background. In the left hand photograph, Ann Martin is being held by her mother, Vera. The right hand photograph shows Ann's younger sister, Lynda, in a pram with Vera alongside:

This next photograph was taken in the front garden of 62 Ware Street in July 1955 and gives a good impression of the view up Ware Street towards Sandy Mount farm. Lynda Martin is the youngest child and stands in front of her cousin, Yvonne Gilbert. Lynda's parents, Fred and Vera are behind them. The Mission Hut is in the background on the right hand side:

All reproduced courtesy of Ann Lampard and Lynda Copsey

By the late 1960s there had been a great deal of development in Ware Street. The Foster family had given up farming at Sandy Mount and a small housing estate was almost complete. The bungalows in Sharsted Way had also been constructed. Further properties in Ware Street continued to be extended or changed in other ways.

There had also been changes at 62-64 Ware Street. Vera Martin's parents, Bertie and Emma Watkins, had moved from the cottages opposite the railway station to No 64 in the mid-1950s. Fred and Vera Martin now owned No. 62, but in 1964, they moved to Romney Close opposite the coachworks on the Ashford Road which he owned. No. 62 was subsequently rented out, and Emma acted as a contact point for the tenants.

During the 1960s, there were minor changes to the properties: for many years there was a substantial wooden garage at the back of No. 62. It was replaced by a brick-built structure at the end of a concrete drive which ran alongside the cottage. The wooden garage is clearly shown on the right hand side of this undated photograph of Lynda playing by an upturned metal bedstead at the back of the property. In the background, the side and rear view of Stocks farmhouse can be seen:

Reproduced courtesy of Lynda Copsey

Around this time, both cottages had gabled porches added and the dormer windows in the roof were removed. At No. 62, a bathroom and separate lavatory was added in a small extension at the back of the house when main drainage was installed in Ware Street. The original 'privy' arrangements comprising a small shed were retained at the bottom of the garden, although it was later converted to a garden store.

There were many internal beams, although none of the tenants seemed aware of the age of the property. The attic extended the entire length of the building and was accessed via a steep flight of stairs behind a door in the front bedroom of No. 62.

Access to the bedrooms at No. 62 was unconventional by modern standards. The master bedroom in the front had a door at the top of the stairs from the ground floor. The other two bedrooms were at the back of the property, with the second accessed from the front bedroom and the third accessed from the second. There was a panel set into the kitchen ceiling which could be removed in order to gain access to the back bedrooms from below. In an arrangement known as a 'flying freehold', much of the third bedroom was effectively in No. 64, sharing two internal walls and located above a room in the other property.

In the last thirty years, the cottage has been bought and sold several times and various renovations, modernizations, and extensions completed. This photograph below was taken in 1999 and shows the results of recent renovations:

Reproduced courtesy of Malcolm Kersey

No. 64 is on the left hand side of the photograph. The lower roofline at the back of No. 62 was once part of the bathroom extension. All the windows are modern replacements of a different design to the original fittings.

Since this photograph was taken, the property has changed hands once more and further work has been undertaken. Another new property now stands on the former garden of No. 64.

Rosemount Dairy Farm and Henry Hodges

Almost directly behind Winter Haw stands the property known as Rosemount. Many people are unaware that not only was this the most recent farm holding in Ware Street but in the first half of the twentieth century, it was also the biggest private building project. The origins of the idea for the dairy began in the 1880s with Henry Hodges; a fiercely determined young man with an overwhelming ambition. His parents, Henry and Mary (née Foster) both came from families that had lived in Thurnham and Bearsted for many generations.

The fulfilment of Henry's ambition began with a gift from Hubert Bensted, an architect living in Thurnham Lane. Hubert was rather taken with Henry, who was working for him as a gardener and gave him a cow as a present.

This undated photograph shows Henry, as a young man, working in Mr Bensted's garden:

Reproduced courtesy of Jean Jones

The cow was the start of a dairy business which Henry managed to build up fairly quickly. He ran it from his home at 1 Ware Street, although the cattle were pastured on rented land elsewhere in Bearsted and Thurnham. Henry's wife, Ellen, had many talents and quickly found that she was especially good at making butter. Jean Jones (née Hodges) often used to watch her grandmother shaping the pats of butter with a pair of wooden 'scotch hands'. Both Henry and Ellen longed to have their own farmhouse and dairy.

120

1 Ware Street was part of the Milgate estate, owned by Walter Fremlin. In addition to the small dairy operation, Ellen ran part of the premises as a small shop. It was her proud boast that you could buy anything there from a pin to an elephant, but she mainly sold confectionery. Although the forge which had been run from the premise had long since fallen into disuse, the shop was still called Old Forge Stores. Jean still has many screw-top sweet jars and Sharps toffee tins that came from the shop.

This picture shows Ellen Hodges outside her shop, accompanied by a member of the Shorter family:

Reproduced courtesy of Jean Jones

Ellen and Henry had two sons, George and Henry[1] who both went to Thurnham School. Henry (usually called Harry) was good at school but like many boys in the village, left when he was aged 14. He achieved a perfect attendance record and was awarded a solid silver medal with seven extra bars: one for each year of attendance during 1904-1910. Whilst he was growing up, he used to toboggan down Sandy Lane in snowy weather. He often visited the donkeys that were kept in a neighbouring field owner and which were used to transport goods to and from the railway station. The owners lived locally.

Henry was able to run a small dairy business from the family home but intended to have proper premises and a house built when he had sufficient capital. The First World War interrupted his business plans as both George and Harry had to serve in the army. Harry was severely wounded during fighting. While a stretcher party was recovering him from the battlefield, gas shells landed nearby and he was badly gassed when the bearers dropped him. Harry was rendered unfit to serve. Following his discharge, he returned to Thurnham and rejoined his father in running the dairy business. George continued in the army and reached the rank of Sergeant Major. His service included a spell in India.

This undated photograph shows Harry in his uniform:

Photograph courtesy of Jean Jones

Eventually, through many years of careful management, dedication and sheer hard work, Henry managed to save £800 in half crown pieces.[2] Around 1921, he bought the plot of land which lay between Winter Haw and the railway line. The purchase included an acre of ground and an oast house which was already on the site.

As part of Henry's grand design, a farmhouse needed to be built on the land to accommodate the Hodges family. It was constructed with bricks made at the brickfield in Ware Street which were transported to the building site by cart. It was probably the last major order for the Bearsted Brick Company. Henry's natural habit of careful management certainly came to the fore during the construction of the house; some of the windows came from Hollingbourne workhouse which had just been demolished. The family moved into their new home in 1923.

Although there was no garden, Ellen was confident that with time and opportunity, there would be one. She achieved this a few years later when she was able to supervise some landscaping and develop her horticultural plans. Once again, the Hodges family habits came into their own as the rose arches were obtained from the Milgate estate dispersal sale. The principles of thrift, economy and recycling wherever and whenever possible were by no means unusual in Ware Street; in nationally hard economic times what money existed in the community during the 1920s and 1930s was earned, as the local saying confirmed, 'the hard way'.

This undated photograph shows Henry and his wife by the house. Note the thatched hayrick:

This photograph of the farm is undated but was taken during winter, possibly from Sandy Lane, and gives a good overall impression of the holding. The farmhouse is in the left hand side with the railway line behind it. Note also the oast house to the right and the cow sheds in front of the farmhouse. In the foreground can be seen the large garden attached to No. 64 Ware Street, which is just visible on the right hand side of the photograph. This view gives an indication of the extent of the holding once called Winter Haw:

Both reproduced courtesy of Jean Jones

Harry's son, also called Harry, married Alice Goodwin from Otham. She had been in service at Barty House, which at that time was owned by the Wallace family. Their first home was a house in Ware Street called Arcady. It was sufficiently close to Rosemount for Harry to continue to assist his father in his business. This detail, from an undated postcard of Ware Street, shows the property.

The winter of 1927 was hard; there were many days of low temperatures and freezing nights. Thick snow had fallen and all the telephone wires were down. Like many small communities, Ware Street was virtually cut off from the outside world. Despite this, farm animals still had to be fed and milked; some how the farmers coped. On Christmas Day there was no respite from the terrible weather. Alice was heavily pregnant and on her way to Rosemount Farm in the snow, when she fell over. She went into labour and with Harry's assistance, returned to Arcady. After two days, the baby had still not arrived and help was clearly needed. A neighbour pulled socks over his boots and walked over to Hollingbourne to summon the doctor, using only a small hurricane lamp to help him find his way. In the event, all was well and Jean safely arrived.

The Hodges and Goodwin families regularly participated in the hop picking at Otham. Despite the hard work, it was a good opportunity to catch up with all the family news. Jean recalled that although the hop gardens were not very far away, it seemed quite distant to Ware Street. This picture shows Jean in 1935, hop picking in Otham with her grandmother Goodwin, Aunt Min, and her cousin, Walter Goodwin:

Both reproduced courtesy of Jean Jones

The family attended services at the Mission Room in Ware Street. It was rather closer and more convenient than St Mary's church in Thurnham Lane. The Mission Room was heated by a farrier's stove which still had an opening in which to place irons before applying them to a horse's hoof. Jean was baptised there.

Jean has many good memories of her family's farm and growing up in Ware Street. On hot summer days it always seemed to be quiet and few sounds, apart from the trains running along the railway line, intruded. It was a place which seemed to have its own rhythm and pace of life despite the gathering storm as events led up to the Second World War.

This is one of Jean's favourite family photographs. She is the small girl being carefully supervised on one of the farm horses by her grandfather, Henry Hodges:

Reproduced courtesy of Jean Jones

During the war, the family were fully aware that the proximity of the railway line might cause problems to them. It was well known that a train engine had to be fully stoked on order to climb the gradient before arriving at the railway station. Harry was concerned that German pilots would attack the railway line as it led to Maidstone, a closed military town.

Harry's fears were justified one night, when a bomb embedded itself in the far side of the railway line before detonating. It was less than thirty yards from the farmhouse. Fortunately, there was no damage caused other than to the embankment and the metal rails, which were twisted and buckled. Robert Skinner, the headmaster of Bearsted School had been on Observer duty that night and from his post, could see matters unfolding. Jean has never forgotten the relief on Robert's face when she walked into school, safe and well, the next morning.

After Harry took over the dairy business from his father, he was able to make further developments. Jean had a brother who also worked for the dairy. A two-wheeled cart with 'Hodges, Rosemount Dairy' written on the side was purchased and used for the milk round. Jean recalled that she used to jump on the back of it, but was wary of tipping it up. Later the deliveries were conducted in a motorbike and sidecar.

125

These two pictures show Harry with the vehicles that were used for deliveries:

Both reproduced courtesy of Jean Jones

The Hodges family ran the dairy at Rosemount Farm for many years but they were in a similar situation to the Foster family at Sandy Mount: as Bearsted and Thurnham began to change in the 1960s. There was little room for a small, family-run dairy business. It was a difficult decision to sell, but the economics which had led to commercial success for her grandfather and her family had changed once more.

Jean continues to live in Ware Street but in recent years, the farm house that had been her family's achievement has now been greatly altered and extended. The oast house has also been converted into a family dwelling.

Aaron Hunt and an off-licence, Ware Street

For many years, there were very few shops in Ware Street and before the second half of the twentieth century, there were relatively few purpose-built, solely commercial premises in Bearsted and Thurnham. The majority of those which existed seem to have occupied only part of the building as it was thought quite usual for shops to comprise just one room of an existing property.

The land upon which a property came to be built and included a one-room shop can be traced back to a map compiled in 1709. This indicates that an area on the north side of Ware Street, located just before a lane (which is now called Chapel Lane) was owned by Peter Atthawes.[1]

Around 1780, the property was owned by the Goldridge family. John Goldridge was noted in a land tax assessment that year as paying twelve shillings quarterly for the property.[2] When he died on 3 March 1785 he left his interests in the property to his children and grandsons.[3] Matters in the estate became complicated as his grandson, also called John, ignored the provisions in his grandfather's will and married two years before achieving his majority. Had the younger John defiantly married Ann Burrows at a church in the City of Westminster in the face of family opposition? This cannot now be ascertained, but by doing so, he forfeited his share of the property. In 1785, the property was occupied by Thomas Brork. He` was succeeded by Richard Bruge, and Anne Masters, the relict and widow of John Beeson.[4]

By 1789, Richard Obee, a bricklayer from Thurnham, was living at the dwelling. He originally paid £40 for the lease, (just under £3,700 today) and, in due course, renewed it.[5] The Goldridge family still owned the premises and the lease document yields information about them. The interested parties included Richard Goldridge of Bearsted and Elizabeth his wife, John Utting of King Street, Southwark, and his wife Sarah, and Elizabeth Goldridge, of West Malling. Richard is described as a carpenter, John was a gunsmith and Elizabeth was a spinster. The lease also indicates that the property had once contained at least two messuages and tenements but was now to be regarded as one messuage. The property was described as lying:[6]

> ...abutting to the King's Highway leading from the town of Maidstone...towards the town of Ashford to the north....

Below are reproduced some of the seals and signatures from the lease:

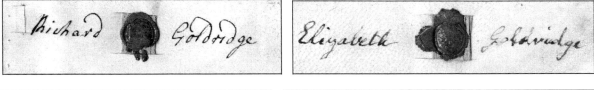

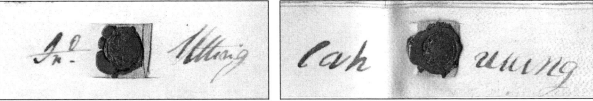

Reproduced courtesy of Michael Perring

Interestingly, the property details specify:[7]

> .....all that one other Messuage or tenement...heretofore used or occupied as two Messuages or tenements together with the Beaufet and Oven Door or Lid with all the shelves therein...

Evidently, there was a part of the premises which particularly merited a description and perhaps therefore indicate a facility that was worth noting on lease documents. However, whether the oven was already being used for commercial purposes; such as for baking bread for sale, remains unknown.

The records for the property recommence with the 1841 census when Thomas Coker was recorded as living there.[8] Thomas was aged fifty five and a baker. Also resident were some of his children, John aged twenty five and a butcher; Mary, aged twenty and a spinster. As Henry was running his bakery business from the premises, there would have been at least one outhouse for baking it. Just three years later, Thomas died and was buried in St Mary's churchyard, Thurnham, on 21 January.[9]

When the tithe apportionment map was drawn up in 1843, although the property is shown on the map, there are remarkably few details about it. The accompanying schedule merely indicates that it was part of a plot of land held by the Rev Charles Cage, vicar of Bearsted. The tenant is not specified.[10]

By 1847 another section of the Cocker family was living in Ware Street. Although it is not clear whether Henry Cocker was Thomas's son, he was certainly earning his living as a baker and shop keeper from the same premises. Henry had been born in West Kingsdown.[11] He was married to Susan, and by the 1851 census Ellen and George, aged four and two, respectively, had been born.[12]

Eight years later, Henry's enterprise had slightly changed as he was described as a grocer, brewer and beer retailer.[13] It is likely that the bakery outhouse was now being used for more than one purpose. By 1861, Henry had three more children: Eliza, John and Kate.[14] In 1862, the property was in the ownership of Charles, Earl of Romney[15] so it is possible that a tenancy agreement was not renewed. Although Henry was recorded in the 1862 parish rate book as liable to pay £17 5s,[16] there is certainly no trace of the family in subsequent records for Thurnham, so it is likely that the Cocker family then moved from Ware Street.

Between the 1871 and 1881 census, Aaron Hunt, and Frances, his wife, and their family moved in to Ware Street. Aaron had been born in Brenchley. By 1874, he was evidently earning a living as trading as a grocer because he was listed under this category in a trade directory.[17]

In the 1881 census returns, Aaron and Frances had four children: Sidney, William, Margaret and Albert. Apart from Sidney, who had been born in Edenbridge, all the children were born in Thurnham. The property was specifically listed as a shop but Aaron's occupation was given as a wheelwright journeyman rather than a fulltime wheelwright.[18] Like many people in Bearsted and Thurnham, Aaron had diversified and ran the shop in addition to his craft or trade.

By 1883, the property had become part of a jointly owned estate which included James Whatman of Vinters Park[19] and was included as lot two in a sale held at the Star Hotel, Maidstone, on 12 April. At the time of the sale, the property already had a licence to sell beer, but consumption on the premises was not permitted.[20] There are no further details about this licence.

The property was bought by Albert Style for £280 and conveyed on 25 June 1883. The Deed of Conveyance includes a good description of the property: [21]

> ..all that messuage, dwelling house, shop and cottage with the stable, cart lodge, and garden thereto belonging as the same are more particularly delineated in the map or plan drawn in the margin of these presents…now in the occupation of Aaron Hunt situate at Ware Street…

Albert Style was part of the Style family that eventually went into partnership with the Winch family in Maidstone. They became known as Style and Winch. The company were well-known for the number of off-licences that they supplied. It is feasible that Albert Style had seen that the property already had an Off-Sales Licence and decided to invest in it.

Below are shown some of the sale particulars: [22]

LOT TWO.

That Freehold Dwelling House,

AND

SHOP AND COTTAGE,

With good Garden, a Stable and Cart Lodge, situate at Ware Street, Thurnham,

The Dwelling house being Licensed for the Sale of Beer to be consumed off the Premises.

The whole is let to Mr. Aaron Hunt, a yearly tenant,

At a Rental of £15 per annum.

THERE IS A WELL OF WATER UPON THE PREMISES.

Certain Fixtures belonging to the Tenant are not included in this Sale.

Reproduced courtesy of the Centre for Kentish Studies

As the twentieth century began, the Hunt family were still living in their tile-hung house and part of the property continued to be run as small shop. By this time, Aaron was assisted by Ethel and Maude. This photograph shows the shop and off-licence. Note the painted sign over the door and the hanging tiles that are just visible on the top left hand side. It is not known who is in the photograph, but it is probably Aaron Hunt and two of his daughters:

Reproduced courtesy of Roger Vidler

The earliest entries in the register of licences held in the Centre for Kentish Studies record Aaron Hunt as the licence holder from 1906 to 1927.[23] Thereafter, the licence passed to Maude Hunt, one of his daughters.[24] Maude held the licence whilst Aaron continued to be listed in trade directories as a grocer for many years.

This undated photograph below shows Aaron Hunt's shop in Ware Street on the left hand side. The weather-boarded house next door was occupied by the Cooper family:

Reproduced courtesy of Terry Clarke

Maude gave up the licence in 1928 and was succeeded by Adelaide Hunt.[25] She was another member of the Hunt family and ran the premises until 1945 when the licence was taken over by Aubrey Brook Winch. He was succeeded by Leonard Vinten.[26]

Many people who grew up in Bearsted and Thurnham during the 1950s, have fond memories of the small off-licence establishment that was universally known as Ma Vinten's. In addition to a small amount of off-sales, sweets, crisps and snacks were sold from the premises. It was frequently rumoured that if Mr and Mrs Vinten ran out of beer, they would keep a customer talking whilst another member of the household ran down to The Bell public house for a fresh supply!

Roy Barham recalled that the Vinten family kept a goat at the property. It used to wander into the bar area and look as if it needed to be served. However, the main reason why Ma Vinten's was particularly attractive for children was purely because Mr and Mrs Vinten were always so accommodating to young people. They always treated them as proper customers who were respected and valued rather than just being viewed as a nuisance. Pamela Message (née Pye) remembered that although she and her friends were too young to drink alcohol, Mrs Vinten would happily serve them lemonade or make them hot blackcurrant drinks in the winter months.

Leonard Vinten held the licence from March 1946 to 1952. Evidently, he was the last licence-holder as it was subsequently not renewed. However, it took some time for the compilers of the Kelly's trade directory to up date their records as Leonard was recorded in the entry for Thurnham as a beer retailer at the premises in 1956.[27]

In the late 1950s the history of the property came to an end. Despite continuous maintenance by the families who lived there, it is likely that by this time they would have needed considerable renovation in order to continue to use them as residences. Demolition followed and the land was later re-developed for further housing.

Ware Mead and the farm in Chapel Lane

In 1709, John Watts was commissioned to draw an estate map for William Cage. Part of the map clearly shows that in the lower part of Ware Street, there was land called Ware Mead. However, this was not part of the manor of Ware. As shown previously, it was not unusual for an arrangement whereby isolated areas of land actually belonged to another manor. This part of Ware Street certainly reflects this arrangement although how it came to be part of the manor of Thurnham is not clear.

Some of the earliest records about the land date from the fourteenth century: in 1374 permission was granted by Sir John de Northwode who held the manor of Thurnham, to John Meggil to use the land for pasture after a hay crop had been taken. Further permission for pasture on the land was agreed by Nicholas Wotton in 1411 to John Meggyll.[1]

Below is shown an interpretation of the relevant section of the map: [2]

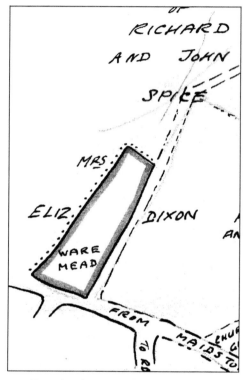

Reproduced courtesy of Michael Perring

Evidently, Ware Mead was surrounded by land held by Mrs Elizabeth Dixon. There is very little information about Elizabeth, but it is evident that she was certainly regarded as a prominent person in the area. She is the only woman specified as a land holder on the map.

By 1742, Ware Mead had become part of the lands owned by John Cage of Coombe in Thurnham. John used it as security to obtain a loan of £700. By 1764, as part of the Manor of Thurnham, it was included in part of the Surrenden-Dering estate, becoming part of the marriage settlement of Deborah Winchester to Sir Edward Dering. In 1842 when the Manor of Thurnham was sold to Dame Mary Hampson, Ware Meadow was noted as occupied by John Beeching.[3]

The map clearly shows a path where Chapel Lane is located today, as it leads north from Ware Street. About 30 yards along the track, on the left hand side, local Methodists built Providence Chapel in 1818.[4,5] Unfortunately, the land chosen was not suitable; flooding was a constant problem due to the close proximity of a stream. By 1849, the congregation had decided that a new building was needed elsewhere but it was not until 1875 that a new site was obtained in Ware Street. The replacement chapel was built virtually opposite a track which is known today as Hog Hill. The original chapel was demolished in 1877.

It is not known when the lane started to be called Chapel Lane, but it is possible that it was informally known as this for many years before passing into everyday usage and official documents.

In 1884, part of the land at Ware Mead facing Ware Street, including that formerly occupied by the chapel, was used to accommodate the railway line between Ashford and Maidstone, which opened later that year. In the twentieth century, part of the remaining land was occupied by Kent Frozen Foods. The railway is carried over Chapel Lane on an arch bridge of very fine brickwork.

There are very few records about Chapel Lane Farm. However, in 1995 Julian Swift appraised the building prior to renovation and restoration. He discovered that there were at least five phases to the current property. Rupert Austin from the Canterbury Archaeological Trust also undertook a survey. Evidence was found which indicated that the first building on the site was probably erected during the fifteenth century and comprised a hall house, largely constructed from oak. At least two mullion windows remain from this phase of construction, as does one bay with particularly low eaves which has been incorporated into one end of the present building.[6,7]

This photograph of the farmhouse, facing Ware Street was taken in November 2005:

Reproduced courtesy of Roger Vidler

The second phase of building probably took place in the early sixteenth century. The rather low roof was removed and the supporting posts raised to the current height of the eaves. At the same time, a hall house with a crown post roof was built. This incorporated part of a fifteenth century bay but also had another two bays to the east of the earlier section. There were new wooden floors made of elm. The trusses and braces for the crown post, the collars and collar purlins are still in the roof. The particularly slender wooden framework of the roof is reminiscent of those found in barns of the same date. A further set of six mullion windows with horizontal sliding shutters was also installed.[8]

During the second phase, a smoke bay was built. Smoke-bays were small areas, divided from the rest of the house with lath and daub panels to contain the hearth. They were open to the roof and formed an integral part of the building. They are believed to be the next stage in the evolution from an open hearth to a completely enclosed fireplace or hearth with a chimney. There are remarkably few dwellings which were of a 'transitional' form which still exist today; Chapel Lane Farm is, therefore, a rare example. Some of the smoke-blackened remnants, together with the rafters remain. In addition to the screens, the hearth would have featured a large timber beam known as a bressumer, which may have looked very similar to that still in place over the later inglenook fireplace.[9]

There was access past the smoke bay at ground level as some original door posts still remain, together with a door frame in the rear wall of the centre bay. There is evidence of a passage at the first floor level. A staircase probably lay behind a partition at the east end of the front of the house.[10]

There were further alterations to the house during the late sixteenth and early seventeenth centuries. It is believed that smoke bays were a brief phase in the development of hall houses, lasting only around a hundred years before being abandoned in preference to continuously floored buildings with chimney stacks. At Chapel Lane Farm, the smoke bay was substantially altered by the insertion of a three flued chimney structure made of bricks with two large fireplaces at ground floor, usually called inglenooks. These are still present, together with the entire brick stack and a first floor fireplace which retained the original hearth and even traces of the original pink lime wash finish.[11] The kitchen fireplace also retained the original hearth. A bread oven was built into the thickened jamb of the main room fireplace and it was designed to be integral to the main chimney stack. It may well have been that at this time that a staircase to the attic was constructed.[12]

Towards the end of the seventeenth century, the roof was altered once more and an attic mullion window in oak was added.[13]

During the mid-eighteenth century, a large proportion of the roof was replaced. The original rafters were renewed with Scots pine using joints copied from the originals. Perhaps this work was undertaken during a scheme of renovation under the direction of Charles, Earl of Romney, who was the owner at that time. Evidently, sufficient timbers were left over to use them in new ceilings and partitions in the property.[14,15]

Later alterations included adding another bread oven and moving the stairs. A modern chimney stack was added.[16]

There are no farm records which would give details of tenancies over many years prior to the 1790s. However, the Akehurst family were evidently at Chapel Lane Farm by 1797; William Akehurst is recorded paying the land tax for the property of £2 8s a quarter from this date.[17]

It is believed that a property near to the farmhouse, known today as St Anne's, may also date from medieval times. However, from the outside, it is evident that the dwelling was altered in the eighteenth century; there is also a rainwater hopper for the guttering which bears the initials E D and date 1797. It is tempting to link this with the Elizabeth Dixon mentioned previously, but there are no records to confirm this suggestion. Perhaps the property, was once part of the holdings for Chapel Lane Farm.[18]

In 1825 a burglary took place at Chapel Lane Farm, but it was a considerable time before a culprit was apprehended and a prosecution took place.

Edward, or Ned, Hart, and his family were like many ordinary people living at Thurnham in the first two decades of the nineteenth century. They were amongst the poorest members of society. When not sporadically employed, they received small amounts of money over many years from the parish overseers to support themselves. Between 1819 and 1824 Edward Hart regularly received payments.[19]

Edward had married Sarah Culley at St Mary's church on 24 August 1823. Sarah was expecting a child at the time of their marriage: their daughter, also called Sarah, was baptised on 5 September. On the next page is shown the marriage entry from the church register.[20]

Evidently Edward and Sarah were struggling financially after their marriage and the birth of their child. Between September and November, Sarah received a total of eighteen shillings in payments from the parish overseer.[21]

Edward and Sarah's marriage entry:

Reproduced courtesy of the Churchwardens and Parochial Church Council of St Mary's church

Edward was a brick layer. It is probable that he would have been employed at, or through, the brick and tile field in Ware Street which had recently been bought by Bidingfield Wise.[22] However, bricks were usually made only in the spring and summer, so although he was a skilled labourer, the work was seasonal. Because of the variability of his trade, Edward would have spent a great deal of time pursuing steady employment, turning his hand to whatever work was available. This is certainly borne out by the payments made to him from the parish as it is recorded that between 1822 and 1823 he was employed to dig and clear fields in and around Thurnham.[23]

Farming was under a great deal of economic pressure in the 1820s: the weather was poor and harvests were not good. The Napoleonic Wars had ended and the south of England had a great deal of spare workforce as soldiers returned from the continent and were discharged from the army. Wages were low, employment was scarce and food prices rose.

These were tough economic conditions for any family, but the pressure on the Hart family deepened when Sarah became pregnant again. It will never be known why Edward chose to burgle William Akehurst's house at Chapel Lane Farm, particularly when William had made payments to the Hart family during his stint as parish overseer in 1819 and 1820. Below is an entry from the parish overseer records, showing a payment made by William and received by Edward: [24]

1820			
29 January	Edward Hart two days lame	1s	6d

It remains open to question whether William thought that the theft was a reward for his assistance. The principal items listed as stolen were food and drink so perhaps it was the desperate action of a man who could think of no other way to provide food for his family. Frustratingly, the records that would show if Edward was still in receipt of poor relief from the parish in 1825 do not exist. The burglary was a catastrophic move: Edward went on the run.

135

Edward evaded arrest for approximately eighteen months before being apprehended on 2 July 1827. Below is shown a transcript of the report published on 21 August in the Maidstone Journal and Kentish Advertiser:

EDWARD HART was indicted with stealing one crock, a stone bottle and other articles, the property of William Akehurst, at Thurnham.

On the 3rd of February 1825, on rising in the morning, Mrs Akehurst found that some of the bricks were taken out of the wall of the house underneath the kitchen window. On going into the dairy, she found the pork all taken away, a ham, a stone bottle of wine, and other articles, to the value of about £2.

On the 4th of February, Mr Forster, the constable, searched the apartments of the prisoner and a man named Smith, and found a hand of pork, a leg and two cheeks, a bottle of parsnip wine and other articles belonging to Mr Akehurst. Hart was at the bottom of the stairs, and on the constable telling him he had a search warrant, he went out of the house. He was missing till the 2nd July last, when the constable overtook him with some soldiers near Maidstone. He was afterwards delivered up to a peace-officer in Maidstone.

Several witnesses gave the prisoner a good character.

Guilty. Sentence not passed.

Reproduced courtesy of Kent Messenger group

After Edward's departure, Sarah had been left heavily pregnant and with a small child to look after on her own. How Sarah coped with the absence of her husband remains uncertain. Edward, their second child, was baptised on 17 April 1825. By a curious quirk of events, Edward's baptism is on the same page of the register as George, the second son of John and Judith Dyke (née Cogger), who was baptised on 15 May. The two families knew each other: John had worked in the same fields alongside Edward.[25] It would be good to think that John and Judith had supported Sarah in her isolation, the later stages of pregnancy and even the birth of her child.

Below is shown the two entries on the same page of the baptism register: [26]

Reproduced courtesy of the Churchwardens and Parochial Church Council of St Mary's church

From the newspaper report, the details of Edward's arrest are ambiguous: was the constable accompanied by some soldiers when Edward was apprehended? Was Edward in the company of some soldiers because he had joined the army? Many of the newspaper reports at this time are not what they first might seem, there was a constant fear of being sued for libel. This meant that the writers of reports employed a great deal of allusion, relying on their readers being already familiar with the matters to which they referred. This makes it quite difficult for modern day readers to understand accurately what the reports might mean.

If Edward was with some soldiers near Maidstone because he had joined the army, his initial survival after leaving Sarah would have been made slightly easier. However, it was a risky step to take as he would not have been able to choose where to go with the army. If manoeuvres had brought him close to Maidstone, he must have been aware that he was running a risk of recognition. Alternatively, he may have been over-confident that because a considerable amount of time had elapsed since the crime, that he would not be caught. It remains open to question if he ever thought of seeing Sarah and the children.

Unfortunately, there are no further details available about the regiment which Edward may have joined, and by which his service with the army could have been traced. The Queens Own Royal West Kent Regiment were stationed in Jamaica from 1825 to 1827, which coincides with the time Edward was on the run, so this may account for his disappearance. Nevertheless, it is interesting to see that civil law had precedence over military law on this occasion; Edward was indicted and convicted for theft rather than army desertion. It was subsequently noted by the gaoler that he was an army deserter.[27]

Edward was committed to appear at the Summer Assizes at Maidstone on 16 August. He was one of a hundred and twenty five cases heard in one day and it did not take long to convict him. He was sentenced to transportation for seven years.[28] From 16 August to 31 August, Edward was then held at Maidstone Gaol before being moved on 1 September and put aboard a prison hulk, or ship, called *The Retribution* anchored at Sheerness.[29]

There is no record of his subsequent arrival in any penal colony, so there is a strong chance that he was not transported. Whatever the truth of the matter, Edward seemingly vanished from the local scene; there are no further records about his family in Thurnham.[30]

It is possible that this burglary had unexpectedly tragic consequences. In 1830, Chapel Lane Farm was one of two farms in Bearsted and Thurnham which were involved in disturbances. On the night of 9 November, the haystacks at the farm were fired. Also targeted were the barn and stable which were part of Otteridge Farm in Yeoman Lane, occupied by Michael Stokes.

It did not take long for the incidents to be considered part of the local social unrest, fully reported in the local newspapers, and quickly dubbed the Swing Riots, after a fictional Captain Swing who was said to be behind them. The unrest included written demands by labourers made under the pseudonym of Captain Swing for increased wages. Hay stacks and barns were set on fire and threshing machines were destroyed because of their potential for putting labourers out of work during the hard winter months.

John Dyke, or Field, was apprehended and charged with the firing and destruction of haystacks at Chapel Lane Farm together with firing the buildings at Otteridge Farm. The case went to trial and the witness statement from the court papers includes one from William, eldest son of William and Sarah Akehurst. Below is a partial transcript of William's statement: [31]

The Examination of William Akehurst the Younger of Thurnham in the County of Kent, Farmer, who says:

…I remember the night of my Father's Fire I was alarmed between 3 and 4 o'clock on Wednesday Morning the 10th November inst. A Deaf Man who then worked for Mr Clarke of Bearsted alarmed us by beating at the front of the House. We spoke to him several times and received no answer. I did not know him at that time. I looked out of the window and saw the man and heard him say Our Stacks were on fire. I believe the time was between 3 and 4 in the morning. Some parts of the stacks were saved by the use of the Engines and the rest was consumed. The stacks were my Father's Property…

Reproduced courtesy of the National Archives

There are several details in this account which are most intriguing. The deaf man that had roused the Akehurst family actually worked for Mr Redburn Clark of Bell House by Bearsted green. There is also a reference to engines attending the fire. It is not known whether Thurnham parish owned a fire engine so it is likely that the engines may have been owned by the Earl of Romney's family. The Earl certainly had the first insurance policy issued by the Kent Fire Insurance Office. Although fire brigades were in their infancy, the Kent Fire Insurance Brigade kept an office and engine yard in Maidstone. The limit of a Maidstone call was twenty miles. Ware Street was well within this distance,[32] but there is no record that Chapel Lane Farm was attended.

Unlike Michael Stokes, it appears that the Akehurst family had not insured the farm or its contents. They had no alternative other than to bear the financial loss from the destruction of the haystacks.

Other witness statements for the trial included one from William Hewitt, a farm labourer. Below is a partial transcript: [33]

...I know John Dyke. I have known him from a child. I remember his coming to my house on the Monday night before the fire at Stokes. I believe it was about 7 o'clock. He came to the Back Door - two of the children let him in - myself and my wife and children were at home. He stayed till about 9 o'clock my wife and he talked a good deal together about there he had been to at different places. I remember my wife asking him about the fires and whether he had joined the Rioters. He said he did not dare to be seen with them but he was a writer, then my wife said what send letters? And he said yes. I knew that he was°a° Deserter.

I remember saying to him 'Mr Stokes was telling me one day as I came along the Road any body might ride along the road and fire into the stacks as they pass'. Dyke made no answer. I then asked him about balls - what they were made of and whether he knew anything about them. He said they were made of gunpowder, spirits of turpentine, spirits of vitriol and a little aqua fortis...

Reproduced courtesy of the National Archives

The trial was fully reported in the local newspapers and below is a partial transcript from the Maidstone Journal, 30 November 1830, of the committal:

COMMITTAL OF INCENDIARIES

During the last fortnight, the police of Maidstone have been actively engaged in tracing an individual suspected of being concerned in some of the late outrages. We have carefully abstained from giving publicity to the different rumours which have prevailed, fearful of impeding the course of justice. We are now, however enabled to state the exertions of the Maidstone magistrates and their offices have been successful in obtaining a conclusive body of evidence against a man named John Dyke, who underwent a long examination, on Saturday last, before Colonel Shaw and W. G. D. Tyssen, Esq. It appears from the evidence of one of the witnesses, named Hewitt, that on the night before the fires at Bearsted, Dyke was at his house, and stayed there until 9 o'clock at night, conversing about the disasters in the county.

Hewitt asked Dyke if he joined the rioters, who replied that he did not, but that he was 'a Writer' doubtless meaning of threatening letters. Hewitt then asked him if he knew how the balls were made which the incendiaries were supposed to use, and he said, of gunpowder, spirits of turpentine, a little spirits of vitriol and aqua fortis. He then spoke of man named Hart, who some years previously, had been transported for a robbery at Mr Ackhurst's and Dyke said 'Hart was a good-hearted fellow'. He left Hewitt's house about 9 o'clock and about 2 o'clock in the morning, Hewitt was awoke by some one rapping at his bedroom window. On rising, he saw Dyke and asked what he wanted. Dyke gave him a dagger which he requested him to take to his grandfather's saying 'There is somebody about'. He then said, 'Ackhurst's stacks are alight and Stokes barn will soon be on fire.' He then went away.

In a few minutes after, Hewitt heard the alarm of fire, and found that Stokes's premises were in flames. Ackhursts's stacks were also on fire at the same time. He afterwards cautioned that circumstance to some gentleman of the neighbourhood and active steps being taken to secure Dyke. He was apprehended at Challock by Mr Fancett, the superintendent of the Maidstone police on Sunday week. On Dyke's person were found several threatening letters, signed 'Swing', which are in Mr Fancett's possession. Dyke is fully committed for trial at the next assize.

Reproduced courtesy of Kent Messenger group

It is interesting that William and Mary Hewitt's depositions for the trial specifically record that in the course of an evening's conversation, the following exchange had taken place: [34]

> ...Then after sitting a little while he said Ned Hart is gone, he was a good bottomed fellow. Ned Hart's name had not been brought up before. My husband asked him whether he knew where Ned was gone, he answered to New South Wales or Botany Bay...

Reproduced courtesy of the National Archives

From the newspaper accounts, Edward's departure was touched upon in the trial proceedings but not examined in depth.

Whether John had fired the stacks at Chapel Lane Farm to avenge Edward's prosecution and his believed subsequent transportation still remains open to question. Even by nineteenth century standards, there was not a great deal of evidence in the witness statements to support the allegation concerning arson at Chapel Lane Farm or at Otteridge Farm.

The charge concerning Chapel Lane Farm was not pursued, but John was convicted of firing the barn and stable at Otteridge Farm and received a death sentence. He was hanged on the gallows at Penenden Heath, 24 December 1830, and buried in Bearsted churchyard. It was the last public hanging on the Heath. As The Maidstone Gazette and Kentish Courier reported, John maintained his protestation of innocence to the end. It was estimated that around 5,000 people had attended his execution and although the Militia were in attendance, there was no trouble from the crowd. Many years later, it was reported that real culprit, on his deathbed, had confessed to setting the hay ricks on fire.[35]

If this confession is true, the details are still open to interpretation as it is not possible to be sure that the hay ricks mentioned in the confession were those at Chapel Lane Farm. The trial documents refer to the destruction of the barn and stable at Otteridge Farm, rather than anything else, but perhaps this is too precise an interpretation of the wording used. However, it would be a savage irony if the real truth of the matter was that John Dyke was convicted and hung for a crime that he did not commit, rather than the act of avenging his friend, Edward Hart, who did not, after all, sail to Botany Bay.[36]

After these dramatic incidents, there is a gap in the records for Chapel Lane Farm but in 1839, the lease for the farm tenancy was due for renewal. A partial transcript of the draft agreement giving details of a new lease between Charles, Earl of Romney and George Hills is shown below.

The package of lands included: [37]

> ...all that messuage or tenement (in two dwellings) with outbuildings, yards, gardens thereunto belonging situate in Ware Street in the parish of Thurnham containing by measure with the suite of buildings, one acre, fourteen perches, more or less. Also a piece or parcel of land called Wents Field situate in Ware Street, four acres, two rods, thirty one perches.
>
> All which parcel ...are now in occupation of said George Hills or his undertenant for the sum of £4 4s 0d at the remit of £20 paid half yearly on 5 April and 10 October in equal payments...

However, subsequent records indicate that George Hills may have been only a prospective tenant. It certainly seems that he did not take on the tenancy as less than five years later William Akehurst was recorded in the tithe apportionment schedule as occupying both Chapel Lane Farm and St Anne's, although the latter was now owned by Bidingfield Wise.[38]

William died in 1846. He had made his will on 31 August 1840, but it sheds no light on the subsequent disposal of the estate: the property or a tenancy is not specifically mentioned.[39]

The family continued to run the farm as the 1851 census shows William's wife, Sarah, still living there, assisted by her sons Robert, John and Thomas. Sarah was described as a farmer of sixty acres. The younger William, was married to Amelia, and lived a little distance from Chapel Lane Farm either in St Anne's or in Ware Street. He was described as a farmer of thirty one acres.[40]

Ten years later, there had been further changes. William was still farming and described himself as a farmer of 36 acres, assisted by Amelia, but they had moved from Ware Street into Chapel Lane. John Akehurst had taken over running the farm, which now comprised fifty seven acres of land and was assisted by a widowed sister in law, Caroline. John had not married but shared the property with his two nephews, John and Lewis and his niece Clara. All three children were under seven years of age.[41]

The 1862 parish rate book for Thurnham shows that both William and Thomas were rated on property and land in Ware Street, although two sections of the rateable holdings were described as owned by Miss Lucy Wise and Edward Hughes. Miss Wise was part of the Whatman family so evidently the ownership of the land and holdings had now passed into other hands. The precise date for this change remains unknown. The amount that the Akehurst family were liable to pay amounted to £76 10s.[42]

In 1866, a map which included Thornham and Ware Street showed the farm name as Pleasant Farm[43] but there are no other records to confirm that it ever bore this name. It is possible that this was an attempt by James Whatman to associate the farm with his other property at Mount Pleasant. However, when later versions of the map were published, the name had reverted to Chapel Lane Farm. Perhaps this is an instance of the local name for the farm prevailing over official usage.

In 1867 James Whatman arranged a mortgage between himself and two other parties: Frederick Woolaston and Stephen Heelis. It not certain if this is the first mortgage arranged with the farm used as security.[44] However, a series of mortgages seems to have been part of the usual financial arrangements within the Whatman family for the greater part of the nineteenth and twentieth centuries.

The 1871 census returns show that John Akehurst, a farmer of sixty acres, was still at Chapel Lane Farm. John had a housekeeper, Faith Meers, but Caroline Akehurst and her family were no longer living there. Instead, the accommodation was shared by George and Mary Marks together with their four sons and a daughter. George was a shoemaker. However, it is not clear if the farmhouse was divided into two properties with separate access arrangements or there was a degree of common consent within shared accommodation. William was still living in Chapel Lane but had reduced his land holding to just seven acres. By this time, he was aged sixty six and Amelia was seventy four.[45]

After the 1871 census and before the next, the Akehurst family decided to give up farming in Chapel Lane. They had weathered the tough economic conditions during the first half of the nineteenth century. They had undertaken their duties as Parish Overseers for Thurnham when their turn arose. They had coped with the stresses and strains of burglary, arson and two court cases, but time had passed and they faced increasing old age with its associated infirmities. After seventy five years working the land it cannot have been an easy decision. It was time to pass the farm on to different hands.

Chapel Lane in later years

During the 1870s there were changes and developments in Chapel Lane. As the area was set slightly apart from the rest of Ware Street, and was not on a main route to anywhere particular in Thurnham, the lane became almost a small sub-hamlet.

At an unrecorded point, but between 1871 and 1874, a new family arrived at Chapel Lane Farm. Henry Barrow was living there and paid a parish poor rate charge of 1s 1d upon it. Evidently, it was a short stay as the 1881 census return recorded the farm as occupied by Thomas Barney and his wife Ann. They were born in Bapchild and Milstead respectively. Their two sons, Robert and James, were also living there and assisting them in agricultural work.[1]

By 1873, a terrace of cottages had been built in Chapel Lane close to St Anne's, as Miss Wise was rated for them that year. They were called Wises Cottages, perhaps an allusion to the owner. Two of them were specifically noted as being occupied by George Marks and Edward Flood. George probably moved there from Chapel Lane Farm.[2]

In 1881 both St Anne's and one of the cottages were unoccupied. However George Marks, now noted as a cordwainer rather than a shoemaker, together with his wife, Mary and their children were still living in the terrace. Their neighbours were Henry and Frances Medhurst; James and Rachel Randall; John and Amy Tilby.[3] Later families to live at the properties included Emily and Edgar Pettipiere. Their daughter, Norah, was born there in 1916 and spent the majority of her early years living in Ware Street.

This photograph was taken in 2005 and shows the properties, which are now called Chapel Lane Cottages:

Reproduced courtesy of Malcolm Kersey

Sometime between 1881 and 1883, the Barney family ceased to run the farm and James Morris became the tenant. In 1883, a sale of some of the lands and properties held by Charles, Earl of Romney took place.[4]

Below are shown some of the sales particulars:

LOT ONE.

That Productive Plot of

FREEHOLD GARDEN GROUND

PARTLY PLANTED WITH CURRANTS,

Situate near the Junction of Weavering and Ware Streets at the four-went way, in the parish of Thurnham, near the Bell Inn, with a frontage to the High Road, and containing

4a. 2r. 23p.,

According to the Ordnance Plan, in the occupation of Mr. James Morris, a yearly tenant at a

Rental of £18 per annum.

KENT.

WARE STREET, THURNHAM.

Particulars & Conditions of Sale

OF VALUABLE

FREEHOLD PROPERTY,

COMPRISING

4a. 2r. 23p.

OF

Market Garden Ground

DWELLING HOUSE,

SHOP, AND ONE COTTAGE,

Having an off Beer Licence, let to yearly tenants,

Which will be submitted to Public Auction,

BY

Messrs. TOOTELL & SONS,

AT THE

STAR HOTEL, MAIDSTONE,

On Thursday, the 12th of April, 1883,

At 3 o'clock precisely, in Two Lots.

Both reproduced courtesy of the Centre for Kentish Studies

The package of land and messuage, previously tenanted by the Akehurst family for so many years, comprised Lot 1 and was bought by James Whatman for £435. James Morris, had planted some of the land with fruit trees which included a quantity of blackcurrant bushes. He was also using part of the land as a garden nursery. The sale was completed on 11 July 1883.[5]

There are many documents which accompanied the purchase but the most important is the draft conveyance for the sale, which included details of a claim.[6] Although Charles, Earl of Romney's late father, (also called Charles) had previously owned a share it was not until 29 March 1862 that sole possession was secured. The other interested parties were the Right Honourable James Henry, Earl of Court Town, County Wexford; The Right Honourable Sir William Hart Dyke of Lullingstone Castle; and Sir Edward Henry Scott of Sundridge Park, Bromley.

As indicated in a previous chapter, during the nineteenth century the majority of the land and holdings in the Chapel Lane area were held by members of the Whatman family. However, at the time of James Whatman's death in 1887, the family was not as wealthy as many people believed. James had spent a great deal of time, energy and finance diverting the railway line to Maidstone and Ashford from running through part of his estate at Vinters Park. From his estate papers, it is evident that James has used his property to secure finance.[7]

In order to begin addressing the muddled nature of the estate, sections were re-mortgaged whilst James' affairs were sorted out and his widow, Louisa secured her income. In the case of Chapel Lane Farm, this property had already been used as security as an indenture had been signed on 22 April 1887 between Louisa Whatman, her two daughters Florence and Louisa, and Alexander Ross.[8] Matters for the family were not helped by a Chancery Court Order which declared that the estate was insufficient to meet both debts and the funeral expenses.[9]

Probably as a result of the financial strain on the estate, barely three years later, the extended family agreed a mortgage between themselves and the Royal Exchange Assurance Company on Chapel Lane Farm. Subsequent, varied mortgages and other transfer arrangements concerning the financial arrangements for the farm made by the Whatman family persisted until the middle of the twentieth century.[10]

When the 1891 census was taken, Alfred Sale was the tenant. He ran the farm with his wife Sarah, aged 50 and their two children, Mary Ann and Ernest, aged 19 and 11. None of the family was born in Bearsted or Thurnham.[11]

The next tenants were probably Minnie and Henry Kemp as they were recorded as living at Chapel Lane Farm when their son, Alexander Kemp was born there in 1895. Alexander was subsequently baptised at St Mary's church. It may have been a brief tenancy though, as the 1901 census return shows Charles and Sarah Vidgeon were living at the farmhouse, with their two children Ethel and Rose. The Vidgeon family eventually had seven children: Ethel, Rose, Amy, Jack, Bertha, Jean, and Charlie.[12]

In 1911, under the provisions of a recent Finance Act, the Whatman family were charged £21 17s 2d for the completion of returns detailing their land holdings, including Chapel Lane Farm. Around this date too, the land agent decided to undertake some repairs on the buildings. The water supply, though, was more than adequate. In 1907 it was recorded that the mains, previously supplied by Walter Fremlin of Milgate, had now been purchased by the Mid Kent Water Company. The Whatman family were charged £1 11s 9d every quarter for the water supply.[13]

In a bundle of documents concerning suggested improvements to Chapel Lane Farm are included some loan forms for The Lands Improvement Company. It is not clear, though, whether they were ever completed. The accompanying schedule shows that the farm was now being run as a small mixed holding as the document mentions a new cow lodge, a granary that had been built, and a herd of pigs.[14]

Below is shown a copy of the schedule:

Estimates – Chapel Lane.

Clean all guttering & paint 2 Coats of White Paint to House & new Cow Lodge & Granary –

Clean down all wood work to ~~House~~ House, Cow Lodge & Granary & paint 3 coats plain colour.

        Labour £ 3

        Materials £ 2   – £ 5   –   –

To tar all wood work previously tarred
1 coat gas tar to Cow Lodge Waggon Lodge
Piggeries & Gates   *Labour £1. 10*

        Materials £1 5   £ 2 15 –

                        £ 7 15 .

Reproduced courtesy of the Centre for Kentish Studies

By 1914, Chapel Lane Farm had become part of the holdings occupied by the Tolhurst and Foster families. After Rose Tolhurst married George Foster, they farmed the land at Chapel Lane but their main holding was at Sandy Mount.

In May 1915 the land agent for the Whatman family filed a report about the farm. Below is a transcript of the report: [15]

Report Chapel Lane Farm and Sandy Mount

4 May 1915

I have inspected the holdings known as Chapel Lane Farm and Sandy Mount. I understand the present rent is £85 per annum plus an extra £5 to cover the interest on the capital expended upon a new cow house, making a total of £90 per annum.

The tenant is farming the land well and in a progressive manner. He has a good head of stock and a sound retail milk business has been built up, which is a valuable asset. If it were diverted from these holdings, the letting value would in my opinion, decrease.

I tactfully approached Mr Foster about an increased rental and without any friction or misunderstanding, after careful explanation of the whole position, he agreed amicably with me to pay an increase of £20 per annum this new agreement to start from Michaelmas 1915 and the 1st payment of an increased rental Lady Day 1916.

I pointed out that the cottages etc should be painted again this year, that the weather boarding of some of the outbuildings should be tarred again without delay. It will add to the life of them considerably.

Signed R H Green

Reproduced courtesy of the Centre for Kentish Studies

During the First World War, land girls came to assist the haymaking. During this time, this delightful photograph was taken:

Reproduced courtesy of Tony and Sheila Foster

At a recent, but curiously un-recorded point in the twentieth century, the tenancy of the farm at Chapel Lane passed from the Foster family. In January 1944, some of the stock was included in the sale of part of the Sandy Mount property, held to reduce the size of the holdings. This extract from the sale catalogue gives an indication of the stock sold: [16]

	CHAPEL LANE FARM	
184	Guernsey Cow, due with 5th calf end of Jan.	35
185	Red Cow, stocked May 21st	36
186	Ditto, due with 3rd calf Feb. 10th	37
187	Ditto, due with 3rd calf Feb. 1st	38
188	Pedigree Shorthorn Dairy Bull, "Maplescomb Zebedee," D.17376, born March, 1942. Licensed	39
189	Ditto, "Maplescomb Witness," D.03078, born July 26th, 1939. Licensed	40
190	Guernsey Heifer	41
191	Ditto	42
192	Roan ditto	43
193	Ditto	44
194	Two Red Heifers	45
195	Two ditto	46
196	Two ditto	47
	The foregoing 10 Heifers are all home-bred and have been running with Pedigree Shorthorn Bull since Oct. 12th last.	
197	Four Roan Yearling Heifers	48
198	Four Red ditto	49
199	Four Red ditto	50
200	Three Weanyer Heifer Calves	51
201	Two ditto	52
202		
203		
204		

Reproduced courtesy of Barbara Foster

The Whatman family continued to own the farm until 1954. Louisa Whatman died in 1950 and her nephew, Lieutenant Colonel A J Trousdell inherited her land holdings. Chapel Lane Farm was not included in an auction of the estate held on 20 May 1954 but was separately conveyed on 28 July. The farm, outbuildings and 43 acres of land were sold for £1,750.[17] The farm was bought by Kathleen Seager who appears to have been running it with William Wingrove as a mixed, but rather large, smallholding for some time before the sale. A trade directory for that year certainly lists William Wingrove as farming there but he also occupied a holding in the Gidds Pond area of Grove Green.[18] It was the start of a long association. William kept several hives of bees for many years at the farm. He was an enthusiastic beekeeper and sold the honey to local people.

In 1973 a section of the farm comprising Pope's Field was sold to Maurice and Daphne Coppin. In 1975 the President of Bearsted Golf Club, Eric Sibley, then indicated to Kathleen that the club might be interested in buying some of the land to extend their course. Negotiations were successfully concluded on 20 April 1976, with the trustees of the golf club purchasing seven acres together with a lease for a further thirty three acres. This acquisition was then incorporated into new landscaping and an extension of the course. On 30 March 1990, the Golf Club purchased the land that it had previously leased.[19]

In 1984 the farmhouse was placed on the listed property register.[20] Kathleen and William continued to run the farm but eventually they decided that in the face of increasing old age, it was time to retire. Although the golf club was initially interested in buying the farm and land, with a view to using the farmhouse as a new club house, the sale did not proceed.

On 20 April 1995, the property was sold and a full historical appraisal of the house undertaken. A subsequent programme of a sensitive restoration and renovation of the farmhouse, granary and outbuildings began. The latest changes to be completed include a small extension at the back of the house. Although new building techniques were used, it was specifically designed to blend sympathetically with the older sections.

Although it is no longer a working farm, a new chapter with fresh owners has opened for Chapel Lane Farm. The property is now reaping the benefits from careful custodianship of a building which has witnessed and reflects many of the social and economic changes in the Ware Street area.

Bell farmhouse, Bell Lane and The Bell Inn

The construction of the railway line through Thurnham and Bearsted in 1884 brought a significant change to the lower end of Ware Street. A bridge was required to span the gap between the embankment in Bell Lane and Chapel Lane. Once the bridge was installed it effectively divided Bell Lane and Bell farmhouse from some other agricultural buildings and the Bell Inn. In time, many people came to regard the bridge as marking the end of the street. However, the full extent of Ware Street today still runs from White Lodge by Chestnut Place, up to the junction of Hockers Lane and the closed-off section of Weavering Street.

Long before the manor of Ware existed, Bell Lane was a hollow way or a sunken lane. There were a number of these sunken lanes in the area cutting across what is now Ware Street, and further on in Thurnham and Bearsted, across The Street. Bell Lane, Sandy Lane, the track which is now called Hog Hill, Thurnham Lane and Water Lane all bear the typical characteristics of hollow ways; steep sides, a distinct cutting where the road descends and the route lined with great trees. The shade provided by the trees provides the right growing conditions for plants such as the hart's tongue fern.[1]

It is thought that the origins of these trackways go back before Saxon times, when the local residents undertook transhumance; that wonderfully evocative phrase to describe the practice of moving swine around to summer and winter pastures. The entry for Thurnham in the Domesday book certainly mentions forty pigs, so there is written evidence which hints that the practice was undertaken in the locality.[2]

The sunken lanes around Bearsted and Thurnham are the results of centuries of erosion, exacerbated by traffic of animal and human feet.[3] There is good evidence that land in Ware Street was used as pasture: as discussed elsewhere, a section of Ware Mead was used as animal pasture from around 1374. Part of Ware Mead was opposite Bell Lane. It is easy to surmise that animals would have been led down the sunken track by John Megill, who had been granted permission in that year to pasture animals in Ware Mead.

It is entirely possible that the original farmhouse for a settlement at Bell Lane was the property that later became the Bell Inn. Any research into property and land holdings in the area though is severely hampered by a lack of information and because the farmhouse was demolished in April 2006. However, the Bell Inn is several centuries older than the property that once occupied the site of Bell farmhouse.

As this photograph below, taken in February 2006 shows, sections of the farmhouse were probably built in the 1800s but may have incorporated parts of an older building.

Reproduced courtesy of Malcolm Kersey

147

The photograph below shows the same area in April 2006. It was taken barely two months after the photograph on the previous page. So efficiently was the site cleared, that it is hard to envisage that Bell farmhouse ever once stood on this site.

A new housing development is currently under construction. It is called The Chimes and comprises a mixture of flats and houses, as shown in this photograph taken in September 2007:

Both reproduced courtesy of Malcolm Kersey

Written records for property in Bell Lane bear a curious obscurity as although dwellings are mentioned the term 'farmhouse' and 'cottages' appear to have been used in an interchangeable manner. It is also highly regrettable that a survey of the farmhouse, which may have clarified periods of construction, was never carried out. It is therefore entirely possible, but unproved, that the building may have been sub-divided and accommodated several families. Some of the census returns for Thurnham certainly record a number of residents in the area.

In 1841 it was recorded that Thomas Woolven and his wife Ann together with their nine children were living there. Their nearest neighbours were William and Mary Vass who shared their accommodation with the daughter, Elizabeth.[4] Both Thomas and William were agricultural labourers. The property was owned by the Earl of Romney.[5]

The enumerator for the 1851 census included Bell Lane in the returns for Ware Street but did not specifically record it under that name. It is not easy to locate who was living in the lane at this time. Ten years later, however, James Kemp and his wife Ann lived in Bell Lane with their daughter, Charlotte. James was an agricultural labourer who came from Eynesford. Their neighbours were James Bridgland, who at 80, was a widower and a retired labourer. He was living with his widowed daughter, Elizabeth Tolhurst and a grandson, William Ambrose. Both Elizabeth and William worked at a paper factory.[6]

In 1871 James and Ann Kemp still resided in Bell Lane but his household now included his widowed daughter, Eliza Crowhurst, together with grandchildren Anne and James. Eliza was born in Maidstone and Anne and James were born in Thurnham. Their neighbours were Alfred and Harriet Hewett together with their son, William. James Bridgland (but actually recorded as Jim) was living nearby with his wife, Elizabeth. Jim came from Hollingbourne and was a farm bailiff.[7]

In 1880 a farmhouse, two cottages and gardens were specifically recorded in the Thurnham parish rate book for Bell Lane. Nicholas Robinson occupied Bell Farm together with some buildings and land. Although the properties were individually rated, the total amount due was 7s 6½d. Between the compilation of the tithe map in 1843 and the parish rate for 1880, the ownership of the property passed from the Earl of Romney to James Whatman. James Kemp and Mr Sherwood each occupied a cottage and thirty perches of land which attracted a rate of 9d,[8] but they are not specifically mentioned in the census return for 1881. The census does show Alfred Hewitt in Bell Lane and Nicholas Robinson, together with his wife Elizabeth and their six children living at Bell Farm. Nicholas came from Boughton Malherbe and was described as a farmer of thirty seven acres.[9] There is no parish rate book for 1882 which might have given further information.

There had been changes in the land holdings of the area by 1891; the Whatman family had disposed of the farm following James Whatman's death in 1887 and a subsequent decline in their financial affairs. There is a curious absence of a farmhouse recorded in the 1891 census return for Thurnham. Just two families were recorded as living in Bell Lane: Thomas and Susan Lurcock and their neighbours, William and Jane Jackson.[10]

In 1901 Arthur Betts, a fruit tree grower from Hollingbourne, was living in Bell Lane with his wife, Mary and their three children. Their neighbours were Thomas and Florence Austin. Thomas was a waggoner. They had some interesting neighbours: widower, George King was also living in Bell Lane together with his daughter Lillian. She was specifically recorded as having been born in Switzerland but was a British subject. Their housekeeper, Annie Clarke, was also widowed and she had a daughter called Caroline.[11]

In the early 1900s Tom Gilbert's family were living in Bell Lane. Their neighbours were the Betts family with at least four sons: Albert, Charles, Ernest and Ernest Edward. During the First World War, only one brother was not in the army: Ernest Edward, who served in the Royal Air Force. Also living in Bell Lane at this time was Frederick Croft who was a gunner in the Royal Garrison Artillery.[12]

In the early 1930s, a woodyard had been opened, and was successfully trading in Bell Lane. It was owned by the Baker family who lived in the farmhouse.[13] In 1934 Grace Baker married Sidney Hunt at Holy Cross church. The photograph overleaf shows Grace and Sidney during their wedding reception at the farmhouse. Note the steep bank behind Grace and Sidney; it formed part of the sunken lane.

Reproduced courtesy of Chris and Sue Hunt

In 1939, a cottage in Bell Lane, named Ashley was described as located in Bell Field. The property was the home of Alfred and Emma Jane King. Their neighbour, Kingsley Drummond, lived in an un-named house next door.[14] By the outbreak of the Second World War, the Luxton family had moved into Bell Lane as two members were recorded as serving in the armed forces. Charles Luxton served in the Royal Artillery, whilst his sister was in the Women's Auxiliary Air Force.[15]

Also living in Bell Lane were part of the Seager family. It is not known whether they had connections with the branch of the Seager family who had owned The Bell public house in the nineteenth century. This earlier branch of the family will be discussed later. In January 1941, Mabel Seager married Arthur May at St Mary's church. Arthur was serving in the Royal Army Medical Corps and had previously narrowly escaped capture during the Dunkirk evacuation. In 1942 he was posted as missing for several weeks before being located in an army hospital in the Middle East.[16]

By 1949, Doctor Ledward and his wife, Peggy, were living at the farmhouse. They stayed there several years before moving to Little Snowfield. Louie Smith recalled that, for a time, Doctor Ledward kept a boat in the garden of her house at 84 Ware Street. Trevor Cleggett could also recall that he looked forward to delivering newspapers at the farmhouse. On Saturday mornings, Mrs Ledward always left sixpence and a slice of cake out for him on a small plate covered by a basin to protect it against the birds. It was a kind gesture and appreciated by Trevor. Although Doctor and Mrs Ledward lived at the farmhouse, part of the land was used by the Bradley Brothers for fruit cultivation.[17]

The woodyard traded successfully for many years, later becoming the premises for Maiford Limited. Its principal business was supplying fencing contractors. However, the volume of traffic using the limited access in Bell Lane was an issue, particularly the large lorries which were collecting and delivering supplies. The site was considered too small for further expansion, so the business re-located and the land was sold for housing.

Despite the problems researching the history of this area, there is some information about the Bell Inn. As indicated previously, it is possible that the property was once the original farmhouse for Bell farm. There is certainly a plaque upon the building which says that it dates from the fifteenth century. This photograph of the property was taken in 2007:

Reproduced courtesy of Malcolm Kersey

The precise date that alcohol first began to be sold at the Bell Inn is not known, but amongst the earliest records for the building is an entry in a register of alehouse keepers. Between 1753 and 1782 the landlord was Richard Bellingham.[18] It would be good to think that the alehouse gained the name the Bell Inn as a pun upon the name of the landlord. There is then a break in the licensing records and when they recommence in 1793, Richard Ledger was listed as landlord.

By 1800, ownership of The Bell had passed through John Seager, William Evernden, Richard Seager and Flint Stacey.[19] Stephen Seager then inherited it through the will of his father, John, in 1801.[20] Both father and son were brewers. For the next twenty five years, Stephen used leases for the property to secure loans and finance for his business interests pursued with John Adcock, John Brenchley and two other members the Brenchley family. All were involved in the brewing trade. In the first of the loan agreements from 1801, a description of the property also included the names of several previous occupiers who are not recorded elsewhere:[21]

> ...all that messuage or tenement, now in three tenements or dwellings with the barn, stable, yard, garden and lands of the same belonging or therewith used with all and singular the appurtenances situate lying and being in the parish of Thornham and formerly in the occupation or tenure of James Fuller deceased, since of John Catt, William Bills and Burgess Masters and now or late in the tenure of Thomas Fisher, his assigns or undertenants...

Thomas Fisher acted as a land tax assessor for many years and in 1801 was recorded as liable to pay a parish rate of four shillings.[22]

In 1806 the lease for The Bell was renewed but by 1825 financial catastrophe had struck Stephen. In a bond of collateral security for that year, it was noted by John Brenchley, William and Courtney Stacey and John Adcock that Stephen had been declared bankrupt. Under the bankruptcy arrangements, John Adcock received The Bell together with other property in Aylesford and East Farleigh in lieu of payment. The latter continued to be used as security by bond of John Brenchley and William and Courtney Stacey but The Bell was re-leased. Licensing records show that in 1826 the landlady was Ann Ledger.[23] It is not known whether Richard (landlord in 1793) and Ann were related.

In 1828, a Court Baron for the Manor of Thurnham was held at the inn: [24]

As To Copyhold
20 October 1828

At a Court Baron of Sir Edward Cholmely Dering, Lord of the Manor of Thurnham, holden at the Bell Inn in Thurnham for the Manor of Thurnham, Kent, this day

The Homage presented (inter alia) as follows:

Thomas Philpot applied to the said court on behalf of the heirs of Francis Armstrong for leave to enclose:

About twelve perches of ground in Ware Street in Thurnham aforesaid, part of the Lords Waste which the rest of the homage recommended the Lord the grand accordingly on payment of the yearly fee of one shilling which was then paid with the entry fee…

It is entirely probable that many such meetings to discuss manorial affairs were held at the inn but this seems to be the only remaining record.

In 1839 George Nelson was noted in a trade directory for Kent as the landlord of the inn and he continued until 1859 when his wife, Ann succeeded him.[25] The census return for 1841 recorded that George and Ann were living at The Bell with their four daughters.[26] Shortly after the census, the tithe map or Thurnham was compiled. The accompanying schedule recorded that the inn occupied two plots and continued to be owned by Messrs Brenchley, Stacey and others. The land surrounding the inn was cultivated as a small wood called a 'shaw' and for other arable purposes such as hop gardens. It would be good to think that the oast house (which remains next to the inn) was constructed by the brewers for a convenient supply of prepared hops and malt.[27]

In 1853 and 1855, the rent from the Bell Inn together with the property and land was included as security in a transfer of mortgage and subsequent conveyance arranged between Edwin Stacey and Henry Morris. Interestingly, the public house is referred to as: [28]

…known by the name or sign of the Blue Bell…

---

but there are no other records which mention this change of name.

Ann Nelson ran the inn until 1874 when George Morgan, from Hollingbourne, took over the business. In 1881 George was recorded in the census return as the publican, assisted by his wife, Martha.[29] He ran the business for many years and was succeeded by John Hodges who was a local man, having been born in Thurnham. The licensing record, around 1900, shows that the inn was classed as an alehouse and was owned by the brewery, Isherwood, Foster and Stacey.[30]

This trade price card from 1920, which was distributed by the brewery, gives some indication of the type of refreshments which were available at the public house:

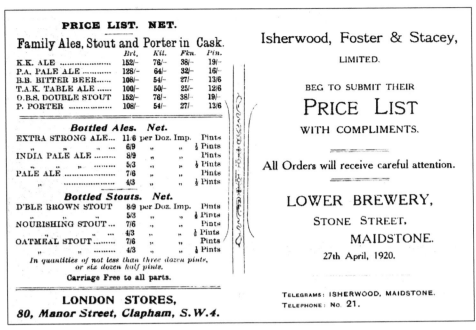

PRICE LIST. NET.					Isherwood, Foster & Stacey,
Family Ales, Stout and Porter in Cask.					LIMITED.
	Brl.	Kil.	Fkn.	Pin.	
K.K. ALE	152/-	76/-	38/-	19/-	BEG TO SUBMIT THEIR
P.A. PALE ALE	128/-	64/-	32/-	16/-	
B.B. BITTER BEER	108/-	54/-	27/-	13/6	**PRICE LIST**
T.A.K. TABLE ALE	100/-	50/-	25/-	12/6	WITH COMPLIMENTS.
O.B.S. DOUBLE STOUT	152/-	76/-	38/-	19/-	
P. PORTER	108/-	54/-	27/-	13/6	All Orders will receive careful attention.

Bottled Ales. Net.
EXTRA STRONG ALE... 11/6 per Doz. Imp. Pints
,, ,, ... 6/9 ,, ,, ½ Pints
INDIA PALE ALE .... 8/9 ,, ,, Pints
,, ,, ... 5/3 ,, ,, ½ Pints
PALE ALE .... 7/6 ,, ,, Pints
,, ,, ... 4/3 ,, ,, ½ Pints

Bottled Stouts. Net.
D'BLE BROWN STOUT 8/9 per Doz. Imp. Pints
,, ,, 5/3 ,, ,, ½ Pints
NOURISHING STOUT... 7/6 ,, ,, Pints
,, ,, ... 4/3 ,, ,, ½ Pints
OATMEAL STOUT......... 7/6 ,, ,, Pints
,, ,, ... 4/3 ,, ,, ½ Pints

In quantities of not less than three dozen pints, or six dozen half pints.

Carriage Free to all parts.

LONDON STORES,
80, Manor Street, Clapham, S.W.4.

LOWER BREWERY,
STONE STREET,
MAIDSTONE.
27th April, 1920.

TELEGRAMS: ISHERWOOD, MAIDSTONE.
TELEPHONE: No. 21.

Reproduced courtesy of Maidstone Museum

In 1927, John Hodges gave up the licence and George Bonner took it over. George ran the inn for many years and it came to be regarded as a family business as in 1949, Sidney Bonner renewed the licence. Sidney had a shorter tenure as landlord but was listed in trade directories until at least 1956. Many other members of the Bonner family also lived at the public house.[31] The inn was evidently a lively place in which to enjoy a pint of beer and in 1937 this photograph of the darts team was taken just before they departed upon an outing. Regrettably, the identities of the people included are not known:

Reproduced courtesy of Norah Giles

During the Second World War, the Bell Inn, like the other public houses in Bearsted and Thurnham, benefited from the custom of the armed forces stationed nearby. It was sufficiently close to Detling aerodrome to become a regular visiting place for the airmen posted there and it was also used by the soldiers camped on Bearsted Golf Course and in Mote Park. In January 1944 it was noted in the parish magazine that £8 had been collected at the public house for the Red Cross and Prisoners of War fund.[32]

In March 1993, the lower section of Ware Street was closed in order to allow the railway bridge to be replaced and the supports strengthened. This photograph, taken during the work reveals a view of the lower section of Ware Street and the Bell Inn which had not been seen for over a hundred years:

Reproduced courtesy of Janet Smith

In the twentieth century, the oast house ceased to prepare hops and the conical roof known as a roundel was removed. It remained as commercial premises and for many years a furniture company was based there. It is currently called Kent House and is occupied by Swift Roofing Limited and Phoenix Roofing Supplies. This photograph, taken in 2007, shows the remaining part of the oast house and its close proximity to the Bell Inn:

Reproduced courtesy of Malcolm Kersey

Louie Smith recalled that in the middle of the 1950s, an area opposite the Bell Inn was occupied by a fruit store owned by Mr Stokes. Around a decade later, Kent Frozen Foods, a company specialising in supplying frozen food to the wholesale and retail markets, took over the site. In the late 1960s, domestic deep freeze appliances became widely available and so the company was able to develop in to this market. Many older local residents can remember visiting the shop at the premises. In terms of modern marketing, the stock of the shop was very remarkably simple: it comprised two large rooms of chest freezers and a manned till. The contents of each freezer were described on a sheet of paper attached to the lid.

By 2005, Kent Frozen Foods had outgrown the site and relocated to Aylesford. Demolition of the former industrial buildings started. In their place, a small housing estate called Ragstone Place was developed by Bellway Homes. The first section to be named in the development was Edelin Road in December 2006, although there is no apparent local reference for this name. Perhaps a future for the Bell Inn[33] beckons which serves the needs of the new residents as a truly local public house.

These photographs of Ragstone Place, the former oast house and the Bell Inn taken in June 2006 and September 2007, respectively, give an impression of this area of lower Ware Street in recent times:

Both reproduced courtesy of Malcolm Kersey

Ware Street in the twentieth century and more recent times

At the end of the nineteenth century very little had altered in Ware Street for many years. Few people would have guessed that the new century would bring two world wars and a new social order which would affect the structure of local communities for ever. Without ever realising it, Tom Gilbert and Mrs Emma Louise Smith (usually called Louie) witnessed the disappearance of many of the old ways of Ware Street as they grew up; Tom was born around 1903. Louie was born a little later. It was not until the late 1980s that the importance of this information was realised and some of it recorded by the now disbanded Thurnham History Group. What emerges from all of the information available about the area is a fascinating portrait of Ware Street, sketches of some of the characters that lived there and the peaceful rhythm and routines of everyday life.

Tom's family moved into a house beyond what was then regarded as the top of Bell Lane around 1900. It was usually very quiet there, with a view which looked out on a meadow as it sloped down to the railway. Two wooded and high banks formed a valley, called Banky Meadow, which joined Romney Hill on the main Ashford to Maidstone Road. At the top of the hill there was a gate which led to a farm and what may have once been old quarry working known as Bell Hole, which even then was overgrown with bushes and trees. This was a short distance from an old cart track which led to some cottages where his family and their neighbours, Mrs Betts and her two sons, lived. Although Tom's house did not have a piped water supply, many houses in Ware Street did enjoy this facility.

Louie came from a well-established local family who have lived in the area for over 150 years. She was born in Smart's Cottages, on the Green in Bearsted but some of her great-grandparents lived in Ware Street. This photograph was taken around 1917 and shows Louie as a small child with her parents Charles Earl, Elizabeth Lydia (née Baker) and her older brother, Charles:

Reproduced courtesy of Louie Smith

Both Tom and Louie could easily recall that there was little to punctuate the stillness on a warm summer evenings, which was particularly appreciated after a day of hard physical work. Near the Methodist Chapel, a nightingale could often be heard singing in the woods and bushes beyond the railway station. There were also occasions when Tom also heard the distinctive call of the nightjar from over a mile away. The bird was in a wooded area beyond the golf course.

It was quite usual for children in Ware Street to roam the fields and woods; the countryside was part of their playground. If they were lucky enough to discover a pheasant or partridge nest, then they would tell Mr Attwood, who was the local gamekeeper. Mr Attwood paid three pence for the information about a nest and was known to pay up to sixpence if the eggs were brought to him.

Prior to the First World War, autumn was a particularly important time. For around six weeks nearly everyone in the village worked to harvest hops. Whole families participated as the joint effort boosted earnings. The cash was used to buy shoes and clothes for the winter. Tom recalled that the local name for receiving the money was 'The Pay Off'. During the war, his father was in the Army. The wages were low, and as many men were serving their country, money was scarce. In 1916, Tom's family decided that he should leave school. He was aged nearly thirteen when he went to work. His first wages were six shillings a week[2] and in the absence of his father, he was regarded as the 'man of the house'. The chores he had to perform included tending the garden and allotment.

A diagram to accompany these memories of the north side of Ware Street appears on the next page.

From the village green on the North Side of Ware Street

Hill House

Many people in Ware Street admired this fine brick built house because of the good views of the area which could be obtained from the grounds. During the 1880s, George Baldwin, an accountant and collector for the Maidstone Gas Company, had lived there with his wife. The house had gas lighting and George was keen to promote the idea to others, although few in Ware Street could afford. When Tom was growing up, Charles Tubb lived there and shared the house with his sister, Louisa.

The Railway Station

Throughout the twentieth century, the railway line and station which serves Bearsted and Thurnham was a backdrop for all the residents of Ware Street. There were eight other previous schemes which were drawn up and rejected before a successful design was achieved. Nearly all of the abandoned schemes involved the railway line crossing the Ashford Road and the location of the station in the vicinity of the Kentish Yeoman public house and Yeoman area of Bearsted.[3] If just one of these plans had gone ahead, the structure of Bearsted would be very different today. The main station building was built on the site of an old sand quarry and pit where donkeys were stabled in between hauling deliveries of sand. In the 1880s, the local sand merchants were John Flood and Frederick Davis. Both lived in Bearsted.[4]

The line was opened on 1 July 1884 and the station was originally called Bearsted and Thurnham, but the name changed to Bearsted in 1980. The stations on the Maidstone East to Ashford line were all built to the same design by Arthur Stride, using dark red and pale yellow bricks. There was also a goods yard with a brick built shed and pound for animals, but it was shut in 1964,[5] becoming a storage yard for Wakefield coal merchants until the 1990s.

By 1900, the regularity of the trains on the line had become part of the background everyday life, with people using the services as an informal time check in the course of their day. The arrival of Tom's family in Ware Street coincided with a train travelling over the railway bridge. He knew nothing about trains and immediately thought that there was a huge monster making a terrible noise. He did not take long to overcome his fear.

Both Louie and Tom could clearly recall the attractive flower beds and gardens at the station that were lovingly tended by the staff. Mr Slingsby was the stationmaster in the early years of the twentieth century and wore a uniform of a frock coat and gold-braided cap with great panache. Around fifteen staff worked at the station.

Below is an interpretation of Tom Gilbert and Louie Smith's memories of the north side of Ware Street:
(not to scale)

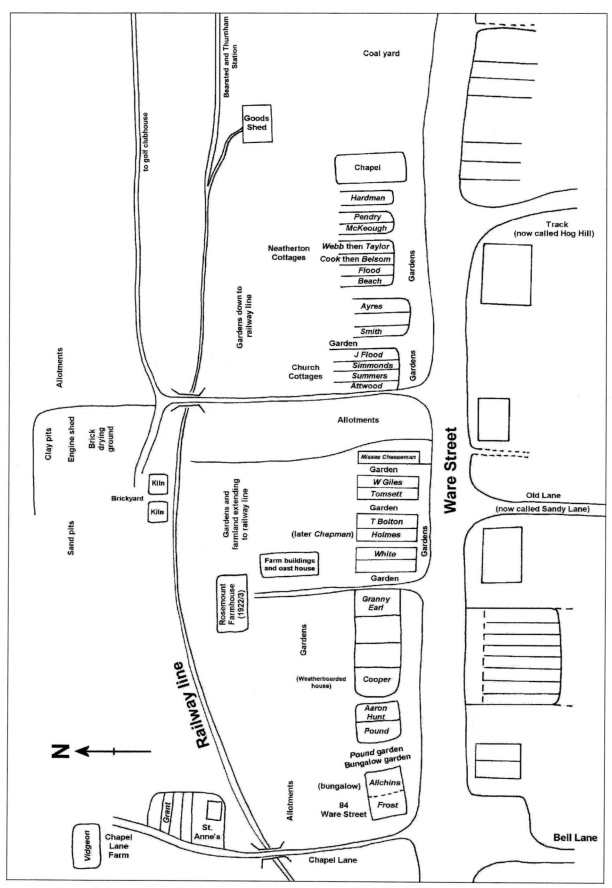

Reproduced courtesy of Malcolm Kersey

In the 1930s, the signalman, Mr Pearson, fulfilled many posts at the station. These included selling tickets and completing the documentation for luggage and the trade for the goods yard. In season, two men loaded baskets of fruit and other crops whilst other workmen bagged coal from the open trucks. The signal blocks were largely kept open for most of the time, except when shunting and picking up vans, as trains to and from Ashford were the only ones in steam. The siding behind the fence by the up-line to London was for horseboxes and there was a small patch of grass kept to reassure the animals when they were being loaded.[6]

This undated postcard shows the station building around the turn of the century. It had changed very little since it opened. Note the wooden gates and the lamp which bore the name Bearsted, rendered as Bearstead!

Reproduced courtesy of Martin Elms

This undated picture shows the lines at the station heading towards Ashford. Note that the goods shed has a separate siding and there is a signal box on the left hand side. Above the signal box, and sited at the highest point, is the club house for the golf course. It is perched on what is believed to be, the remnant of one of the sandbanks which was formerly part of a quarry.[7] For many years, there was a corresponding sandbank fragment on the other side of the line, in the area which is now the main station car park.

Reproduced courtesy of Jean Jones

The down line was accessed either by a small footpath from Thurnham Lane or by carefully walking over the line. The line was electrified in 1961.

The Methodist Chapel

The chapel was built at one of the highest points in Ware Street. Louie, and many older residents of Ware Street were able to recall that Miss Tolhurst, a generous supporter of the Methodists had sold the site to them for £30. It cost £250 to build the chapel which was opened in August 1877.[8]

It was well known, too, that although the previous site for the chapel in Chapel Lane was abandoned due to flooding, that there had also been problems building the new chapel. The site comprised a mound of soft sand, nearly twenty feet deep. The building was erected on piers, three to each side and each wall was supported by a slab of concrete.

This photograph of the chapel was taken in December 2006. The extension on the right hand side of the photograph was opened in 1985.

Reproduced courtesy of Malcolm Kersey

A great many of the congregation during the twentieth century that Louie could recall were very well respected members of the community in Bearsted and Thurnham: the Perrin, Goodenough and Holtum families all attended services. They also thoroughly supported the work of the Wesley Guild.

During the Second World War and for several years afterwards, the chapel was used as an extra schoolroom for the children at Bearsted School. After the evacuees from Plumstead arrived, all the accommodation had to be shared. The extra space was greatly appreciated by all the staff and the Headmaster of Bearsted School, Mr Skinner.

In the 1960s the congregation had suffered a reduction as several families who were stalwart supporters had moved out of Bearsted. However, the new houses that were being constructed in the area brought new families to the chapel and in 1977 the Centenary of the building was celebrated. In 1985, after further underpinning of the building, the facilities at the chapel were further improved with an extension to incorporate a schoolroom and church offices. Since then, there have been further refurbishments of the building which were completed in 2007.

Golf Course

A golf course was opened in 1896 behind the railway on land owned by Sir George Hampson. It was designed by Hubert Bensted but it was not known as Bearsted Golf Club until 1914. Ella Cardwell was a member of the golf club for many years. As she grew up in Ware Street, the golf course seemed a natural part of her surroundings. She had been a very small child in 1923, when a new eighteen hole golf course had been opened. The well-known golfer, Harry Vardon was invited to play an exhibition match to mark the occasion. Prior to playing, Harry drank what seemed to be a vast quantity of whisky but to widespread amazement, still managed to win the match.[9]

The first hole of the golf course was in the corner next to the railway and on the bank above there was a man-made pond, known as 'Cal Pond'. Chris Hunt could remember that during the 1950s, great crested newts lived by the pond. The newts were regularly caught there by small boys. West of Cal Pond the ground and clay bank looked as if it had once been excavated. Stories persisted that house tiles had once been made there. The sand pit at the entrance to the golf course was quite deep and formed a fairly high cliff.

Brick Field and Sand Quarry

By 1900, the brick fields and kilns of The Bearsted Brick Company were located beyond the railway. In the first decade of the twentieth century the main brick makers were Richard and Charles Norman. They had taken over the business from Benjamin and Eleanor Warman.

The making of bricks had not changed over many centuries. They were always made in the spring and summer. During the winter the clay was turned over to expose it to wet and frost. Ashes were added to the clay in the ratio of one fifth ashes to four fifths clay. They were well mixed by digging, watering and raking backwards and forwards with a pronged hoe.

The mixture was then taken to the pug mill which comprised a barrel containing a series of blades and was powered by horse or a steam engine. The blades cut and reduced the clay to a fine blend before it was emptied into wet sacking. The sacking kept the mixture, now called stock clay, from drying out. Pieces of the clay, approximately the size of a brick were cut and dusted with sand before being thrown into a wooden brick mould. Excess clay was then trimmed from the mould before the soft brick was removed and placed on a pallet board. When the board was full, the bricks were again dusted with sand and laid in two rows with a small space between them to allow the air to circulate.[10] When the bricks were partially dried, they were known as green bricks.

There were two kilns at the brick field, each held thousands of bricks. The green bricks were loaded into the kilns with spaces between them. The kilns were really furnaces which each held six or seven fires. The fire covers were swung into position over the furnace openings and sealed with a slurry mixture of clay and Fullers Earth, before firing. The clay and Fullers Earth mixture was an efficient sealant. Both ingredients were obtained from a nearby meadow. The fires burned for some days.

Tom worked at the brick field for a short while in the 1920s. Although it is not altogether clear when it closed, it is last mentioned in a trade directory for 1937.[11] It is likely that many of the houses in Ware Street were built with bricks supplied by this company.

Today, barely eighty years after The Bearsted Brick Company closed, there is little to show at the site to suggest that it was once an industrial area which can be traced back over four centuries. The evidence of brick drying grounds, the clay pits, and the kilns indicated by Tom in his sketch plan of the north side of Ware Street has been largely erased. There is now an abundant growth of alder saplings and brambles taking advantage of the light sandy soil. Odd fragments of brick, tile and lumps of kiln waste are scattered around, perhaps only disturbed by the wildlife. The majority of the site has been levelled and now awaits another use.

Only one structure remains to indicate a previous use for the site: a partially collapsed shed, measuring approximately forty feet by twenty five feet. This may have been the engine shed which Tom included in his sketch plan. The brick-built ends of the shed and some fragments of wall remain, indicating that there were at least three bays to the building. The remains of the corrugated iron roof have collapsed both inwards and backwards on to the bank of soil behind it.

These next two photographs, taken in 2006, show the remains of the shed. This first picture gives a good indication of the extent of the building. The remnants of a brick-built side end are visible in the background through the saplings:

This picture below shows a close-up of the interior of the building. Note the collapsed parts of the roof comprise corrugated iron and wooden timbers, together with the remains of one of the brick bays:

Both reproduced courtesy of Malcolm Kersey

Neatherton Cottages

This is a pair of cottages which are today known as 10 and 12 Ware Street. An ornamental stone plaque on the front of them gives the date of building as 1879, but nothing is known about the original owner. Tom recalled that 10 Ware Street was occupied by Mr Webb and two sisters called Esther and Sally. 12 Ware Street was occupied by Mr and Mrs Cook and two daughters.

Around 1938, Harry and Gladys Rumble moved there with their family. They had three daughters: Eve, June and Maureen. Harry worked for Charles Foster at Sandy Mount farm. Bryan and Malcolm Salvage recalled that milk was delivered to the cottages from Foster's farm. Whilst Harry and Gladys lived there, they only had an outside toilet half way down the garden. Most of the garden was taken up by vegetables which Harry grew. Until mains drainage was laid on, the only water available was from an outside tap on the rear wall of the end cottage in the block which was shared by all the cottages in the block.

This undated photograph, was taken from outside the Methodist chapel and shows Neatherton cottages on the right hand side and the Mission Hut in the distance on the left hand side:

Reproduced courtesy of Malcolm Kersey

Church Cottages

Tom recalled that these were occupied during the greater part of the twentieth century by four families whose names were Flood, Simmonds, Summers and Attwood.

Ware Street by the road next to the Golf Course

Some of the land was used for allotments. Nearby were two houses, the second of which was the home of the Misses Cheeseman who ran a small laundry. Their neighbours were the Giles and Tomsett families and Tommy Bolton. Tommy was a local carrier who undertook daily journeys to Maidstone. His garden was really a jumble of buildings and these were used to accommodate his horse and cart. He had three children: a daughter known as 'Topsy' and twin boys, whose nick-names were 'Alike' and 'Similar'. The Holmes family lived next to the Bolton family. Mr and Mrs Chapman and their daughter, who was known as Rene were also neighbours.

Roger Vidler could recall that in the 1950s, the Smith family were one of three families that lived in the properties which had been altered to accommodate them. Below is a detail taken from an undated photograph of Ware Street which shows these dwellings. The white-washed end wall of 62 Ware Street can be seen on the left hand side of the picture. The Smith family lived in the end of the property on the right hand side :

Reproduced courtesy of Roger Vidler

This next photograph was taken from just below the last property towards the middle of the photograph above. It shows the view looking up Ware Street from opposite the Mission Hut and Mount Pleasant.

Reproduced courtesy of Jean Jones

By 1939, Louie, was married to Jack Smith, and they were living at 48 Ware Street. The house was owned by Mr Hodges of Rosemount Dairy and Jack was working on the farm. He earned seventeen shillings a week as a waggoner, milking the cows and delivering milk. Louie was able to work in the fields of local farms whenever the demands of her family allowed. She was particularly skilled in putting up the strings on wooden poles for such vegetable crops as peas and runner beans.

The ground floor of 48 Ware Street comprised one large downstairs room with a scullery at the back. There was still an iron pump for water but it was not used as the house had a piped supply. There was no electricity and no mains drainage. Meals were cooked on an iron range. There was an outside lavatory which was emptied on a Saturday morning by a vehicle known as a 'honey wagon'. It was operated by two men who undertook this operation whilst cheerfully eating their sandwiches; quite oblivious to the awful smell! Louie recalled that the inhabitants of other properties in Ware Street sorted out sewage matters for themselves. This usually meant that the men of the family dug an enormous pit at the bottom of the garden for the lavatory drainage and when it was full up, another one was dug. Luxuriant rhubarb usually grew on the top of the filled pits.

Further down Ware Street were three cottages and garden by a track leading to the Rosemount Dairy. The yard for the dairy was adjacent to a house which was occupied by an old lady known as 'Granny Earl'; Louie's great grandmother. She lived in the house with a son and grandson. Her grandson, Charles, was Louie's father. In the summer, Granny Earl sold lemonade from her house. Later occupants were Frederick and Mary Bodiam, who moved there after Frederick retired. He had been a coachman for Walter Fremlin at Milgate and lived at Milgate Lodge. He had also worked for Mr Hampson at Commonwood. After Frederick's death in 1936, Mary moved further up Ware Street, to Winter Haw.

Around 1930, Tom's family moved into one of these houses. He could recall that at the end of their property was a weather-boarded house which was occupied by the Cooper family. Next door to them, on the right hand side, was a rather dilapidated house believed to date from medieval times, presumably this was where Granny Earl had lived for a time, but the name of the occupant when Tom lived nearby was not recorded. On the other side of the Cooper's house was a tile-hung property run as a shop by Aaron, Ethel and Maude Hunt. All the properties on the left hand side of the picture below (including the weather-boarded dwelling) were demolished in the 1950s. New houses were then built on one section of the cleared land.

Reproduced courtesy of Terry Clarke

These two undated photographs show Mrs Cooper outside her house, and a group of four ladies which includes Maude Hunt.

Both reproduced courtesy of Jean Jones

Close neighbours to the Gilberts were the Pound family with their children: Harry, Daisy and Albert. Mr Pound's garden was along the west of the house and joined the garden of a small bungalow. Between the garden and the railway line was a large piece of ground that Tom's family used as an allotment. He recalled that a bungalow nearby was rented by the Allchins family but is not certain whether he actually meant 84 Ware Street.

One intriguing property which did survive from earlier times, and the later demolition of adjacent properties, is No. 70 Ware Street. This is included in the picture on the previous page as the house with half-timbers in the upper storey and a long roof with a chimney in the middle of it.[12] After extensive renovation and the addition of a small extension during the last two decades of the twentieth century, it came to be called Stocks House. This photograph of the property was taken in 2006:

Reproduced courtesy of Malcolm Kersey

The property is believed to have been built some time between 1475 and 1500. It is a listed building that was subject of an architectural survey undertaken in 1989. It was built in the Wealden hall house style with a central section that was originally a one bay open hall with a lower end of two bays. There are several particularly intriguing features in the property: there is still a division, known as a dais partition, in the hall which would have marked the slightly raised area in which distinguished guests were seated. The partition includes an almost complete screen, called a spere, which bears evidence for a doorway for access to the front of the property. There is also a vaulted stone cellar which may have been contemporary with the main construction. The jambs of the arches of the vaulted sections have chamfered edges and overall, it was built to a high standard.[13]

Such a substantial property would have cost a great amount of money to construct. Unfortunately, its history remains enigmatic; there are few clues in the manorial documents to indicate who might have decided to build it.

Although there are no specific records in the Centre for Kentish Studies,[14] it is possible that a reference in Robert Shornden's will of 1599 to 'the Stockhouse' may relate to the property. Perhaps that was the original name and alluded to a previous agricultural function. Later members of the Shornden family certainly held property on the south side of Ware Street near the Methodist chapel but there is no direct link to Stocks House.[15]

This photograph is undated but was taken around 1890 and shows Stocks House in the centre and the lower end of Ware Street towards the railway bridge. Note also how the railway line is clearly visible in the background and appears to be a recent construction.

Reproduced courtesy of Malcolm Kersey

Photographs of some properties in Ware Street are remarkably elusive. A glimpse of the one-storey property a few yards east of 84 Ware Street is found on the left hand side of this undated photograph below. The detail has been taken from another postcard which is fully reproduced elsewhere.

Reproduced courtesy of Roger Vidler

167

Little is known about the property which has now been demolished, but it was once attached to a house called Arcady which was adjacent to 84 Ware Street. Louie could recall Mrs Cronk lived there in the middle years of the twentieth century. Mrs Cronk was a good customer of the shop at 1 Ware Street; Roger Vidler recalled that her favourite purchase from his family's shop was Passing Cloud cigarettes.

It is not known when Arcady was built. In 1939, Harry and Richard Birch lived there for a while.[16] It was eventually demolished towards the later half of the twentieth century. This undated photograph from the early 1920s shows the close proximity of the two properties. No. 84, is on the left of the picture and Arcady is the property with black timbers and white decoration.

Reproduced courtesy of Terry Clarke

Louie and Jack moved to 84 Ware Street in 1958 but had little idea that the house had been built many years previously. Jean Jones recalled that when her family owned 84 Ware Street, the deeds indicated that at one time the site had been occupied by a property which had been left to 'the poor of Thurnham parish'.[17] This is confirmed by a memorandum dated 1742 drawn up Rev Henry Rand, who was vicar of Bearsted between 1733 and 1765.[18] The document gives details of a £200 bequest by Luke Phillips, a gentleman from Herefordshire, to augment a small vicarage within ten miles of Maidstone. The trustees of Mr Phillips had given the money to a charity called Queen Anne's Bounty which was used to boost the income of poor clergy. The charity had then added a further £200. Henry Rand used the money to purchase a package of land which included: [19]

> ...a House and two acres of Meadowland adjoining Ware pond in the parish of Thurnham...

Ware pond and an adjacent property are clearly shown on the 1843 tithe apportionment map as plots 50 and 50a, located on the corner of what is now called Chapel Lane.[20] Both plots were described as in the accompanying schedule for the tithe map, as held by the Vicar of Bearsted, Rev Charles Cage.[21]

In 1919, the house was sold, along with the other property in Maidstone. The total sum realised, £3,500, was placed once more with Queen Anne's Bounty. The property at Ware Street was sold to Mr Lushington.[22]

At an unknown date, but after the sale to Mr Lushington, the property was renovated and was incorporated into one building. During the course of the work, radical changes were made. The right hand side of the property was slightly heightened, dormer windows were inserted into the roof and the upper half was tile-hung. The section of the property on the left hand side was reduced to one storey and a small wooden structure was added to the side.

This undated photograph shows the changed appearance:

Reproduced courtesy of Louie Smith

For many years, Louie used the wooden section of the property as an informal bathroom and as a useful storage area. However, in 1999 it was demolished during renovations and a new section at the back of the house was constructed to provide a permanent bathroom.

This photograph, taken in 2005, shows that the end of the dwelling is slightly lower on the left hand side of the property, with a single chimney pot. Note the bricked up doorway which once led to the wooden structure.

Reproduced courtesy of Malcolm Kersey

169

This photograph, taken in 2005, shows the front of 84 Ware Street:

Reproduced courtesy of Malcolm Kersey

During recent repair work on the roof, a small cache of papers was discovered underneath the tiles. Although some documents were disintegrating, they were legible. They comprised a series of orders and receipts dated 1915 to 1927 from a wholesale merchants called Midmore and Hall, 24 Stone Street, Maidstone to Mr Frost, who was living at the house.

This is the most complete document:

Reproduced courtesy of Louie Smith

The hole through the middle was probably caused by filing the paid bill on a metal spike. Mr Hickmott is noted as the local carrier, and he used a Ford car for deliveries. Mr Frost ran a bicycle store and repair shop at 84 Ware Street and also sold small items such as tobacco, matches, shoe polish and pins. He may have used the wooden building as a small premise. Louie was able to confirm that at one time, Mr Frost even had a small steam engine stationed in the garden.

Adequate drainage at the lower end of Ware Street was difficult to achieve for many years. Louie's house has been flooded several times. In 1968, after many days of torrential rain, water poured down Chapel Lane. It accumulated underneath the railway bridge and by the lower properties in Ware Street. This picture shows the flood and two stranded cars in the water on the far side of the bridge. The occupants of the cars managed to escape.

As the bad weather and rain continued, water then poured through Louie's garden as shown in this photograph below. Barely a day later, an entire garden from a neighbouring property slid down to 84 Ware Street. After the water had drained away, it was decided to leave the remains of the garden where it had come to rest. There is a step down into Louie's house as the level of the ground outside is now raised.

Both reproduced courtesy of Norah Giles

Chapel Lane

On the right hand side of Chapel Lane there were allotments. One house, called St Anne's was set back from the lane. There were also some cottages. One family Tom remembered living there was called Grant and there were six children: Kate, May, Fred, Frank, Bert and George. The farmhouse at Chapel Lane was occupied by the Vidgeon family with their children.

Beyond the farmhouse were other buildings, cow-sheds and fields which were all part of Sandy Mount farm run by the Tolhurst family. The rest of the farm was located between the two lanes leading from the south side of Ware Street up to Roseacre Lane. Some of this area is now called Windmill Heights.

The South Side of Ware Street from the Green

A diagram that accompanies these memories from Tom and Louie about Ware Street can be found on the next page.

The left hand side of the hill was a wooded area and part of the Snowfield estate. Around 1908, Snowfield was the home of Baroness Orczy. After the First World War, she sold it to Major Craig who was the brother of the Prime Minister of Ireland. In 1934 the property was sold once more and the Litchfield-Speer family came to live there.

The first house next to the wooded area was 1 Ware Street, virtually opposite the station. It was occupied by Mrs Hodges who ran a shop from the premises. Next door to the Hodges lived the Watkins family who had children called Alf, Les, Vera and Doris. Doris married Tom's brother, Cyril Gilbert. Mr Watkins was a local shoe repairer.

This undated postcard shows 1 Ware Street on the left hand side and the roof of the Methodist Chapel at the top of the incline on the right hand side.

Reproduced courtesy of Jean Jones

There were two blocks of cottages a short distance from 1 Ware Street. In the first of these lived Mr and Mrs Parks. Mr Parks was the railway signalman. The second block of cottages was slightly higher up and steps were required to reach them. These were occupied respectively by Mr and Mrs Ollett, Mr and Mrs Beach and their three sons: Percy, Len and Mac, and the Elliott family.

An interpretation of Tom Gilbert and Louie Smith's memories of the south side of Ware Street: (not to scale)

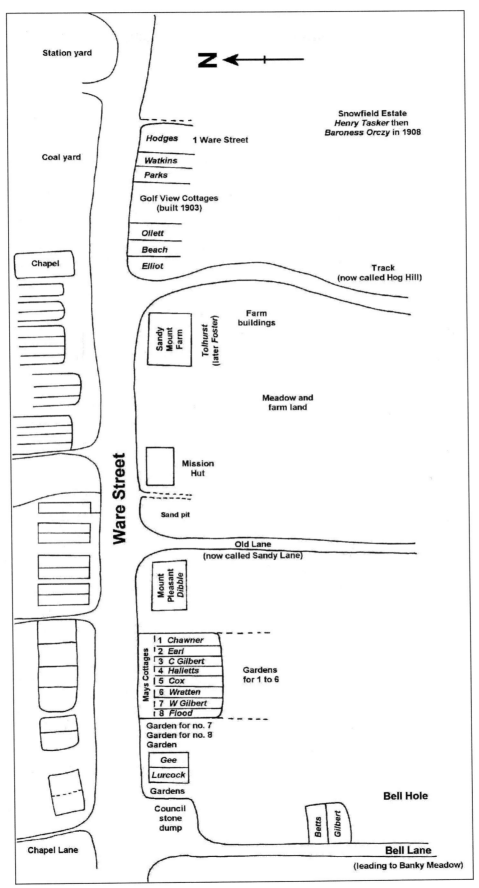

Reproduced courtesy of Malcolm Kersey

Golf View Cottages were built in between these two blocks of cottages in 1903. Towards the middle of the century, Mr and Mrs Beer lived at 2 Golf View Cottages. After a death in Ware Street or in Bearsted and Thurnham, Edward Beer's wife would lay out the body prior to the vicar and undertaker visiting to arrange the funeral. By all accounts, Mrs Beer's duties were on an unofficial basis but were largely regarded by the community as a much valued service offered in a time of need.

There are very few photographs of the south side of Ware Street. This view is undated but includes Golf View Cottages and the properties on either side:

Reproduced courtesy of Janet Smith

Behind the main part of Mr Tolhurst's farm at Sandy Mount were the outbuildings and yard. A track led to them which was later developed into a proper road and became called Hog's Hill.

A little further down Ware Street was a gate beside the Mission Hut. This gate led to a field by Sandy Mount farm where sand had been dug from the bank. The excavations had formed a cliff and many sand martins nested there. At the end of the field there was a short grassy slope and the lane next to it was known as Old Lane. Today it is called Sandy Lane.

Beyond Old Lane was a large house called Mount Pleasant, where the Dibble family lived. When Louie was fourteen in 1929, she left school. She spent some time at Mount Pleasant, working for Mrs Dibble and her daughters; Grace and Doris. She particularly remembered that there was a massive water pump and very long ceramic sink in the scullery.

'Miss Grace', as Louie called her, was a teacher in Nigeria but came home regularly. During one home visit, she invited a family to tea and then consulted Louie about the menu. She usually employed servants in Nigeria and so had very little practical experience of what to cook for such an occasion. Louie suggested that if a hot meal was required, perhaps a meat pudding would be acceptable but it would need to be boiled in a cloth or a basin. Louie showed Miss Grace what needed to be done. However, to this day, Louie has never found out how the meal was received by the guests.

This old, undated postcard shows the view from the field at Sandy Mount farm. Neatherton Cottages are towards the middle of the picture on the opposite side of the road. Behind them is part of the golf course and some properties in Thurnham Lane leading up to Castle Hill are just visible:

Reproduced courtesy of Jean Jones

Mays Cottages

These were situated a short distance from Mount Pleasant. The property comprised eight small terraced cottages. They were usually known as either Mays Cottages or The Bank but were also known for a short time as Barracks Row. Rents were paid weekly and were collected by Mr Brooks who cycled out from Maidstone. At the start of the twentieth century, the cottage windows were regularly taped up due to outbreaks of Scarlet Fever.

Tom particularly remembered Mr and Mrs Teddy Chawner who lived at the first cottage with their daughters Emily, Ada and Lily. Louie recalled that their other children were Sid, Nellie and Bob.

Mr and Mrs Earl with their children: Harry, John, Aubrey, George and Winny lived next door. Some other children in this family were called Jim, Charlie, Fanny, Eva, Sid and Clarence. George later changed his name to Horace.

Mr and Mrs Charles Gilbert (Tom's uncle) and their children Minnie, Amy and Arthur lived at No. 3 Arthur was a surviving twin. Their neighbours at No. 4 were Mr and Mrs Halletts, with their children Joe, Bill and Mary. Mr Halletts was a retired railwayman. When Mary became seriously ill, straw was laid on the road outside to deaden the noise of the passing horses and carts.

No. 5 was occupied by Mrs Cox with her children Bobby and Stephen. Their neighbours at No. 6 were Mrs Wratten and one of her sons. No. 7 was home for another branch of the Gilbert family and their neighbours at No. 8 were Mr and Mrs Flood and their children, Caroline and Edward. Later occupants of No. 7 were Harry and Gladys Rumble before they moved to Neatherton Cottages.

There was no running or piped water into the houses at Mays Cottages but one tap was situated half way up the passageway that ran along the back of the properties. This made it quite difficult for the residents to keep things clean. Privies were emptied with buckets and the contents were buried in the small patch of garden as there was nowhere else. The gardens for these houses were not laid out in a straightforward manner as the back gardens situated directly behind the houses stopped at No. 6. The garden for No. 7 was at the side of the house, so the garden for No. 8 was situated next door to the garden of Mr Gee who lived in the last semi-detached house before the railway bridge.

This photograph of Mays Cottages was taken in 2006:

Reproduced courtesy of Malcolm Kersey

Mr Gee's neighbours were Mr and Mrs Lurcock who had one daughter and a son called Bernard. The council stone dump for the road was situated by the Lurcocks' house. Stones were dumped there and a man would come out and build them into a neat block rather like a dry stone wall. Another man called a 'stone knapper' would then break the rocks into small pieces for road repairs.

Kate Swain later occupied one of these cottages. She was usually known by the residents of Ware Street as Old Kate. She was very eccentric and frequently stood outside her house in all weathers, as if she was waiting for someone or something to arrive. One or two people thought she was waiting for a fiancé who had been killed in the First World War but no one seemed to be entirely sure. She certainly hated the traffic and was known to stand in the middle of the road by the railway bridge and abuse it, often waving a stick. Occasionally she leaped out in front of vehicles, risking serious injury and causing the driver to brake very hard. Quite unexpectedly, one day she left Ware Street for ever: it was later discovered that she had taken a post as a housekeeper.

This photograph of the two houses was taken in the winter of 2005 from the garden of 84 Ware Street:

Reproduced courtesy of Janet Smith

This undated photograph from the early years of the twentieth century shows Ware Street looking up from the railway bridge. Mr and Mrs Lurcock's house is the property on the right hand side:

Reproduced courtesy of Jean Jones

This photograph shows the same area of Ware Street in 2006. Note the new property under construction in the garden of the adjacent house which was also recently extended. Within living memory, the percussion of the stone knapper at work nearby has now become a forgotten sound.

Reproduced courtesy of Malcolm Kersey

Envoi

As the twenty first century begins, the most obvious changes to Ware Street are the recent arrivals of the housing developments at Ragstone Place and in Bell Lane. Once more, the area has begun to adapt to economic change and circumstance.

These pages have attempted to chronicle at least part of the history and origins of Ware Street that can be traced back over six hundred years. The sunken lanes are an indication of the land use which took place before the Norman Conquest, and which continued well into the medieval period. To this shaping of the landscape, can be added the witness found in the written records. How curious it is that the copies of some fourteenth century manorial transactions were recorded in the seventeenth century.

It is plain that the income gained from the manor of Ware was never substantial. Between the sixteenth and eighteenth centuries, the residents evidently had a lifestyle which sufficed for their immediate needs. It was not a particularly prosperous period, but by the beginning of the nineteenth century, the residents were experiencing financial and economic pressure. Some of the poorest members of long-established families in Bearsted and Thurnham came to live in the cheaper accommodation available in Ware Street. Perhaps it was this change of circumstance that helped to save some of the older properties. Did the owner of Mays Cottages decide not to demolish them simply because they were just more convenient to retain? We shall never know.

The early years of the twentieth century saw the start of world wide social and economic change. Several families emigrated to Canada and explored the wider world prior to the Great War in 1914. Farm work continued to employ the largest number of people in Ware Street, but there was still sufficient capacity in the community to support a diverse variety of occupations. The closure of the brick field and tile kiln in the 1920s meant a loss of one form of employment, but there were jobs available further afield.

The identity of Ware Street as a separate manor has long since passed out of recognition by the local community. But, even after six hundred years, glimpses of Ware Street as a place and a community which long ago met economic and social changes with relative equanimity can still be found. Even on a busy day the experience of past centuries seems to be very close; a true social richness which first became apparent when I came to live in the area over thirty years ago.

Kathryn Kersey

Appendix One

Transcriptions of the original Latin records for the Manor of Ware

Document One

A Court of the Prior and Convent of Rochester Cathedral, held at Ware on the Thursday next before the Feast of Saint Dunstan in the third year of the reign of King Richard

Cur(ia) Prior(is) et Convent(us) Eccl(es)ie Cathedral(is) Roffen(sis) tent(a) apud Ware Die Jovis p(ro)x(ima) ante festu(m) s(an)c(t)e Dunstani Anno Regni Regis Ric(ard)i [secundi omitted] t(e)rcij

Symon Sucenor ven(it) et [blank] rel(evium) suu(m) de terr(a) p(er)quis(ita) [blank] De Sheller,

et est rel(evium) suu(m) [blank],

Pre(ceptus) est Levar(e) de [Thorneham Thomas interlined] Whyce de terr(is) p(er)quis(itis) Joh(ann)is [blank] et de hered(um) Ric(ard)i [blank],

et est Rel(evium) suu(m) [blank],

Joh(ann)es Burbache Rog(e)r(us) de Cynton Wili(elmus) de [blank] in m(isericord)ia D(omi)ni p(ro) Defalt(a) Cur(ie),

Pre(ceptus) est [blank] will(elmu)m [blank] p(ro) terr(is) p(er)quis(itis) de will(elm)o Suconer Hamon(em) Mors Jacobu(m) Monk(es) Rob(er)tu(m) Arnolde Rog(e)rum de Chelisfeilde Will(elmu)m Bedell p(ro) rel(evijs) et fidel(itatibus) decent(ibus),

[blank] Joh(ann)em de Northwoode et Thom(am) Whyce p(ro) rel(evijs) [et omitted] fidel(itatibus) decent(ibus),

[No(m)i(n)a sectar(iorum) interlined] Cur(ie) de War,

Joh(ann)es Sherstede
Symon Sucener modo Rob(ertus) Morrel
Joh(ann)es Springe modo Jo(hannes?) Meggys
Thomas Whyce
Ric(ard)us Burbache
Johanna Chapman
Joh(an)na Dunne

Isti sunt Tenentes sup(r)a menc(i)onat(os) qui tenent(es) de ten(ementis) [quod written in error for quondam] Hugo(nis) De Thorneham pr(e)d(i)c(t)am? p(er)tin(entibus) ad Capellam be(a)te Marie De Rochester videlicet D(omi)na de Northwoode p(ro) ten(emento) Cynton(i) Rogerus De Syntoner Will(elmu)m Heyes Ham(onem) Mars Jacob(um) Monek(es) Rob(er)tus Arnolde Rog(e)rus de Chelesfeild Will(elmu)s Bedell,

Isti om(n)es tenentes tenent p(ro) iiij acr(is) terre in parcell(is) pr(e)te(r) D(omi)nam de Northwoode,

Et debent int(er) eos iiij s(olidos) iij d(enarios) pr(e)ter ix d(enarios) De D(omi)na de Northwood p(ro) e...d(e)m? [eisdem?],

179

Document Two

In the thirteenth year of the Reign of Richard II of England

Anno R(egni) R(egi)s Ric(ard)i s(e)c(un)di [blank] Angl(ie) terciodecimo

Esson(ie),

Joh(ann)es Bracok Joh(ann)es Barstede et Joh(ann)es Burbache p(er) Joh(ann)em Spring,

Prec(eptus) est Joh(ann)i Gy Bedell(o) distr(ingere) Joh(ann)em wrecocke q(uo)d sit ad p(ro)x(imam) Cur(iam) ad respondend(um) D(omi)no de fidelitat(e) et rel(ev)io p(ro) j rod(a) terr(e) [de Joh(ann)e F] p(er)quis(ita) de Joh(ann)e Fleg(es),

et est Rel(evium) ob(olum),

Pr(eceptus) est Bedell(o) distr(ingere) Joh(ann)em Clyve Hamonem Maas Rog(e)r(um) Chelisfeild Will(elmu)m Bedell et Alic(iam) Cyntone [de Rel(ev)ie, q(uo)d sint interlined] ad p(ro)x(imam) Cur(iam) ad respondend(um) D(omi)no de fidelit(ate) et rel(ev)io p(ro) terra et ten(ementum) p(er)quis(itis) et eis access(itis) [De D(omi)no] et ad sanand(um) Defect(us) [secte omitted] Cur(ie),

Et Alicia(m) in m(isericord)ia ad respondend(um) D(omi)no de fidelitat(e) et rel(ev)io p(ro) terr(is) Joh(ann)is Maas de Joh(ann)e Beneyt,

et Joh(ann)em Roo p(ro) terr(a) [blank] filius de Rog(e)ro Cynton,

Pr(eceptus) est Bedell(o) distr(ingere) Joh(ann)em Clyve Rob(er)tum Morrell D(omi)nam de Northwood Hamonem Maas Jacobu(m) Monke Rog(e)rum Chelisfeild Rob(er)tu(m) Arnolde ar(migerum)? Alic(iam) Cynton et Will(elmu)m Bedell q(uo)d [sunt written in error for sint] ad p(ro)x(imam) Cur(iam) ad respondend(um) D(omi)no p(ro) Defalt(a) sect(e) Cur(ie),

Sum(m)a huius Cur(ie), [blank],

[heading blank]

Ad hanc Cur(iam) [omitted] ad fac(iendum) D(omi)no fidelit(atom) p(ro) terr(is) p(er)quis(itis) de Will(elm)o Cynton et de Rog(e)ro Chelisfelde,

ij d(enarios),

[p(ro), blank] no(n) ven(it) ad fac(iendum) D(omi)no fidelit(atem) De terr(a) p(er)quis(ita) De Will(elm)o Cynton et q(uo)d Levar(e) de Will(elm)o Bedell,

ij d(enarios),

[blank] no(n) ven(it) ad fac(iendum) D(omi)no fidelit(atem) De terr(a) p(er)quis(ita) De eodem Will(elm)o Cynton,

Et no(m)i(natus) Distr(ingere) pr(e)d(i)c(t)i Hamo Rog(er)us et Will(elm)us Bedell p(ro) fidelitat(ibus) fac(iendis) cont(r)a p(ro)x(imam) Cur(iam),

Et ad sanand(um) Defect(us) eos sect(e) Cur(ie),

Ad Cur(iam) preced(entem) pr(eceptus) fuit Bed(ellum) Distr(ingere) Joh(ann)em Bacheler et Aliciam ux(or)em eius p(ro) fidelit(atibus) D(omi)no fact(is) De v rod(is) terr(e) eidem Alicie access(itis), post mortem Joh(ann)is Beneyt p(at)ris sui,

Et bed(ellum) [blank] nulla(m) fec(it) exec(utionem) in m(isericord)ia,

Et no(m)i(natus) [al(ias) interlined] distr(ingere) p(ro) eodem cont(r)a p(ro)x(imam) Cur(iam),

Pr(eceptus) est Bedell(o) sic al(ias) Distr(ingere) Joh(ann)am D(omi)nam de Northwoode Joh(ann)em Clyve [blank] non ven(erunt) et Will(elmu)m Bette p(ro) plur(ibus) Defect(ibus) co(mmun)is sect(e) Cur(ie),

Et Bedell(o) in m(isericord)ia [blank] no(n) Distr(inxit) Alicia(m) Cynton p(ro) fidelit(ate) D(omi)no fac(ienda) &c(eter)a,

Et no(m)i(na)t(us) distr(ingere) p(ro) eodem cont(r)a p(ro)x(imam) Cur(iam),

Pr(eceptus) est Bedell(o) distr(ingere) Hamo(n)e(m) Maas Rog(er)um Chelisfeild Rob(er)tum Arnold Alic(iam) Cynton will(elm)um Bedell Rog(er)um Cynton cont(r)a p(ro)x(imam) Cur(iam) p(ro) plur(ibus) Defalt(is) co(mmun)is sect(e) Cur(ie)

Document Three

A Rental of the Rents of le Ware in Thornham
1390-1398

Rentale Redituum in le Ware in Thurnham 1390-1398

Rentale redd(it)u(um) in p(ar)ochia de Thorneh(a)m [sic] pertinent(ium) ad Capellam s(an)c(t)e Marie v(ir)g(in)is Eccl(es)ie Cathedral(is)

H(oc) N(umer)o

Roff(e)n(sis) renovat(um) p(er) om(n)es Tenentes ib(ide)m tempore f(rat)ris Rog(er)i de [blank] Monachi et Custodis dicte Capelle Anno D(omi)ni Mill(esi)mo Trecentesimo [altered from Sexcentesimo] Nonagesimo Annoq(ue) Regni [quinto, vero interlined] Regis Ric(ard)i post Conquestum s(e)c(un)di vicesimo tercio

Solvend(orum) ad Festa [An(n)unciac(i)o(n)is b(ea)te Marie virginis et interlined] S(an)c(t)i Mich(ael)is Archangeli p(er) equates porc(i)o(n)es,

Primo de eodem Redd(it)u apud Le Ware in Thornh(a)m pr(e)d(i)c(t)a,

[blank],   ij s(olidos) vj d(enarios),

De Johanne [Spring interlined] de Berghestede p(ro) una pec(ia) terr(e) voc(ata) welteghe croftes cont(inenti) v [accr(as) written in error for acr(as)] terr(e) iac(entes) [iuxta; int(er) interlined] terr(as)

[Joh(ann)is Sharsted et hered(um) Ric(ard)i Burbach v(er)sus South et regia(m) strat(am) v(er)sus interlined and extends into right-hand margin]

[added in margin: North] et terr(am)]

d(i)c(t)or(um) heredum et Will(elm)i Wrecock(es) v(er)sus [B, East interlined] et ad Northrokesacrestrete v(er)sus West,

Ad eosdem terminos,   xx d(enarios),

De Hered(ibus) Ric(ard)i Burbache p(ro) iij m(essuagi)os cont(inentibus) iij rod(is) et Di(midia) [Daiwork(es)] terr(e) quondam Rob(er)ti Beneyt Pet(ri) Roksacre et Rob(er)ti ate Welle iac(entes) int(er) terr(as) Joh(ann)is [Spring interlined] v(er)sus South et West et Regiam stratam v(er)sus North et ad terr(am) Will(elm)i Wrecok(es) v(er)sus East,

ad eosdem t(er)minos,   iij d(enarios),

De eisdem [p(er) written in error for p(ro)] iij rod(is) terr(e) iac(entibus) in loco voc(ato) Ferrays int(er) terr(as) Joh(ann)is Sharsted v(er)sus North et West et terram pr(e)d(i)c(t)or(um) heredu(m) v(er)sus South et ad Northrokesacrestrete v(er)sus Boream,

ad eosdem t(er)mi(n)os   iij d(enarios),

De Rob(er)to Morrell [~~Elizabeth Cokir?~~] [p(er) written in error for p(ro)] iij rod(is) terr(e) iac(entibus) in loco voc(ato) Ferrays int(er) terr(as) Joh(ann)is Sharstede v(e)rsus South [altered West] et North et ad Northrokesacrestrete v(er)sus East,

ad eosdem t(er)mi(n)os   iij d(enarios),

De Johanne [abbreviation marked in error] Sharstede et Joh(an)ne Meggyll p(ro) una rod(a) terr(e) quond(am) will(elm)i wrecock(es) iac(enti) apud Le weltighe int(er) terr(as) heredu(m) Ric(ard)i Burbache v(er)sus South et west et terr(am) will(elm)i wrecok(es) v(er)sus East et ad Regiam stratam v(er)sus North,

ad eosdem t(er)mi(n)os,   j d(enarium),

It(e)m de eodem redd(it)u apud Thornh(a)m streete infer(ius) monte(m)

De Her(edum) Joh(ann)is Clyve p(ro) ij acr(is) terr(e) iac(entibus) apud Le Slede et Stuper int(er) terr(am) Rob(er)ti Arnold v(er)sus East et terr(am) Joh(ann)is Wookherste v(er)sus west et terr(am) vicar(ij) De Thornh(a)m v(er)sus South et ad terr(am) will(el)mi Bedill v(er)sus North,

ad eosd(e)m t(er)mi(n)os,   vj d(enarios),

De eisdem p(ro) una acr(a) [terr(e) interlined] iac(enti) atte [~~Reg?~~ [perhaps, Rog] Berne al(ias) voc(ato) Le uphouse int(er) terram pr(e)d(i)c(t)or(um) heredum v(er)sus South et terr(as) vicar(ij) De Thornh(a)m v(er)sus North et west et ad terr(as) Alexandri Birland et Will(el)mi Bedill v(er)sus East,

ad eosd(e)m t(er)mi(n)os,   iij d(enarios),

De Edmundo Arnolde p(ro) ij acr(is) terr(e) iac(entibus) atte Forhell int(er) terr(am) heredum Joh(ann)is Clyve v(er)sus west et terr(as) will(elm)i Bedyll et Joh(ann)is Broun(e) v(er)sus East et terr(am) vicar(ij) de Thornh(a)m v(er)sus South et ad Regiam viam v(er)sus North,

ad eosdem t(er)mi(n)os,   vj d(enarios),

De eodem p(ro) iij rod(is) terr(e) iac(entibus) in Le Eastcombe int(er) terr(as) Margar(ete) [altered from Marger(ie)] Maas v(er)sus South et East et terr(am) Will(elm)i Bedyll v(er)sus West et ad terr(am) Alicie de Ayntone v(er)sus North

ad eosdem t(er)mi(n)os,   ij d(enarios) q(uadrantem),

De eodem p(ro) una croft(a) voc(ata) Littlecroftes cont(inenti) unam rod(am) terr(e) iac(entem) sub mes(suagio) suo

v(er)sus West et terr(as) Rog(er)i Chelisfeilde et [~~Ha~~] Hamo(n)is Maas v(er)sus East et terr(am) Joh(ann)is Broun(e) v(er)sus North et ad [~~terr(am)~~] regiam viam voc(atam) Dunstrete v(er)sus South

ad eosdem t(er)mi(n)os,   ob(olum) q(uadrantem)

De eodem p(ro) Di(midia) acr(a) terr(e) iac(enti) apud Le Hunost? al(ias) voc(atum) Lewente,

ad eosdem t(er)mi(n)os,   j d(enarium) ob(olum)

De Jacobo Monk(es) p(ro) una acr(a) terr(e) Josesacre quond(a)m Hamo(n)is Maas iac(enti) iuxta Dunstreete v(er)sus South et terr(am) Rog(er)i [Colisfield? Chelisfeld interlined]

[added in right hand margin Chelisfeild]

v(ersus North et Croft(es) Rob(er)ti Arnolde v(e)rsus west et ad terr(am) will(elm)i Bedill v(er)sus East,

ad [altered] eosdem t(er)mi(n)os,   iij d(enarios),

De eodem p(ro) una acr(a) terr(e) iac(enti) apud Degherislond [altered] int(er) terr(am) will(elm)i Bedill [altered] v(er)sus North et regiam viam v(er)sus Sowth et inter terr(as) Gi(s)l(e)b(er)ti Braunch v(er)sus west et East,

ad eosdem t(er)mi(n)os,   iij d(enarios),

De eodem p(ro) iij rod(is) terr(e) de (terris) Hugon(is) de Thornham quond(am) Joh(ann)is Beneyt iac(entibus) in Berashcombe inter terr(am) Joh(ann)is Beneyt pr(e)d(i)c v(er)sus North et terr(am) Joh(ann)is Bedill v(er)sus South et terr(am) vicar(ij) de Thornh(a)m v(er)sus East et ad terr(am) Ric(ard)i Bushe senior(is) v(er)sus West,

ad eosdem t(er)mi(n)os,   ij d(enarios) q(uadrantem),

De Symone Cotev(er) [perhaps Coten(er)] al(ia)s Cotebie p(ro) ij rod(is) terr(e) quond(am) Hamo(n)is Maas iac(entibus) apud Breche int(er) terr(am) Rog(er)i Chelisfelde v(er)sus West et terr(am) Will(elm)i Bedyll v(e)rsus East et terr(am) vicar(ij) de Thornh(a)m v(er)sus South et ad terr(am) Rog(e)ri Chelisfeld pr(e)d(i)c(t)i v(er)sus North,

ad eosdem t(er)mi(n)os,   j d(enarium) ob(olum),

De eodem p(ro) iij rod(is) terr(e) quond(a)m Hamo(n)is Maas iac(entibus) in Le Eastcombe ad terr(am) Marger(ie) [altered] Maas v(er)sus South et terr(am) Joh(ann)is Chelisfeilde v(er)sus North et terr(am) Edmundi Arnolde v(er)sus West et ad terr(am) Margar(ete) [altered from Marger(ie)] Maas pr(e)d(i)c(t)e v(er)sus East

ad eosdem t(er)mi(n)os,   ij d(enarios) [ob(olum)] q(uadrantem),

De Rog(er)o Chelisfelde p(ro) una acr(a) terr(e) iac(enti) in Le Eastcombe capit(a) ad terr(am) Will(elm)i Bedyll v(er)sus South et terr(am) voc(atam) [Ga...latelond] Ganelatelond? [perhaps Gavelatelond] v(er)sus North et terr(am) pr(e)d(i)c(t)i Rog(er)i v(er)sus West [ad] terr(am) Will(elm)i Bedyll v(er)sus East

ad eosdem t(er)mi(n)os,   iij d(enarios),

De eodem p(ro) iij rod(is) terr(e) iac(entibus) in loco voc(ato) le Chermer al(ias) voc(ato) Shottfor int(er) terr(am) Joh(ann)is Bedyll v(er)sus South et terr(am) d(i)c(t)i Rog(er)i v(er)sus North et terr(am) Will(elm)i Bedyll v(er)sus West et ad terr(am) Alexandri Dirland v(er)sus East,

ad eosdem t(er)mi(n)os,   ij d(enarios) q(uadrantem),

De eodem p(ro) una rod(a) et Di(midia) terr(e) iac(entibus) apud Le Breche int(er) terr(as) pr(e)d(i)c(t)i Rog(er)i v(er)sus North et South et terr(am) Symo(n)is Cotev(er)? [perhaps Coten(er)] al(ias) Cotebie v(er)sus East et ad terr(am) Alexandri Dirland v(er)sus West, ad eosdem t(er)mi(n)os,   j d(enarium) di(midium) q(u)a(drantis)

De Johanne Chelisfelde p(ro) una acr(a) et una rod(a) terr(e) quond(am) Alic(ie) de Ayntone iac(entibus) in Le Eastcombe int(er) terr(am) Will(elm)i Bedyll v(er)sus West et terr(am) pr(e)d(i)c(t)i Joh(ann)is v(er)sus East et terr(am) Rob(er)ti Arnolde v(er)sus South et ad terr(am) Rog(er)i Chelisfeild v(er)sus North,

ad eosdem t(er)mi(n)os,   iij d(enarios) ob(olum) q(uadrantem),

De Joh(ann)e Bachelor p(ro) una acr(a) et una rod(a) terr(e) de terr(is) Hugon(is) de Thornham quond(am) Joh(ann)is Beneyt iac(entibus) in Berashcombe int(er) terr(as) Joh(ann)is Bachelor pr(e)d(i)c(t)i v(er)sus North et South et terr(am) heredum Joh(ann)is Clyve v(er)sus East et ad terr(am) Joh(ann)is Foxe v(er)sus West,

ad eosdem t(er)mi(n)os,   iij d(enarios) ob(olum) q(uadrantem),

De will(el)mo Bedill Edmundo Arnolde et Margar(ete) [altered from Marger(ie)] Maas p(ro) xij Daywerc(is) et Di(midia) et octava p(ar)te uni(us) Daywerc(e) terr(e) ubi mes(suagium) Hugon(is) de Thorneh(a)m olim constructu(m) fu(er)at iac(entibus) apud Thornehamstreete v(er)sus West et terr(am) Joh(ann)is Broun(e) v(e)rsus East et [terr(am)] mes(suagium) Will(elm)i Whytewonge v(er)sus North et ad [terr(am)] mess(uagium) Margar(ete) [altered from Marger(ie)] Maas pr(e)d(i)c(t)e v(e)rsus South;

ad eosdem t(er)mi(n)os,   j d(enarium),

De Alexandr(o) Dirland p(ro) una pec(ia) terr(e) ubi grangia Joh(ann)is de Aynetone quondam constructa [fura] fuerat cont(inenti) unam rod(am) terr(e) iac(entem) int(er) terr(as) heredu(m) Joh(ann)is Clyve v(e)rsus South et West et terr(am) Will(elm)i Bedyll v(e)rsus North et ad regiam viam v(e)rsus East,

ad eosdem t(er)mi(n)os,   ob(olum) q(uadrantem),

It(e)m de eodem redd(it)u sup(r)a montem apud Ainetone

De D(omi)na Johanna D(omi)na de Northwoode p(ro) uno gardino ubi messuag(ium) Rog(e)ri de Ainetone olim constructu(m) fu(er)it cum una(m) pec(iam) terr(e) adiacent(em) in crofto voc(ato) Ayntonscroftes al(ias) voc(ato) Eastbynne quond(am) Rog(e)ri et Will(elm)i de Aynetone cont(inentes) in toto iij acr(as) et iij rod(as) terr(e) iac(entes) int(er) terr(am) pr(e)d(i)c(t)e D(omi)ne in crofto pr(e)d(i)c(t)o v(e)rsus South et viam ducentem v(e)rsus Aynetone Daue v(e)rsus East et Ayntonstreate [word divided between two lines] v(e)rsus West et ad croft(am) voc(atam) Northayntonescroftes [v(e)rsus West] et [ad croft(am)] silvam voc(atam) yppintonswoode v(e)rsus North,

et p(ro) una pec(ia) terr(e) voc(ata) Aldiflonde cont(inenti) iij acr(as) et Di(midiam) quond(am) Rog(e)ri et Will(elm)i de Aynetone pr(e)d(i)c(t)or(um) iac(entes) ad viam Regiam v(e)rsus North et West et Le Brome [et interlined] Skelkisdale al(ias) voc(atum) Cokkisdaue v(e)rsus East et ad Eastdowne v(e)rsus [South interlined],

et p(ro) una acr(a) et Di(midia) terr(e) quond(am) Rob(er)ti et Joh(ann)is De Aynetone iac(entibus) in Skelkisdale al(ia)s vocat(am) Colkisdale iux(t)a viam v(e)rsus North et ad terr(as) pr(e)d(i)c(t)e D(omi)ne v(e)rsus West, East et South

ad [t(er)mi(n)os] eosdem t(er)minos,   xv d(enarios),

Sum(ma) huius redditus   x s(olidos) ij d(enarios) ob(olum) q(uadrantem) et di(midium)

Document Four

A Court of the Prior and Convent of Rochester held there
in the Thursday next after the Feast of Saint Luke the Evangelist
in the fifteenth year of the reign of King Richard II

[Ware]

Cur(ia) Prior(is) et Convent(us) Roffen(sis) tent(a) ib(ide)m Die Jovis p(ro)x(ima) post Festu(m) s(an)c(t)i? [Luco? Luce interlined] Evangeliste An(n)o Regni Regis Ric(ard)i s(e)c(un)di quinto Decimo

Joh(ann)es Spring de co(mmun)i sect(a) p(er) Joh(ann)em Sharstede,

Bedell(us) in m(isericord)ia p(ro) [non Jo] no(n) [blank] Joh(ann)em wrecock ad respondend(um) D(omi)no de fidelit(ate) p(ro) una rod(a) terr(e) p(er)quis(ita) De Joh(ann)e Flegg(es),

Et no(m)i(na)t(us) Distr(ingere) p(ro) eodem cont(r)a p(ro)x(imam) Cur(iam),

Pr(eceptus) [est omitted] Bedell(o) q(uo)d Levar(e) fac(iat) De Joh(ann)e Clyve de rel(ev)io p(ro) terr(a) p(er)quis(ita) de Will(elm)o Synton,

et est rel(ev)ium,   iiij d(enarios) ob(olum),

Et no(m)i(na)t(us) [p(ro) fidelitat(e)] distr(ingere) p(ro) fidelitat(e) fac(ienda) cont(r)a p(ro)x(imam) Cur(iam),

Et de Hamone Maas de rel(ev)io p(ro) terr(a) p(er)quis(ita) de Will(elm)o Cynton,

Et est rel(ev)ium,   iij d(enarios) q(uadrantem),

Et de Rog(e)ro Chelisfeild de rel(ev)io p(ro) terr(a) p(er)quis(ita) de pr(e)d(i)c(t)o will(elm)o,

                                                iij d(enarios) q(u)a(drantem),

Et de Will(elm)o Bedyll de rel(ev)io p(ro) terr(a) p(er)quis(ita) de pr(e)d(i)c(t)o Will(elm)o,

                                                q(u)a(drantem),

Et de Alic(ie) Cynton de rel(ev)io,   ij d(enarios),

Et no(m)i(natus) Distr(ingere) om(n)es p(ro) fidelitat(ibus) fac(iendis) cont(r)a p(ro)x(imam) Cur(iam),

Et ad sanand(um) Defect(us) sect(e) Cur(ie),

Prec(eptus) est Bedyll q(uo)d Levar(e) fac(iat) De will(elm)o Bette de rel(ev)io p(ro) iij rod(is) terr(e) p(er)qu(i)s(ita) de Alano Bette,

Et ip(s)e antea de Joh(ann)e Weneytt,

Et est rel(ev)ium duplex   ij [denarios omitted] ob(olum),

Et no(m)i(na)t(us) distr(ingere) p(ro) fid(elitate) fac(ienda) cont(r)a p(ro)x(imam) Cur(iam),

Et de Joh(ann)e Bachelor et Alic(ia) ux(or)e eius de rel(ev)io p(ro) v rod(is) terr(e) eidem Alic(ie) [access] access(itis) post morte(m) Joh(ann)is Beneyt p(at)ris sui,

         iij d(enarios) ob(olum) q(u)a(drantem),

Et no(m)i(n)at(us) distr(ingere) p(ro) fidelitate fac(ienda) cont(r)a p(ro)x(imam) Cur(iam) et p(ro) Defalt(a) sect(e) Cur(ie),

Ad hanc Cur(iam) venit Rob(er)tus Morell et ponit se in m(isericord)ia p(ro) Defalt(a) sect(e) Cur(ie) ut sup(r)a,

Pr(eceptus) est Bedyll q(uo)d Levar(e) fac(iat),

De Hamone Maas,	ij d(enarios),
Jacobo Moncke,	ij d(enarios),
Rog(e)ro Chelisfeild,	ij d(enarios),
Rob(er)to Arnold,	ij d(enarios),
Alicia Cynton	ij d(enarios),
Will(elm)o Beddell	ij d(enarios),
Joh(ann)e Burbache	ij d(enarios),

et Joh(ann)e Meggyll p(ro) Ric(ard)o Burbache   [blank],

p(ro) Defalt(a) sect(e) Cur(i)e,

Et no(m)i(natus) distr(ingere) p(ro) eodem cont(r)a p(ro)x(im)a(m) Cur(iam),

Pr(eceptus) est Bedell(o) sic plur(es) distr(ingere) Joh(ann)am al(ias) D(omi)nam de Northwode, Joh(ann)em Clyve et Will(elmu)m Bette q(uo)d sint ad p(ro)x(imam) Cur(iam) ad respondend(um) D(omi)no p(ro) Defalt(a) sect(e) Cur(ie),

Sum(ma) huius Cur(ie),   ij s(olidos) xj d(enarios) ob(olum)

Document Five

The Court of Ware, held there on the Thursday next before the Feast of Saint Dunstan in the [blank] year of King Richard II

Cur(ia) de ware tent(a) ib(ide)m Die Jovis p(ro)x(ima) ante festum s(an)c(t)e Dunstani Anno [blank] R(egni) R(egi)s Ric(ard)i s(e)c(un)di &c[(eter)a],

De Simo(n)e Cutever? [perhaps Cutener] de rel(ev)io,	j d(enarium) ob(olum)
Pre(ceptus) est Levar(e) de Thoma Whyce De terr(is) Perquis(itis) de Joh(ann)e Burbache et de her(edibus) Ric(ard)i Robasar de Rel(evio),	iij d(enarios)
De Joh(ann)e Burbache p(ro) Defalt(a),	iij s(olidos) ij d(enarios)
De Rog(e)ro Cyntoner p(ro) ead(em),	ij d(enarios)
De Will(elm)o de Helles p(ro) ead(em),	ij d(enarios)
De Will(elm)o de Helles p(ro) ead(em) [repeated]	ij d(enarios)
Sum(m)a,	[blank]

Pre(ceptus) est [blank] will(elmu)m Dyche de terr(is) p(er)quis(itis) de Rog(e)ro Cutever? [perhaps Cutener] Hamone Mars Jacobu(m) Monek(es) Rob(er)tu(m) Arnolde Rog(e)ru(m) de Chelisfeild et Will(elmu)m Bedell p(ro) rel(evijs) et fid(elitatibus) decent(ibus),

[blank] pr(eceptus) est D(omi)nam Joh(ann)am De Northwood et Thomas Whyce p(ro) Rel(evijs) et fidelitat(ibus) decent(ibus),

Rental(e) de Thorneham,

[A added] Joh(ann)es Sharstede,	ij s(olidos) vj d(enarios)
[A added] Joh(ann)es Sprynge,	xx d(enarios)
[A added] Rog(e)rus Burbache,	[blank]
[A added] Thomas Whyce,	vj d(enarios)
[A added] Johanna Chapman,	iiij d(enarios)
[A added] Johanna Donne [1 Day]	
[A added] D(omi)na Johanna De Northwoode p(ro) [blank] de execuc(i)one	ix d(enarios)

Document Six

A Court held there on the Wednesday next, after the Feast of Saint Mark the Evangelist, in the twenty second year of the reign of King Richard II

Cur(ia) tent(a) ib(ide)m Die [et] Martis p(ro)x(ima) post festum s(an)c(t)i Marci Evangelisti Anno R(egni) R(egi)s Ric(ard)i s(e)c(un)di Anglie vicesimo s(e)c(un)do],

No(n) [blank] essoinatus fu(er)it bis,

Rob(er)tus Morell p(er) Ric(ard)um Carde,
Joh(ann)em Meggill p(er) Joh(ann)em Sharstede,
Joh(ann)es Spryng(es) p(er) Edmundu(m) Arnolde,
de co(mmun)i sect(a),

Distr(ingere) [est] prec(eptus) est bedello sic al(ias) dis(tringere) D(omi)nam Johannam de Northwood q(uo)d sit ad p(ro)x(imam) Cur(iam) ad respondend(um) D(omi)no p(ro) plur(ibus) Default(es) sect(e) Cur(ie) sanand(o),

Et Rob(er)tum Arnald p(ro) plur(ibus) Defalt(es) co(mmun)is sect(e) Cur(ie) sanand(o),

Et ad hanc Cur(iam) venit Ed(mund)us Arnold et posuit se in m(isericord)ia D(omi)ni p(ro) plur(ibus) Defalt(es)co(mmun)is sect(e) Cur(ie) p(er) eundem Rob(er)tu(m) fact(um) &c(eter)a,

Prec(eptus) est bedell(o) Leovar(e) ad opus D(omi)ni de bonis et catallis Rob(er)ti Morell ij d(enarios) faciend(i) Defaltu(m) ad hanc Cur(iam),

Et [blank] pr(e)cept(us) est bedell(o) dis(tringere) eund(u)m Rob(er)tu(m) cont(r)a p(ro)x(imam) Cur(iam) ad respondend(um) D(omi)no p(ro) plur(ibus) Defalt(es) co(mmun)is sect(e) Cur(ie) sanand(o) &c(eter)a,

Prec(eptus) est bedell(o) dis(tringere) Joh(ann)em Carde Rob(er)tus Arnolde et Joh(ann)em Chelisfeild q(uo)d sint ad p(ro)x(imam) Cur(iam) ad respondend(um) D(omi)no p(ro) plur(ibus) Defalt(es) co(mmun)is sect(e) Cur(ie) sanand(o) &c(eter)a,

Ad'

Document Eight

Court Book entries for the Manor of Ware
1613-1647

Folio 13

Manerium de ware in Thornham

Cur(ia) Baronis Decani et Cap(i)t(u)li p(re)dict(orum) tent(a) ib(ide)m Die Jovis videlicet xxij o Die Septembr(is) Anno R(egni) R(egis) Jacobi Angl(ie) &c(etera) xij o et Scocie xlviij o p(er) Joh(ann)em Somer Seneschallu(m) p(re)fat(o) Decano Subdecano Mag(ist)ro Collins et Mag(ist)ro Barnwell tunc p(re)sen(tibus),

Esson(ie)

Rob(er)tus Barling Johanna Tilden et Georgi...? [ending lost in binding] Coulter,

Homag(ium)

Joh(ann)es Crompe gen(erosus) modo Maior de Maidstone,

Ric(ard)us winter,

Gillamus [sic] Snowe iure ux(or)is,

Rob(er)tus Coulter

Folio 14

Qui dicunt sup(er) sacr(u)m suu(m) q(uo)d w(illelmu)s Coulter Joh(ann)es Spice [blank] Shernden et [blank] Vidgyn sunt Tenen(tes) huius Man(er)ij et debent sect(am) ad Cur(iam) p(re)d(i)c(t)am, et non comparuer(unt) ad hanc Cur(iam) sed pardonant(ur) eor(um) absencia p(ro) eo q(uo)d non p(re)munit(i) fuer(unt),

It(e)m p(re)sentant q(uo)d cit(r)a ultimam Cur(iam) Ric(ard)us wynter p(er)quesivit [de quodam Georgio Page interlined] unu(m) mesuagiu(m) cum uno gardino et unam rodam terr(e) iacen(tia) et existen(tia) in ware p(re)dict(o) in d(i)c(t)a paroch(ia) de Thornham [antehac mesuag(ium) et terr(am) cuiusdam will(elm)i Coulter interlined] abbuttan(tia) sup(er) regiam stratam ib(ide)m v(er)sus Boream ad terr(as) Joh(ann)is Crompe v(er)sus orien(tem) occiden(tem) et Austrum,

p(er) fidelitatem sect(am) Cur(ie) et ann(u)al(em) reddit(um) j d(enarij) ob(oli),

et p(re)sens hie in Cur(ia) fecit D(omi)nis fidelitatem et vadiavit eis tot(um) reddit(um) p(re)dict(um) no(m)i(n)e elevij videl(ice)t

j d(enarium) ob(olum),

et admissus fuit Tenens et po(s)itus fuit in homag(io),

It(e)m p(re)sentant q(uo)d Gillamus Snowe iure Johanne ux(or)is eius [filie et hered(is) Soror(is) interlined] Rob(er)ti Shernden [tenet de D(omi)nis] [quiquidem Rob(er)tus p(er) ult(imam) volun(tatem)] tenuit de D(omi)nis interlined] huius man(er)ij ut de hoc Maner(io) tres pecias sive parcell(as) terr(e) et bosci cum p(er)tin(encijs) iacen(tes) et existen(tes) apud ware p(re)dict(um) (ro)pe quandam venellam ib(ide)m vocat(am) Ferrys Lane abbuttan(tes) ad d(i)c(t)am venellam v(er)sus orient(em) ad terr(am)   Will(elm)i Artridge v(er)sus Austrum ad terr(am) Rob(er)ti Barling v(er)sus occiden(tem) et ad terr(am) hered(um) Joh(ann)is Spice v(er)sus Boream,

p(er) fidelitat(em) sect(am) Cur(ie) et ann(u)al(em) reddit(um)

vj d(enariorum) ob(oli)

et [modo quiquidem Rob(er)tus p(er) voluntatem suam in scriptis dedit easdem terr(as) eidem Johanne duran(ti) vita sua et postea will(elm)o Eaton et Agneti Eaton fil(ie) interlined]

[p(re)sens in Cur(ia) fecit D(omi)nis fidelitat(em) etvadiavit eis no(m)i(n)e]

[eiusdem]

[Johanne et p(re)d(i)c(t)us Gillamus modo p(re)sens in Cur(ia) fecit D(omi)nis fidelitatem et vadiavit interlined]

[eis no(m)i(n)e] relevij tot(um) reddit(um)videlicet

vj d(enarios),

et [fecit D] admissus fuit inde Tenens et po(s)itus fuit in homag(io),

It(e)m p(re)sentant q(uo)d Rob(er)tus Coulter est Tenens huius man(er)ij sed p(ro) eo q(uo)d nesciunt c(er)titudinem terr(as) quas clamat   [tenere de hoc manor(io) interlined] Ideo dies dat(us) est eidem Rob(er)to et cet(er)is Tenen(tibus) huius Man(er)ij ad p(ro)tulend(um) in scriptis [om(n)e] c(er)titudinem [onn.? written in error for omnes] terr(as) et ten(ementa) que quil(ibe)t eor(um)clamat tenere de hoc maner(io) usq(ue) p(ro)x(imam) Cur(iam),

[Memorand(um) that this Court hath been kept for many years past by the Farmer of the Dean and Chapter, and therefore I have hereunder written the rent(s) now paid in Court]

Inprimis,

of Johane Tilden, for 3 years rent now due	ix d(enarios)
of John Crompe, for the like	v s(olidus) vj d(enarios)
of Rob(er)te Barling, for the like, and for his relief	ix s(olidus)
of Georg Coulter, for the like, being heretofore the land of John Cromp	ij s(olidus) iij d(enarios)
of Rob(er)t Coulter and Edward Coulter, being the land(s) of Rob(er)t Sawyers, for 3 years rent now behind	iiij s(olidus) ij d(enarios)
of Gillam Snowe, for 3 years rent now behind	xviij d(enarios)

Folio 24

Maneriu(m) de Ware in Thurnham,

Cur(ia) Baronis ven(er)abil(ium) Decani et Cap(i)t..? [document torn away] p(re)dict(orum) tent(a) ib(ide)m Die et Anno ultim(is) menc(i)on(atis) coram p(re)fat(o) Joh(ann)e Somer Senescallo Mag(ist)ro Doctore Tillesley Archideacono Roffen(sis) et Receptore Eccl(es)ie Cath(edral)is p(re)dict(e) tunc p(re)sen(tibus)

Esson(ie),

Ed(wa)r(d)us Coulter et Georgius Coulter,

Homagium,

Joh(ann)es Crompe

[Gillanus written in error for] Gillamus Snowe

Ric(ard)us Wynter

W(illelmu)s Spice Attorn(atus) p(ro) Johanna Tilden vid(ua)   }   iur(ati)

Henr(icus) Coulter

Rob(er)tus Barling

Rob(er)tus Coulter

Qui dicunt sup(er) sacr(u)m suu(m) q(uo)d nihil est infra hoc Maner(ium) ad hanc Cur(iam) ad eor(um) noticiam p(re)sentabile,

An Entry of the Rent(es) now paid in Court

Payed by Robert Barlyng for 3 years ending at Michaelmas next	vj s(olidus) ix d(enarios)
by W(illia)m Spice for Johane Tilden for 2 years ending at Michaelmas next	vj d(enarios)
by Richard Wynter, for 2 years ending at Michaelmas next	ij d(enarios)
by Georg Coulter, for 3 years ending at Michaelmas next	ij s(olidus) iij d(enarios)
by Robert Coulter and Edward Coulter for 3 years ending at Michaelmas next	iiij s(olidus) j d(enarios)ob(olum)
by Gillam Snowe for 2 years ending at Michaelmas next	xij d(enarios)
by Henr(y) Coulter, for his part for 3 years rent ending at Michaelmas next	ij s(olidus) vj d(enarios)
by Robert Coulter, for his part for 3 years rent ending at Michaelmas next, being for land(s) late W(illia)m Coulter, their father,	xix d(enarios) ob(olum)
by m(aste)r John Crompe, for 2 years ending at Michaelmas next	iij s(olidus) viij d(enarios)

Elegerunt Gillamu(s) Snowe Bedellum huius Maner(ij) p(ro) Anno sequen(ti) qui sacr(u)m p(re)stitit officiu(m) suu(m) fidelit(er) exequend(um).

Document Nine

Court Book entry for the Manor of Ware, 1648

Maner(ium)de Ware in Thurnam vid(e) lib(rum) quintu(m)

Curia Baron(is) Decani et Capit(u)li Eccles(ie) Cath(deral)is Roffen(sis) ib(ide)m tent(a) decimo sexto die Januarij Anno regni dom(in)i nostri Car(oli) nunc Regis Anglie &c(etera) vicesimo quarto cora(m) Petro Buck Arm(igero) ib(ide)m Sen(eschal)lo 1648

Homag (ium)   Nicholaus Muddle
                 Richard(us) Hatch   } Jur (ati)

Qui sup(er) sacramenta sua dicunt et pr(e)sentant q(uo)d Jane Coulter vid(ua) Jacobus Wood Tho(m)as Crump Th(m)as Allen in iure uxor(is) sunt liberi tenent(es) huius maner(ij) et debent secta(m) ad hand cur(iam) ad hunc diem et fecerunt defalt(am).

ideo quilibet eoru(m) est in m(isericord)ia quatour denar(ios)

Alienatio
Item pr(e)sentant q(uo)d Rob(er)tus Coulter qui tenuit de hoc maner(io) quanda(m) terra(m) p(ro) fidelitate sect(a) cur(ie) et annual(is) redit(us) servit(io) un(i) solid(i) et undecem denar(iorum) citra ultima(m) cur(iam) alienavit pr(e)d(ictam) terra(m) Janae Coulter vid(ue) unde accidit domi(nis) pro alienatione totus redit(us) secundu(m) consuetudine(m) huius maner(ij)

et pr(e)ceptu(s) est balivo [des] destringere &c(etera)

Me(moran)d(um) ad hanc cur (iam) q(uo)d pred(icta) Jana Coulter est arretro in redity p(ro) 6 annos

Alienatio
Item pr(e)sentant q(uo)d Tho(m)as Bills qui tenuit de hoc maner(io) quondam parcellam terrae vocat(am) Weltes p(ro) fidelitate sect(a) cur(ie) et annual(is) redit(us) servit(io) un(i) solid(i) et dece(m) denar(iorum) citra ultima(m) cur(iam) alienavit et vendidit pr(e)d(ictam) parecella(m) Jacobo Wood unde accidit dominis pro alienatione secundu(m) consuetudine(m) huius maner(ij) totus redit(us) videlicet un(um) solid(um) et dece(m) denar(ios)

Et pr(e)ceptu(s) est balivo destringere &c(etera)

Alienatio
Item pr(e)sentant q(uo)d Willielmus Roades qui tenuit de hoc maner(io) tres acres terrae iacen(tes) iuxta quanda(m) terr(am) vocat(am) Braces p(ro) fidelitate sect(a) cur(ie) et annual(is) redit(us) servit(io) novem denar(iorum) citra ultima(m) cur(iam) alienavit et vendidit pr(e)d(ictas) tres acr(as) Thomae Crump unde accidit Domi(nis) pro alienatione secundu(m) consuetudine(m) huius maner(ij) totus redit(us) videlicet non(m) denar(ios)

et pr(e)ceptu(s) est balivo destringere &c(etera)

Alienatio
Item pr(e)sentant q(uo)d Henric(us) Muddle Richard(us) Hatch

et

Elizabetha Bell qui tenuerunt de hoc maner(io) un(um) messuag(ium) et un(am) rooda(m) terrae iacen(tia) ad terra(s) Jacobi Wood versus Borea(m) orient(em) et Austru(m) et ad venella(m) vocat(am) Ferris Lane et ad terra(m) Tho(m) ae Brewer versus occident(em) p(ro) fidelitatem sect(a) cur(ie) et annuali(is)..[end lost in binding] servit(io) un(i) denar(ij) citra ultimam cur(iam) alienavit pr(e)missa Nicholao Muddle unde accidit domi(nis) pro [tribus interlined] alienationibus secundu(m) consuetudine(m) huius maner(ij) totus redit(us)videlicet tres denar(ios)

quos pr(e)d(ictus) Nicholaus in curia solvit

Sheet M5 Folio 6

Alienatio
Item pr(e)sentant q(uo)d Henric(us) Muddle qui tenuit de hoc maner(io) p(ro) fidelitate sect(a) cur(ie) et annual(is) redit(us) servit(io) triu(m) dena(iorum) un(um) messuag(ium) un(am) acr(am) terrae vocat(am) Ferris iacen(tia) ad terra(s) Daniel(is) Godfrey versus Borea(m) et occident(em) ad terra(m) Annae Eaton versus Austru(m) et ad venella(m) vocat(am) Ferris Lane versus orient(em) citra ultima(m) cur(iam) alienavit et vendidit pr(e)missa Richard(o) Hatch unde accidit Domi(nis) pro alienatione secundu(m) consuetudine(m) huius maner(ij) totus redit(us) videlicet tres denar(ios)

quos pr(e)d(ictus) Richard(us) in cur(ia) solvit

Item pr(e)sentant q(uo)d (Richard(us)) Thomas Allen in iure uxoris eius tenet de hoc maner(io) un(um) messuag(ium) in quo curia tent(a) est p(ro) fidelitate sect(a) cur(ie) et annual(is) redit(us) servit(io) un(i) denar(ij)

Fidelitate(m) facient(em)

Ad hanc cur(iam) Nicholaus Muddle et Richard(us) Hatch fidelitate(m) fecerunt et in homage(io) posit(i)

Sheet M5 Folio 14

Ware Thurnha(m) al(ias) 5

It(em) pr(e)sent(ant) q(uo)d Willi(el)m(us) Shornden tenet de hoc Maner(io) tres pecias terr(e) et bosci iacen(tes) et exiaten(tes) apud Ware pr(e)dict(um) p(ro)pe quanda(m) venella(m) ib(ide)m vocat(am) Ferriss Lane p(er) annual(em) reddit(um)vi d(denariorum) que fuerunt quondam(m) Rob(er)ti Shornden

pr(e)dict(us) Willi(el)m(us) fuit admiss(us) in Homag(io) solvit reddit(um) aliena(ti)o(ni) u(ni) sol(idi)

al(ias)

Joh(ann) es [Bills interlined] venit et cog(novit) se teneri de hoc Manr(io) unu(m) Messuag(ium) unu(m) Gardinu(m) et una(m) roda(m) terr(e) iacen(tia) et existen(tia) in Ware predict(o) p(er) annual(em) redd(itum) i d(enarij)

solvit reddit(um) et po(s)itus in Homag(io)

Elegerunt Joh(ann)em Bills pr(e)dict(um) Bedellu(m) Huius Maner(ij) p(ro) anno sequent(i) qui sacru(m) pr(e)stitit officiu(m) suu(m) fidelity(er) exequend(um)

194

It(em) pr(e)sent(ant) hered(m) de Godden p(ro)pt(e)r terr(am) quondam(m) Guliel(mi) Coulter que ten(et) de hoc Maner(io) p(er) annual(em) reddit(um) xix d(enariorum) ob(oli)

It(em) pr(e)sent(ant) hered(m) de Solhurst p(ro)pt(e)r terr(am) iacen(tem) et existen(tem) p(er) 4 wents olim terr(am) Roberti Sawier tenet de hoc Maner(io) p(er) annual(em) reddit(um) xvj d(enariorum) ob(oli)

[In margin] *6? lib(rum), fo(lia) 32,59,60*

[English] Rents payd in Court, & the ten(an)ts Names

No(m)i(n)a Tenen(tium)

...lib(rum) fo(lia) 11,24,54

Guliel(mus) Cage miles p(ro) duob(us) reddit(ibus)
Jacob(us) Wood
Guliel(mus) Shornden
Joh(ann)es Bills
[~~Tho h...~~]
Heres Joh(ann)is Godden p(ro) duob(us) reddit(ibus)

Appendix Two

Further information about Edward Hart

Edward Hart was convicted on 16 August 1827 at the Summer Assizes at Maidstone. After receiving a sentence of transportation for seven years, he was held at Maidstone gaol until his removal to a prison hulk. The cost of keeping him at the gaol for two weeks and two days, between 16 and 31 August, amounted to 5s 8½d.[1]

This picture, by George Shepherd, gives an impression of Maidstone gaol around 1829:

Reproduced courtesy of Malcolm Kersey

On 1 September 1827, Edward was put on board a prison hulk, called *The Retribution*, which was moored at Sheerness.[2] The hulk was previously called *The Edgar* and had been launched in 1779. She was converted to a prison hulk in 1813 and re-named *The Retribution* in 1814. By the time Edward was on board, she held six hundred men and was in the last decade of service before being broken up in 1835.[3]

Prison ships, or hulks, had been introduced in the eighteenth century as a temporary expedient in response to a need to accommodate an increased number of convicts. The vast majority of the hulks were de-masted and broken down old warships. It did not take long for them to become a permanent institution and a famous sight for onlookers at places such as Woolwich and Sheerness. The smell of rotting woodwork, the remnants of rigging and seaweed-festooned ropes combined with the stench of the river added to the oppressive conditions in which the prisoners were held. Due to their location on the estuary mudflats, the hulks were isolated and difficult to access. Family visits to prisoners were permitted but seldom attempted.[4]

Many years before Charles Dickens wrote his vivid picture of the convict, Magwitch, in Great Expectations, it was widely acknowledged that the conditions on board the hulks were not good. On arrival at the hulk, convicts were stripped and washed and put in either chains or irons. Each convict was given a linen shirt, brown jacket and breeches to wear. The clothes were often of a very poor quality and did not last long reflecting the corruption of the authorities who took the money from the government and fraudulently supplied clothing of a lesser standard.[5]

The authorities were under great political pressure to keep the costs of the prisons down. They were also keen to avoid accusations of giving prisoners a better life than poor people who did not commit crimes. As a result, the diet was heavily limited. It largely comprised ox-cheek, which was boiled or made into a watery soup, pease pudding and bread or biscuit. Frequently, the meat was almost rotten or regularly substituted with poor quality oatmeal and cheese.[6]

The prisoners were kept in cells, or wards, on board the hulk. There was a passage forming a corridor along the middle of each deck and the cells were to either side. The passage was lit by a lantern held in a metal framework. Although the arrangements varied, there was an average of twelve cells on each of the upper and lower decks and eighteen cells in the orlop deck. Each cell, which held up to sixteen prisoners, opened on to the passage by a door with a grille which was used by the guards for inspection.[7]

The accommodation on board was very crowded: the average area of each deck measured 125 feet long by 40 feet in width. The height of the ceilings was just less than five feet. James Hardy Vaux, a former convict who had served part of his sentence on board a hulk, gave a contemporary description of the conditions on board *The Retribution* in his memoirs: [8]

> ...There were confined in this floating dungeon nearly 600 men, most of them double ironed; and the reader may conceive the horrible effects arising from the continual rattling of chains, the filth and vermin naturally produced by such a crowd of miserable inhabitants, the oaths and execrations constantly heard amongst them....

On the next page is a transcript of a summary of a timetable for convicts on board a hulk in the 1830s. It should be noted that this was drawn up for the prison hulk *The Leviathan* located at Portsmouth, but can be accepted as typical of the day on board other hulks. It is in an indication of the regime to which Edward was subjected.[9]

In the 1820s, there was very limited reform for the hulk system. During this time, convict labour began to be more effectively organised. Convicts still undertook hard labour, but if work decreased in one place, they were frequently transferred to another. The convicts at Medway were employed in the dockyards at Sheerness and Chatham and those with skills were particularly valued.[10] Despite the circumstances, Edward Hart may have been able to use his bricklaying skills.

This transcript below of a further portion of James Hardy Vaux's recollections gives a vivid picture of the reality of supplying convict labour: [11]

> ....Every morning, at seven o'clock, all the convicts capable of work or, in fact, all who are capable of getting into the boats, are taken ashore to the Warren [at Woolwich], in which the royal arsenal and other public buildings are situated, and there employed at various kinds of labour, some of them very fatiguing; and while so employed, each gang of sixteen or twenty men is watched and directed by a fellow called a guard.
>
> These guards are commonly of the lowest class of human beings; wretches devoid of all feeling; ignorant in the extreme, brutal by nature and rendered tyrannical and cruel by the consciousness of the power they possess; no others, but such as I have described, would hold the situation, their wages being not more than a day labourer would earn in London. They invariably carry a large and ponderous stick, with which, without the smallest provocation, they will fell an unfortunate convict to the ground, and frequently repeat their blows long after the poor sufferer is insensible...

Timetable for *The Leviathan*

3.00am
Cooks rise to prepare prisoners' breakfast.

5.30am
All hands called.

5.45am
Muster on deck, breakfast.
One of the three decks is washed. The deck chosen to be cleaned is selected on an alternate basis.

6.45am
Each prisoner brings his hammock, stows it away on deck and proceeds to labour.
On leaving the hulk, the prisoners irons are examined by the guards, who also search the prisoners to prevent anything improper being concealed. In the event of anything being afterwards found upon a prisoner, the guard that searched him is made responsible.
The prisoners are divided into sections of ten, each of which is sub-divided as required, and delivered into the charge of the dockyard labourers.
The prisoners are overlooked by the First and Second Mate, who patrol the yard, not only to prevent them from straying, or attempting to escape, but to make all parties attend strictly to their duties.

12.00 noon
Prisoners return for dinner.
All convicts are subject to a search to prevent any public stores being brought out of the dockyard; after which, a general muster takes place.
Dinners are served by officers and the prisoners are locked up in their wards to eat it. A watch, consisting of an officer and half the ship's company, is set on and between decks, where they remain until 12.40pm, when they are relieved by the other half of the watch.

1.20pm
Prisoners return on shore for labour.

5.45pm
On board again. Irons are examined and their persons searched as in the fore-noon.

7.30pm
Prayers in the chapel, then all prisoners mustered and locked in their wards for the night.

9.00pm
Lights out.

On Saturday evenings:
Each prisoner must wash and shave himself in preparation for Sunday.

Sunday:
All hands are called and mustered at the same time as on working days, the hammocks are brought up and stowed and the decks cleanly swept, after which the prisoners returned to their wards and breakfast is served.

9.00 am
All prisoners are mustered in divisions on the Main Deck for the purpose of seeing that their persons and linen are clean and their clothes kept in proper repair.
Attendance of Divine Service by all on board, the Service to be taken by the Chaplain.

During the week
The steward to see that the repair of clothing is not neglected and clothing issued to those in need.

The official view of the hulk system was, of course, markedly different from that of James Hardy Vaux. The system continued to be used until the late 1850s. It is particularly interesting that this extract below is taken from a government account published in the Sydney Herald, Australia, in 1834: [12]

> ...Upon their arrival the convicts are immediately stripped and washed, clothed in coarse grey jackets and breeches, and two irons placed on one of the legs, to which degradation every one must submit, whatever may have been his previous rank and station in the world. They are then sent out in gangs of a certain number to work on shore, guarded by soldiers.
>
> Out of each shilling earned for the government by the convict, he is entitled to one penny, which is carried to his credit: but of this he receives only one-third weekly, the remainder being left in hand to accumulate until the end of the term which he is doomed to serve; thus it sometimes happens that a man who has been six or seven years at the hulks, on his discharge is put in possession of £10 or £15 beyond which he is supplied with an additional sum of money to defray his travelling expenses home, be it ever so remote.
>
> The diet daily is a pound and a quarter of bread, a quart of thick gruel morning and evening, on four days of the week a piece of meat weighing fourteen ounces before it is cooked, and on the other three days in lieu of meat, a quarter of a pound of cheese, also an allowance of small beer, and on certain occasions when work peculiarly fatiguing and laborious is required, a portion of strong beer is served to those engaged in it...

It has been difficult to trace Edward's subsequent movements after being transferred to *The Retribution* and to confirm whether he was transported to Australia, as John Dyke clearly believed. The records for the penal voyages to Australia do not list a convict named Edward Hart, sentenced to seven years transportation in England, whose details corroborate with a conviction in 1827 and the rest of the known facts about him. [13]

On the face of it, serving a sentence on board a hulk in England, having actually been sentenced to transportation to a penal colony for seven years, seems rather curious. However, a gap between removal to a hulk and transportation, or not being transported at all, was by no means unusual. One interpretation of the delay is that convicts with seven year sentences were of less priority for transportation than those with life or fourteen year sentences. Such prisoners may have been slotted into the ships wherever there was room on board.

The hulks were regarded as prisons in exactly the same manner as other land-based establishments, so it was not unknown for convicts to serve all of their sentences on board before release. [14] This is exactly what happened to Samuel Jarman who was convicted at the same assizes for theft and received the same sentence as Edward. Sadly after his release, Samuel re-offended, was caught and convicted. [15]

It is known that Edward served some of his sentence in a hulk as there are entries for him in the indices to the registers of prisoners on *The Retribution*. One of the gaoler's reports particularly noted that he was a deserter from the army, [16] thus reinforcing the suggestion that he had joined the army whilst on the run between 1825 and 1827.

From another register of hulk prisoners, there is the following information: [17]

Edward Hart	aged 24
Convicted:	Larceny at Maidstone
Received from Maidstone	1 September 1827
How and when disposed of:	Bermuda 1 November 1828

Reproduced courtesy of the National Archives

Despite this entry, a thorough search of records for convicts arriving at Bermuda between 1823 and 1863 has failed to find any entry for Edward Hart. It is therefore likely that he either did not sail or did not survive the journey.[18,19]

Perhaps the truth of the matter is found in a second register and which probably completes Edward's story. However the document is muddled and the precise nature of the information recorded is unclear. The document description indicates it comprises an index to a register of prisoners on *The Justitia*, moored at Woolwich. The following information was included: [20]

Edward Hart	Dead	Gaolers Report:	Good

Reproduced courtesy of the National Archives

There is no date for this entry and the surname is not uncommon but there are only few entries in the indices under Edward Hart. Perhaps Edward had been transferred to *The Justitia* but there is nothing to confirm this suggestion. It is interesting to note that the gaoler reported his conduct as 'Good'.

It was widely acknowledged that the authorities were unable to prevent epidemics of dysentery and gaol fever on the hulks. The latter disease is now believed to be a form of typhus spread by vermin. The convicts were also susceptible to malaria.[21]

Given that there was a very high mortality rate, it is therefore entirely feasible that Edward succumbed to one of these diseases. Even after death there were two further potential indignities for a convict: the grisly attentions of anatomisers or the circumstances of burial. The latter was infinitely preferable despite the lack of organised graveyards for convicts. The bodies were interred in a nearby patch of rough ground rather than a dedicated and consecrated cemetery. It is not known if clergy were present to perform even a perfunctory ceremony. No records were kept.[22]

In 1856, Henry Mayhew, a chronicler of Victorian social underclasses, published a description of a visit to Woolwich. Perhaps it is appropriate to leave the last comment about the convict burial area to Henry, in the transcript which is shown below: [23]

We approached a low piece of ground - in no way marked off from the rest of the marsh - in no way distinguishable from any section of the dreary expanse, save that the long rank grass had been turned in one place lately, and that there was an upset barrow lying not far off. We thought it was one of the dreariest spots we had ever seen. 'This,' said the governor, 'is the convicts' burial ground'.

We could just trace the rough outline of disturbed ground at our feet. There was not even a number over the graves. The last, and it was only a month old, was disappearing. In a few months the rank grass will have closed over it, as over the story of its inmate.

And it is perhaps, well to leave the names of the unfortunate men, whose bones lie in the clay of this dreary marsh, unregistered and unknown. But the feeling with which we look upon its desolation is irrepressible...

Appendix Three

Some other references to Ware and Ware Street

In this section are included some references to Ware Street and land in Ware which were recorded in local newspapers, land transactions and advertisements. With one exception, they remain unlocated.

A slightly edited transcript from the Kent Messenger, 11 July 1891:

BEARSTED POLICE COURT

MONDAY - Before C Whitehead Esq (chair-man), R J Balston Esq., and E L Pemberton Esq.

SERIOUS CHARGES AGAINST A THURNHAM WOMAN

Harriet Medhurst was summoned for allowing her child, while suffering from scarlet fever 'to be exposed', the summons being taken out under the Infectious Diseases Notification Act. Mr Russell, barrister, instructed by Mr G. Hurn, clerk to the Hollingbourne Authority, appeared in support of the information, and narrated the facts, stating that the Bench must come to the conclusion, after hearing the evidence that the defendant had committed a very serious offence, and ought to be made an example° of.

Dr Tuckett, house surgeon at the West Kent General Hospital, stated that on the 22nd June the defendant came to the hospital with her child, which was about eight years of age. He asked the mother what was the matter with the child, and she replied, 'It had scarlet fever about a fortnight ago.' Witness next said, 'Who told you that the child was suffering from scarlet fever?' She answered 'The doctor who attended her.' The Chairman: The child was an outpatient? Witness: Yes, and she remained in the waiting room, were there were as many as 120 other out-patients. Dr Meredith was present when the conversation, which I have just mentioned took place. The Chairman: How long do you think the child was in the waiting-room? Witness: It must have been nearly two hours. The child's skin was peeling all over the body, and it was apparent that she must have had the disease two or three weeks. I afterwards forwarded a certificate to Dr Tuke, medical officer of health to the Hollingbourne Authority.

The chairman: What condition was the child in on this occasion? Witness: Scarlet fever, as is well known, is highly infectious, when the skin begins to peel. Dr Meredith, honorary physician at the West Kent Hospital, corroborated the evidence of the last witness, and said, in reply to the chairman, that the defendant also stated that her doctor told her to take the child to the hospital 'as soon as the scarlet fever was better.'

In reply to the chairman, the witness said that the infectious cases were not admitted to the West Kent Hospital. Dr Tuke stated that in consequence of receiving a note from Dr Tuckett, he visited the defendant's house, at Ware Street, Thurnham, and saw the child in question playing in the front room, where sweets were sold. Persons were passing in and out of her house at the time. The child was undoubtedly suffering from scarlet fever, as its skin was peeling. He told the mother that she must either close the house, or have the child removed to the infectious hospital. The chairman: Do you consider that the child, when you saw her, was in a dangerous state? Witness: Yes. This was the case for the prosecution. Defendant in reply to the charge, pleaded that she thought the child had recovered from scarlet fever when she went to the hospital.

The Bench convicted and the Chairman told defendant that she committed a very serious offence in taking a child suffering from scarlet fever into a hospital where there were a large number of other persons all of whom might have contracted the malady. Had she been in a better position in life she would have been fined the maximum penalty, £5. She was then fined £1 and 11s costs, or, in default of a distraint, a month's imprisonment.

William Medhurst, father of the last named defendant, was then summoned for failing to notify to the medical officer that the child was suffering from an infectious disease. Mr Russell said the prosecution had decided not to go on with this case, having obtained a conviction in the previous case. The Bench accordingly allowed the case to be withdrawn.

Le Hode in Ware in Thurnham, 1551[1]

> ..A piece of land estimated at four acres, called le Hode at Ware in Thurnham purchased of James Knight 1551...

Four Wents, 1648 and 1839

In 1648, in the Court Book for the manor of Ware[2], this entry was made to record a payment: [3]

> ...the heir of Solhurst on account of the land lying and being at Four Wents, once the land of Robert Sawier, which he holds of this manor for a yearly rent of 16½d...

The word 'went' is normally taken to mean a course, path, way, or passage, so an area specifically called Four Wents could describe the location of a place where four such tracks came together. Such a junction existed at the meeting point between Ware Street, Bearsted Road, Weavering Street and Hockers Lane until relatively recently. The junction of Weavering Street is now closed to traffic.

A similar use of the word 'went' to describe an area near to a path or passage also appears in a draft agreement dated 1839 between the Earl of Romney and George Hills which mentions: [4]

> a piece or parcel of land called Wents Field situate in Ware Street....

In the tithe apportionment schedule for Thurnham, George Hills is listed as a tenant for the Earl of Romney and farming plots 55 and 56. This parcel of land is almost certainly plot 55 which fronts Ware Street and plot 56 lies directly behind it. Both of them are one field away from the junction of Hockers Lane, Detling and Ware Street.[5]

Messuage at Ware, 1703[6]

On 14 October 1703, an agreement was signed between: John Davis of Hawkhurst and Elizabeth his wife; Thomas Oliver of Maidstone, husbandman, and Suzann, his wife; Mary Lewis of Chatham, a spinster; Nathaniel Collington of Pluckley and Mary his wife; Daniel Trigg of Chart next Sutton Valence, yeoman; John Pandhurst of Teston, bricklayer, and Elizabeth Dixon of Maidstone, spinster.

The land concerned included:

> ....all that messuage, or tenement, with the barns, stables, bank sides, outhouses, yards, ...garden, orchard, and the piece of parcel of land containing by estimation two acres...lying and being in the parish of Thurnham in the said country of Kent in or near a place there called Ware now or late in the tenure or occupation of Edward Eastling....

Messuage and Shop at Ware Street, 1760[7]

On 20 and 21 August 1760 a lease and a re-lease were signed. The parties involved were William Russell of Bearsted, wheelwright, and Catherine his wife; Thomas Allman of Bearsted, wheelwright, son of said Catherine, and Thomas Southerden, butcher.

Thomas Southerden paid four shillings for:

> ...All that Messuage or tenement with the shop, yard and garden and appurtenances thereto situate lying and being in the parish of Thurnham abutting to the King's common highway and part of the waste lands belonging to the Manor of Thurnham aforesaid towards the north, east and south and to the lands late of Edward Watts, deceased, towards the west or howsoever wise the same or any part thereof doth abut or bound and now or late in the possession tenure or occupation of the said William Russell...

By 1778 the property was owned by Elizabeth Allmann of Boxley, a widow of Thomas Allman late of Boxley, deceased. Davis Sale of Sundrish, a yeoman, agreed to take a lease on it for a total of £250 5s 0d. Below is the property description:

> ...All that messuage or tenement in the said County of Kent with the shop yard garden and appurtenances belonging situate lying and being in the parish of Thurnham abutting to the King's common highway and part of the waste lands belonging to the Manor of Thurnham aforesaid towards the north, east and south and to lands late of Edward Wattes, deceased, towards the west or howsoever otherwise the same or any part thereof doth abut or abound late in the tenure of William Russell and now of Robert Clifford and assigns...

Ware House, Thurnham, 1823[8]

A transcript of an advertisement which appeared in the Maidstone Gazette, 26 August 1823:

> **WARE HOUSE, THURNHAM**
>
> *A neat Cottage Residence and Land, within two Miles of Maidstone*
>
> **TO BE SOLD BY AUCTION**
>
> *BY CARTER & MORRIS*
>
> On THURSDAY 18th SEPTEMBER 1823, at the BULL INN, MAIDSTONE, at Three o' Clock
>
> A VERY Desirable COTTAGE RESIDENCE, called WARE HOUSE with nearly three Acres of orchard and garden Ground, detached wash–house, stable, cow house, small barn, poultry house, piggery, & c. situate at THURNHAM, about two miles from Maidstone.
>
> The House measures 31 feet in front and 28 feet in depth, and comprises good cellars, two parlours, kitchen dairy, four bed rooms and two large attics; the garden is partly walled in, the land extremely good, and the situation very pleasant and healthy, forming a very desirable property for a small Respectable Family.
>
> May be viewed and further particulars had on application to Mr Ottaway, Solicitor, Staplehurst; Mr John Springett, Linton; Mr John Rayner, Loose; or to the Auctioneers, Week Street, Maidstone.

Reproduced courtesy of Kent Messenger group

Notes

A brief overview of Ware

1   Bearsted may have been included in another local land holding such as Leeds. For further details see: pp.11-12
A History of Bearsted and Thurnham
Bearsted and Thurnham History Book Committee 1978, revised 1988

2-3   *The History and Topographical Survey of the County of Kent*
Edward Hasted
1798, reprinted EP Publishing 1972

Court Roll Documents

Document One

1   i   The court was held 17 May 1380

      ii   Manor of Ware Court Book 1631-1647
           CCRc reference M8   169402

Document Two

1   i   The court was held between 22 June 1389 and 21 June 1390, at Ware

      ii   Manor of Ware Court Book 1631-1647
           CCRc reference M8   folio 1 onwards   169402

2   See glossary for the meaning of 'essoin'
The general interpretation here is that the people named in this section were summoned to the court but their attendance had been excused on this occasion by John Spring.

3   See glossary for the meaning of 'distrain'. For further details of the distraint process see p.61
Old Title Deeds
N W Alcock
Phillimore & Co 2001

Document Three

1   Manor of Ware Court Book 1631-1647
CCRc reference M8   169402

2   I am indebted to Dr Peter Franklin for the following information concerning the date:

The Rental has two dates: 1390 and the 23rd year of the reign of Richard II.
Both the fourteenth century and the seventeenth century clerks would have counted the year AD as beginning on the Feast of the Annunciation of St Mary. AD 1390 therefore ran from 25 March 1390 to 24 March 1391. Richard II's twenty third regnal year was shortened by his overthrow and ran from 22 June 1399 to 29 September 1399. The date 1398 is only found here and can be taken as an error.

The details were renewed twice between 1390 and 1399. See page 39 for further information.

3   Vicar of Thornham: the term, 'vicar' was used here instead of Rector.
At the time covered by the rental, the rector of Thornham is believed to have been Roger Horton.
see p.170, *A History of Bearsted and Thurnham*

4   Margaret has been amended from Margery here but later on in the rental the two names seem interchangeable.

5   The wording is unclear here.

6   Colisfeild and Chelisfeld were both written and deleted here.

7   In the original document, the Latin word 'gardino' was used which may also indicate an orchard here.

Document Four

1   i   The Court was held 19 October 1391

      ii   Manor of Ware Court Book 1631-1647
           CCRc reference M8   169402

2   This should be interpreted that John Spring was 'essoined of common suit' i.e. absent, but excused.

Document Five

1   i   Although this document is undated, Richard II reigned from 1377 to 1399

      ii   Manor of Ware Court Book 1631-1647
           CCRc reference M8   169402

Document Six

1   i   The Court was held 29 April 1399

     ii   Manor of Ware Court Book 1631-1647
         CCRc reference M8 169402

Document Seven

1-2   Manor of Ware entry Court Book 1573-1677
      Abstract and transcription of rental details
      CCRc reference M11 169404

      This rental document is in a very bad condition: the parchment is battered and worn, the ink and surface of the document is very creased and flaking in places.

      George Roper also held property in Sutton Street, Thurnham. In 1692, a map of the Milgate Estate noted that his heirs held land adjacent to the Milgate estate in Bearsted and Thurnham.
      see Map of the Milgate estate 1692, CKS reference U1258 P1

Document Eight

1   i   Regrettably, there is no day and year specifically recorded but the regnal year given confirms the court was held in 1614.

     ii   Manor of Ware Court Book 1613-1637
         CCRc reference M4 folios 13-14 and folio 24 169400

2   John Crompe was Mayor of Maidstone in 1613 and 1621.
      The Crompes were a distinguished family as John's brother, Thomas, was vicar of Langley. One of Thomas Crompe's sons, John, was vicar of Thurnham 1614-1661. Amongst his other children were Benjamin and Thomas Crompe. Benjamin (born c. 1610-1611, died 1664) married Dorothy. Their son, John, was Chapter Clerk at Rochester Cathedral before his death in 1718.

Document Nine

1   Manor of Ware Court Book covering 1613-1647, 1637-1728, 1661-1671
      CCRc reference M5 folios 5-6 and folio 14 169401

2   The clerk would have counted the year AD as beginning on 25 March at the Feast of the Annunciation of St Mary, so 16 January 1648 would actually be 1649. This is confirmed by the regnal year recorded.

3   See glossary for the meaning of 'alienation'.

4   William Shornden probably inherited this land through a relative.
      Although the exact relationship to William is unclear, a Robert Shornden certainly made a will in 1599 in which land adjacent to Ferriss Lane is mentioned. The circumstances are unclear because the initial bequest was made to Robert Shornden, who may have been William's father.
      Robert Shornden will, 1599
      CCA reference DCb-PRC 17/51/371

5   I agree here with Dr Franklin's interpretation of this entry which he takes to identify 'Four Wents' as a place name, citing the *Oxford English Dictionary* which describes 'went' as a course, path, way or passage.

Document Ten

1   Parliamentary Survey Part 3, 1649
      Transcript of p.83
      CCRc reference M8 folio 83

Document Eleven

1   Entries for Ware 1668 and 1669 in Court Book 1573-1677
      Abstract and transcript
      CCRc reference M11 169404

2   i   See glossary for the meaning of 'dayworks'.

     ii   'Elnor Arnor' could be derived from the name of a former owner, not recorded in these documents.
         James Moore noted that Alianora Arnor donated 12d to the Light of St John the Baptist at St Mary's church, Thurnham in 1502, see Will of Eleanor Arner of Thurnham, 1502
         CCA reference DCb-PRC17/8/206

Document Twelve

1   Entries for Ware, Court Book 1673–1742
    Abstract and transcript
    CCRc reference M16 169409

The Early Manor of Ware

1   p.16, *A History of Bearsted and Thurnham*

2   For further details about the Charters of Combwell Priory see pp.194-222
    The Charters of Combwell Priory (particularly Charters V and XX)
    Archaeologia Cantiana Volume V: 1863
    Kent Archaeological Society

3   Manor of Ware Court Book 1613-1637
    CCRc reference M8 169402
    Transcribed and translated by Peter Franklin from the original documents and Latin.

4   *ibid.* Manor of Ware Court Book
    Court held 17 May 1380

5   i   *op.cit.* Manor of Ware Court Book 1613-1637

    ii One source that might have been assumed to have been of assistance here is the Custumale Roffense, published by John Thorpe in 1788. However this appears based on an original manuscript held in Medway Archives under reference DRc/R2. There is evidence it was compiled after 1228 but earlier than 1235. The earliest document for the manor of Ware is 1380. In addition, Colin Flight argues that that Thorpe did not print a full copy of the original document.

        For further details about the Custumale Roffense manuscript see pp.83-84,
        The Bishops and Monks of Rochester 1076-1214
        Colin Flight
        Kent Archaeological Society 1997

6-8 Manor of Ware Court Book 1631-1647
    CCRc reference M8 folio 1 onwards 169402

9   i   Unpublished correspondence between Peter Franklin and Kathryn Kersey.

    ii Undated article by Felix Hull concerning the Lost Manor of Ware written for the Thurnham History Group.

10 *op.cit.* Manor of Ware Court Book 1631-1647

11 p.40, *Continuity and Colonization: the evolution of Kentish settlement*
    Alan Everitt
    Leicester University Press 1986

12-13 *op.cit.* p.101, *Old Title Deeds*

14 p.12, *A History of Bearsted and Thurnham*

15 i   The entries in Domesday should not be regarded as indicating the total population or value of the settlements. It was not a complete stock-taking and population census but determined the amount liable for tax. For further details see: p.34
    Village Records
    John West
    Phillimore 1997

    ii *ibid.* p.49

16 i   In a rental for East Malling, dated 1410 the value of land is clearly assessed on fertility and the description varies from 'best' to 'worst or poor'. For further information see *A Rental of the Manor of East Malling c. 1410*
    Edited C L Sinclair Williams
    Included in: *A Kentish Miscellany*, Kent Records (Phillimore) 1979

    ii For a fascinating insight into the early history of woodland in Kent see:
    The Woodland Economy of Kent 1066-1348
    K P Witney
    Volume 38, 1990, Agricultural History Review

17 *op.cit.* Manor of Ware Court Book 1613-1637

18 *op.cit.* article by Felix Hull

19 pp.521-522, *The History and Topographical Survey of the County of Kent*

20-22 *passim., op.cit.* Felix Hull
    Also several undated conversations with Michael Perring concerning the possible location of the manor of Ware.

23   There is a document which lists the field names from 1581 in Thurnham area in the Gordon Ward collection, Kent Archaeological Society

24   *op.cit.* Manor of Ware Court Book 1613-1637

25   A Survey of Boxley and Thurnham, Millgate and Howcourt and other lands lying in the parishes of Bearsted, Thurnham, Leeds and Hollingbourne, being the estate of William Cage Esq. drawn by John Watts, 1709.
      Copy held in private papers of Michael Perring

26   *op.cit.* Manor of Ware Court Book 1613-1637

27   i   A Hugh de Thornham is mentioned as an escheator for the king in the entries for Kent in the Hundred Rolls of 1274-1275.

      ii   *op.cit.* Felix Hull

28-29 *op.cit.* Manor of Ware Court Book 1613-1637

30   For details of documents concerning lands held by the Aineton family between 1370 and 1379
      see pp.154-167, volume 21
      Codex de Kent: Calendarium Cartularii de Surrenden
      Transcribed by Rev Lambert Larking
      CKS reference U1823/105

31   *op.cit.* Hasted

32   i   *op.cit.* Felix Hull

      ii   Until the fourteenth century the settlement Eynton is well recorded. Lambert Larking's researches, published in works such as Codex de Kent: Calendarium Cartularii de Surrenden, mention related names such as Eyntonstreet, Eyntoncrouche, Eyntonfield, Eyntondown and Eyntoncroftes.

           op.cit. Codex de Kent

      iii There are several references to Eynton located in one further bundle of later documents:
           Eynton Feilde is found in a marriage settlement from 1598 and in a land transaction, 12 March 1604.
           'Eynton Feildes withal and singular' is included in a land purchase of Binbury, 29 May 1622.
           CKS reference U55 T571

33   *op.cit.* Felix Hull

34   *ibid.*

35   i   *ibid.*

      ii   For a fascinating discussion of Court roll entries that indicate lost rents and vacant holdings see:
           Lost Rents, Vacant Holdings and the Contraction of Peasant Cultivation after the Black Death
           John Titow
           Volume 42, 1994, Agricultural History Review

36   Other records for the Manor of Ware:

      i   Manor of Ware Court Book 1613-1637
           CCRc reference M4 folios 13-14 169400

      ii   Manor of Ware Court Book 1637-1728
           CCRc reference M5 folios 5-6 169401

      iii Manor of Ware Court Book
           CCRc reference M8 folio 83 169402

      iv   Manor of Ware Court Book 1573-1677
           CCRc reference M11 169404

      v   Manor of Ware Court Book 1673-1742, 1682-1690
           CCRc reference M16 169409

37   Manor of Ware Court Book 1637-1728
      CCRc reference M5 folios 5-6 169401

38-39 Manor of Ware: Dean and Chapter Rochester Estate Book c. 1649
      CCRc reference E4/108189 Volume 3

The Court of the Manor of Ware at Work

1   p.47
     Using Manorial Records
     Mary Ellis
     Public Record Office 1997

2   *passim., ibid.* p.50

3 *passim., ibid.* p.47

4 *passim.* pp.2-83
Manorial Records of Cuxham, Oxfordshire c 1200-1329
Edited PD A Harvey
HMSO 1976

5 *op.cit.* p.50, *Using Manorial Records*

6 i Manor of Ware Court Book covering 1613-1647, 1637-1728, 1661-1671
CCRc reference M5 folios 5-6 and folio 14 169401

ii p.83
Parliamentary Survey Part 3, 1649
CCRc reference M8 folio 83

7 Document eleven: Entries for Ware 1668 and 1669 in Court Book 1573-1677 includes a reference to a John Allen but there is nothing to link him with Thomas Allen.
CCRc reference M11 169404

8 Manor of Ware Court Book 1613-1637
CCRc reference M4 folios 13-14 and folio 24 169400
Transcription and translation undertaken by Dr Peter Franklin.

9 *op.cit.* p.52, *Using Manorial Records*

10 *ibid.* p.53

11 The court was held between 22 June 1389 and 21 June 1390, at Ware
Manor of Ware Court Book 1631-1647
CCRc reference M8 folio 1 onwards 169402
Transcription and translation undertaken by Dr Peter Franklin.

12 *passim., op.cit.* p.52, *Using Manorial Records*

13 *passim., ibid.* p.53

14 Manor of Ware Court Book 1613-1637
CCRc reference M4 folios 13-14 and folio 24 169400

15 *passim., op.cit.* p.54, *Using Manorial Records*

16 *passim., ibid.* p.56

17 *passim., ibid.* p.58

18 Manor of Ware Court Book 1613-1637
CCRc reference M4 folios 13-14 and folio 24 169400

19 *ibid.*

20 *passim., op.cit.* p.58, *Using Manorial Records*

21 *op.cit.* Manor of Ware Court Book 1613-1637

22 *passim., op.cit.* pp.59-60, *Using Manorial Records*

23 *ibid.*

24 *passim., ibid.* p.64

25 Ware was slightly ahead of its time as by the beginning of the nineteenth century, the abolition of copyhold tenure or conversion to freehold tenure was beginning to be considered.

Land tenure in the Manor of Ware and Ware Street: copyhold, freehold or gavelkind

1 Lecture on Copyhold in Kent given by Arthur Ruderman
Kent Archaeological Society Library, Maidstone Museum, 19 March 2005

2-3 *ibid.*

4 Document eight
Manor of Ware Court Book 1613-1637
CCRc reference M4 folios 13-14 169400

5 Document two
Manor of Ware Court Book 1631-1647
CCRc reference M8 folios 1 onwards 169402

6 Document nine
  Manor of Ware Court Book 1648
  CCRc reference M5 folios 5-6 and folio 14 169401

7 Particulars and conditions of sale of some freehold estates 1858
  CKS reference U1569 T15

8 Documents concerning the Armstrong sale, 1858 Whatman estate papers
  CKS reference U289 T43

9 i For further information on gavelkind see: http://en.wikipedia.org/wiki/Gavelkind

  ii For a very thorough discussion concerning the date and adoption of gavelkind as a legal custom in Kent see:
     The Codification of the Customs of Kent
     C L Sinclair Williams
     Archaeologia Cantiana Volume XCV 1979
     Kent Archaeological Society

     John de Berwyke and the Consuetudines Kancie
     Felix Hull
     Archaeologia Cantiana Volume XCVI 1980
     Kent Archaeological Society

  In the latter paper, Felix Hull discussed a strong tradition which states that during the reign of Edward I, a royal charter enrolling the customs which was dated at Canterbury on the feast day of St Alphege, 19 April 1292-1293, was handed to Sir John de Northwode of Thurnham for safe-keeping. John was Sheriff of Kent 1291-1292 and probably, 1292-1293. No trace can now be found of this charter but it is good to note that a family from Thurnham was involved in national matters!

10 *op.cit.* Arthur Ruderman

11 Further Abstract of Title re Armstrong Sale 1858
   Herst Lands 1858-1859
   CKS reference U348 T7

12 *op.cit.* Arthur Ruderman

A Yeoman's Tragedy: The Bedell family in Ware and Thurnham

1-5 Manor of Ware Court Book 1631-1647
    Medway Archives reference CCRc reference M8 169402

6 *op.cit.* Codex de Kent
  1/279   Manor 1411

7 i *ibid.*
    6/7   Parish and church 1434

  ii p.171, *A History of Bearsted and Thurnham*

8 *passim.* p.111
  Jack Cade's Rebellion of 1450
  I M W Harvey
  Clarendon Press 1991

9 passim., *ibid.* pp.74-75

10 *passim., ibid.* pp.54-63

11 *ibid.* p.73

12 *passim., ibid.* p.111

13 *passim., ibid.* pp.89-101

14 *ibid.* pp.153-155

15 p.247
   Some Ancient Indictments in the King's Bench referring to Kent 1450-1452
   R Virgoe
   Volume XVIII Kent Records 1964
   Kent Archaeological Society

16 passim., *op.cit.* pp.153-155, *Jack Cade's rebellion of 1450*

17 *ibid.* p.157

18-19 *op.cit.* p.247, *Some Ancient Indictments in the King's Bench referring to Kent 1450-1452*

20 *op.cit.* Codex de Kent
   6/8, 11   Manor 1451

21   *op.cit.* p.157
      Jack Cade's rebellion of 1450

22   *op.cit.* Codex de Kent
      6/11   Vicarage 1519
      6/13, 20, 21, 23   Manor 1553
      6/15, 17   Manor 1553
      6/19   Manor 1554

23   i   *op.cit.* Codex de Kent
            1/208   Manor 1651 to 1652
            1/210   Manor & c 1652

      ii   There are two further, but isolated, references to land called Bedles or Bodles both found in a bundle of documents about the Manor of Thurnham 1542-1844.
            CKS reference U348 T1/1

The Later Manor of Ware

The Forge in Ware Street

1-3   i   Smiths Forge in Ware Street, 1742
            7 June 1765
            CKS reference U415 T4

      ii   9 October 1790
            Messuage at Ware Street, 1716-1840
            CKS reference U1379 T15

4   Land recovered Hilary Term 2 George III 1762
      Messuage and Land 1750-1835
      CKS reference U82 T151

5   *op.cit.* Messuage at Ware Street, 1716-1840

6   i   Abstract of Conveyance, 5 October 1855
            CKS reference U1282 E3

      ii   The subsequent property description enables the location of the wood to be pinpointed as one of the most northern points of Thurnham parish. At some time after this, the name of Mark Beech Wood fell into abeyance and now appears to be lost. It certainly does not seem to feature on any subsequent maps.

7   Tithe apportionment schedule for Thornham, compiled 1843
      CKS reference IR 29/17/39

8   1851 census for Bearsted
      NA reference HO 107 1616

9   1861 census for Bearsted
      NA reference RG9 499

10   1871 census for Thurnham
      NA reference RG10 949

11   1881 census for Thurnham
      NA reference RG11 0933 118

12-13 1891 census for Thurnham
      NA reference RG12 685

14   Sale particulars of building land 1882
      CKS reference U1401 Z3

15   Sale of Milgate and of the estate of Walter Fremlin 1925
      CKS reference BX88106753, C150549779

16   Equivalent sums today would be £79,787 and £11,369 respectively.

17   Ironically, the new proposed branch of Sainsbury's, or indeed, any other supermarket or shop, was never built on The Landway estate. A branch of Tesco supermarket was eventually built on the housing estate at Grove Green but this was another two decades or so into the future.

Weltighe Crofts and Weltes landholdings

1   i   National Monument Record listing for Stocks House
Monarch Uid 503598
NBR Index Number 8700

    ii   William's holdings are mentioned in the Manor of Ware Court Book entries for 1648 see:
CCRc reference M5 folios 5-6 and folio 14 169401

2   Will of John Pokyll 1483
Transcript made by L L Duncan, available on Kent Archaeological Society website: www.kentarchaeology.org.uk

3   Will of Thomas Pokyll 1508
CCA reference DCb-PRC 17/9/339

The Pokyll family were a well established family that owned land in and around Bearsted and Thurnham. Several further wills from the family remain:

William Pokill 1490, CCA reference DCb-PRC 17/5/167
Philip Pokyll 1510, CCA reference DCb-PRC 17/11/309
Thomas Pokyll 1520, CCA reference DCb-PRC 17/14/252

4   p.46
Thomas Hendley's Book 1529-1585
CKS reference U1044 F1

5   *Kent Chantries*, Kent No 28 (7) 1548,
Kent Records 1935, Volume XII
Kent Archaeological Society

6   pp.454-455
The Stripping of the Altars
Eamon Duffy
Yale 1992

7   i   Entry 2 September 1548 Hatfelde Brodeoke
Calendar of Patent Rolls Edward VI, Volume 1, 1547-1548
HMSO 1920

    ii   Entry on Patent Roll 1548
NA reference CC66/811 Membrane 39

8   i   *op.cit.* Thomas Hendley's Book

    ii   Confusingly, the Hendley family occupied another area of land also called Weltie near lands called Little Chalky Otham stream. See entries 39 & 40:
Stewards Papers Manor of East Court and West Court, Detling
CKS reference U991 E34

9   Dean and Chapter of Rochester, estate leases, related documents, and purchases of new estates 1576-1861
CCRc reference DRc Ele BB02

10   Dean and Chapter of Rochester, estate leases, related documents, and purchases of new estates 1576-1861
CCRc reference DRc Ele 005 2

11   Dean and Chapter of Rochester, estate leases, related documents, and purchases of new estates 1576-1861
CCRc reference DRc Ele 005 4

12-13 Messuage at Ware Street, 1576
CKS reference U713 T76-77

14   Marriage register for All Saints church, Hollingbourne
CCA reference P187/1/1

15   Marriage licence register for All Saints church, Hollingbourne
CCA reference DCb/L/R/13

16   Messuage at Ware 1642-1675
CKS reference U1823/24 T114

17   *op.cit.* Court Book entry for the Manor of Ware 1648

18-19 i   An equivalent sum today is £8

    ii   Manor of Ware 1668-1669
Michaelmas 1669
CCRc reference M11 169404

20   Messuage at Ware 1642-1671
CKS reference U1823/24 T114

21   Deed and partition between William, John, Edward, Henry and Thomas Godfrey 28 October 1657
      CKS reference U289 T42 part 1

22   *op.cit.* Will of William Godfrey 1691

23   *op.cit.* Lease for a year 26 February 1709

24   A Survey of Boxley and Thurnham, drawn by John Watts, 1709

25   Messuage and land 1750-1835
      CKS reference U82 T151

26   *ibid.* 2 January 1762 Mr Edward Watts to Mr William Twopeny, attested copy and re-lease

27   *ibid.* Certified extract Catherine Watts will

28   *ibid.* 2 January 1762 Mr Edward Watts to Mr William Twopeny

29-30 *ibid.* 19 November 1800 Mr and Mrs Armstrong to Mr Brenchley, attested copy of a covenant to levy a fine

31   For an explanation of the gavelkind inheritance system, see p.51 of this book

32   Herst Lands 1858-1859, Further Abstract of title re Armstrong Sale 1858
      CKS reference U348 T7

33   Particulars and conditions of sale of some freehold estates 1858
      CKS reference U1569 T15

34   Documents concerning the Armstrong Sale
      CKS reference U289 T43

35   *op.cit.* Further abstract of title and copyhold

36   *op.cit.* Particulars and conditions of sale of some freehold estates 1858

37   1841 census return for Thornham
      NA reference HO 107/463/2

38   Tithe Apportionment schedule for Thornham, compiled 1843
      NA reference IR 29/17/39

39   1851 census return for Thornham
      NA reference HO107 1618 98-111

40   i   Particulars and conditions of sale of some Freehold Estates 1858
           CKS reference U1569 T15

      ii   Parish Rate Book for Thurnham 1862
           CKS reference Q/GFr12/102 and 103

      iii Equivalent sums today would be £28,854 for lot eight and £29,541 for lot nine

41   Particulars and conditions of sale of some freehold estates 1858
      CKS reference U348 T15

42   18 December 1858
      Draft Conveyance of Freehold messuage, land and hereditaments situate in the parishes of Bearsted and Thurnham.
      CKS reference U348 T7

43-44 i   *ibid.* Hersts Land 1858-1859

      ii   1861 Census return for Thornham
           NA reference RG 9/524 101-116

45   i   An equivalent sum today is £564

      ii   *op.cit.* Parish Rate Book for Thurnham 1862

46   1871 census return for Thornham
      NA reference RG10 946

47   1881 census return for Thurnham
      NA reference RG11 0933 118 2

48   1891 census return for Thurnham
      NA reference RG12 691

Sandy Mount in the twentieth century

1   i   1881 census return for Thurnham
          NA reference RG11 0933 118 2

    ii   1891 census return for Thurnham
          NA reference RG12 691

    iii 1901 census return for Thurnham
          NA reference RG13 770

2   The earliest surviving record which formally records a version of the name as Hog Hill, is a lease from 1791 which gives the location of Bearsted windmill. See:
        Dean and Chapter of Rochester, estate leases, related documents, and purchases of new estates 1576-1861
        CCRc reference DRc Ele 006 1

3   'everything found' is a phase used in these circumstances to indicate that the clothing for work, payments for board and lodgings and utilities were paid by the employer and were therefore not included in the wages.

4   Holy Cross parish magazine, December 1945
        CKS reference P18/28/20

5   p.69
        Maps for Family and Local History
        Geraldine Beech and Rose Mitchell
        National Archives 2004

6-8 Return for Sandy Mount farm, August 1941
        NA reference MAF 32/1040/77

Mount Pleasant

1-2 Messuage at Ware 1642-1671
        CKS reference U1823/24 T114

3   Document dated 30 March 1736, Messuage at Ware Street 1716-1840
        CKS reference U1329 T15

4   *ibid.* Document dated 16 December 1736

5   *ibid.* Document dated 11 November 1785

6   *ibid.* Document dated 9 October 1790

7   *ibid.* Document dated 4 February 1840

8   Tithe map apportionment schedule for Thornham, compiled 1843
        CKS reference IR 29/17/39

9   1841 census return for Thurnham
        NA reference HO107 463

10   1851 census return for Thurnham
        NA reference HO107 1618

11   Abstract of Conveyance, 5 October 1855
        Whatman Estate 1821-1876 concerning the Maidstone-Ashford railway
        CKS reference U1282 E3

12   For further information about Alfred Mynn see:
        Alfred Mynn and the Cricketers of his time
        Patrick Morrah
        First published Eyre and Spottiswoode 1963, Cambridge University Press

13   1861 census return for Thurnham
        NA reference RG9 504

14-16 *op.cit. Alfred Mynn and the Cricketers of his time*

17   1871 census return for Thurnham
        NA reference RG10 946 18

18   1881 census return for Thurnham
        NA reference RG11 0933 121

19   Entry under Thurnham, Kelly's Trade Directory 1882

20   1891 census return for Thurnham
        NA reference RG12 691 101

21   i   1901 census return for Thurnham
               NA reference RG13 770

      ii   Sale particulars and outline history of Mount Pleasant 10 April 2000, written and prepared by James Moore. Copy held in private papers of Michael Perring.

22   *No Return Tickets*
      L Grace Dibble
      Stockwell Books 1989

23   i   Indenture 5 August 1915 agreeing sale of land situate in Thurnham, Bearsted and Boxley included in bundle of documents largely about The Rose public house 1835 to 1927.
               CKS reference U1833

      ii   *op.cit.* Sale particulars and outline history of Mount Pleasant, 10 April 2000

24-25 *ibid.*

Church Cottages and Sharsted Way

1   A Survey of Boxley and Thurnham, drawn by John Watts, 1709

2   Undated notes and conversations between Felix Hull and James Moore compiled by James Moore for private research.

3   Manor of Ware Court Books 1631-1647
       CCRc reference M8 169402

4   John Sharstede's name was also recorded in the 1390-1391 rental. See Manor of Ware Court Book 1631-1647
       CCRc reference M8 169402

5   A diagram of the Sharsted family tree can be found in the Yeandle Papers.
       CKS reference U1401 Z3

6   p.529, *The History and Topographical Survey of the County of Kent*

7   Conversation with Michael Perring about Thurnham church estate, 3 May 2006.

8   i   An equivalent sum would be around £17,400 today.

      ii   Origins of Thurnham Church Estate
               CKS reference P369/6/18-20

9   i   Thurnham file
               Gordon Ward Collection, Kent Archaeological Society Library

      ii   National Monument Record Listing for 30-36 Ware Street
               Monarch Uid 503596
               NBR Index Number 8698

10   Miscellaneous receipts for St Mary's church, Thurnham, 1852 to 1923
       CKS reference P369/6/3

11   Thurnham file
       Gordon Ward Collection

12   *op.cit.* Origins of Thurnham Church Estate

13   i   'Bearsted Cottage Allotments Report' in *Maidstone Journal, Kentish Advertiser and South Eastern Intelligencer*, 22 October 1844

      ii   It is possible that the Churchwardens of St Mary's decided to act upon the provisions included in the Allotment Extension Act of 1882 which required trustees holding charity land for the use of the poor to set apart a portion for use as allotments. See p.214, *The Allotment Chronicles*
               Steve Poole
               Silver Link Publishing Limited 2006

14   *op.cit.* p.42

15   Church Cottages and allotments, Ware Street 1891-1929, St Mary's church property, Thurnham
       CKS reference P369/6/1-2

16   *op.cit.* Thurnham file, Gordon Ward collection

17   *op.cit.* Church Cottages and allotments, Ware Street 1891-1929

18   i   An equivalent sum would be £8 today.

      ii   *op.cit.* Miscellaneous receipts for St Mary's church, Thurnham 1852 to 1923

19   Thurnham parish rate book 1873, Thurnham parish chest records
       CKS reference P369/14/1

20   1881 census return for Thurnham
NA reference RG11 0933 119

21   i   An equivalent sum would be £134 today.

       ii   *op.cit.* Miscellaneous receipts for St Mary's church, Thurnham 1852 to 1923

22   i   An equivalent sum would be £12,857 today.

       ii   *op.cit.* Origins of Thurnham Church Estate

       iii Conveyance of piece of land and right of way in Ware Street, Thurnham 1886
CKS reference U348 T14

23-24 i   An equivalent sum would be £2,337 today.

       ii   *op.cit.* Church Cottages and allotments, Ware Street 1891-1929

25   *op.cit.* Miscellaneous receipts for St Mary's church, Thurnham 1852 to 1923

26-27 *op.cit.* Church Cottages and allotments, Ware Street 1891-1929

28   Equivalent sums would be £42,930 and £42,697 today.

29   i   *op.cit.* Church Cottages and allotments, Ware Street 1891-1929

       ii   p.65
'Dutifulness and Endurance' Bearsted and Thurnham 1914-1918, 1939-1945
Kathryn Kersey 2005

30-32 *op.cit.* Church Cottages and allotments, Ware Street 1891-1929

33   i   Conversation with Michael Perring about Thurnham church estate, 3 May 2006

       ii   p.119
A School at Bearsted
Kathryn Kersey 2003

       iii *op.cit.* pp.112-115, *'Dutifulness and Endurance' Bearsted & Thurnham 1914-1918, 1939-1945*

34   *op.cit.* Thurnham Church Estate
CKS reference P369/6/18-20

35   pp.62-63
Bearsted and Thurnham Remembered
Kathryn Kersey 2005

Winter Haw

1   National Monument Record listing for 62-64 Ware Street
Monarch Uid 503597
NBR Index Number 8699

2   List of Churchwardens and parish officers for St Mary's Church, Thurnham
CKS reference P369/1/1

3   Inventory for John Chrisfield or Kersefield, 2 April 1684
CCA reference DCb-PRC 11/87/21

4   i   Messuage in Thurnham Street 1685
CKS reference U30 T24

       ii   The Chrisfield family name continues to occur in the parish records for many years after the sale of the property

5   Messuage in Thurnham Street 1705
CKS reference U47/38 T26

    Land in Thurnham Street 1710
CKS referenceU838 T412

6   Lease for a year, 30 October 1767
Hampson Papers re Ware Street 1767-1848
CKS reference U348 T2

7-8   *ibid.*

9   *ibid.* 31 October 1767 Mr Sale to Mrs Duckesbury

10-12 i   Will of Hodsall Sale of Bearsted, 1768
see: http://worldconnect.genealogy.rootsweb.com for further details. This site also gives the following reference: PCC Will 1803, Volume 1398, folio 727

    ii   *op.cit.* Hampson Papers
24 July 1768 Lease to Thomas Punnett

13   *op.cit.* Hampson Papers
4 May 1770 Assignment and Indenture re Thomas Punnett, Hodsall Sale and Mary his wife and Mary Drewery of East Farleigh

14   *ibid.* 29 June 1789 Hodsall Sale to Christopher Hull

15   *ibid.* 29 April 1791 Indenture of lease and re-lease between Hodsall Sale, Richard Webb of Bearsted, Mary Duckesbery his wife and Mrs Mary Drewery

16   *ibid.* 29 April 1799
Lease between Richard Webb, Mary Duckesbery to Jesse Webb and John Budds

17   *ibid.* Mary had died 20 March 1803

18 i   *ibid.* 26 February 1825 Indenture

    ii   *ibid.* Document detailing entries for baptism for the children of Richard and Mary Webb extracted by Charles Cage, lists all their children and their dates of baptism:

        Mary, 28 August 1791;   Richard, 20 November 1793;   Jane, 5 August 1794;
        Elizabeth, 10 March 1797;   Anne, 16 October 1799;   Jesse, 15 December 1801;
        Sarah, 22 February 1804

19 i   A sale notice was published in *Maidstone Gazette*, 6 June and 17 August 1824 and also appeared in the *Maidstone Journal and Kentish Advertiser*, 24 August 1824

    ii   A plan of land situate at Ware Street, Thurnham belonging to the Heirs of the late Mr Richard Webb, 1824
CKS reference U348 P1

20   *ibid.* 26 February 1825 Indenture

21   *ibid.* 14 December 1842 Appointment and Re-lease

22 i   *ibid.* 15 December 1842 Mortgage between Thomas Taylor and Henry Robert Coulter

    ii   A comparative sum would be £27,400 today.

23   Tithe Map and accompanying schedule for Thurnham 1843
NA reference IR/29/17/39

24   *op.cit.* Hampson Papers
1848 Hampson Trust: 16 October 1848 Draft re-conveyance

25   1883 Map of Hampson estate
CKS reference U1431 P4

26 i   Marriage register for St Mary's church
CKS reference P369/1/1

    ii   Parish Rate Books for Thurnham 1873-1878, Thurnham parish chest accounts
CKS reference P369/4/1

27   Thurnham parish chest accounts, St Mary's church 1824-1929
CKS reference P369/6/1/2

28   *op.cit.* pp.81, *'Dutifulness and Endurance' Bearsted & Thurnham 1914-1918, 1939-1945*

29   *op.cit.* Thurnham parish chest accounts, St Mary's church 1824-1929

30   Entries for Thurnham, Electoral Roll for Maidstone, 1939
Held at CKS, Maidstone

Rosemount Dairy Farm and Henry Hodges

1   1901 census return for Thurnham
NA reference RG13/770

2   An equivalent sum would be £30,395 today.

Aaron Hunt and an off-licence, Ware Street

1 i   Even in 1882, the shops at Chestnut Place in Bearsted were built with accommodation above them.

    ii   A Survey of Boxley and Thurnham, drawn by John Watts, 1709

2   The value of this tax payment is around £57 today.

3-7   i   Two Messuages in Whier Street
                 Lease for a year, 28 September 1789

          ii   Two Messuages in Whier Street
                 Re-lease 29 September 1789

           Both documents in private collection of Michael Perring

8   1841 census return for Thurnham
          NA reference HO107/483

9   Burial register for St Mary's church
          CKS reference P369/1/1

10   Tithe Apportionment map and schedule for Thurnham 1843
          NA reference IR 29/17/39

11   Entry for Bearsted and Thurnham
          History, Gazetteer and Directory of the County of Kent 1847
          Samuel Bagshaw
          Kent Archaeological Society Library

12   1851 census return for Thurnham
          NA reference HO107/1618

13   Entry for Thurnham, Kelly's trade directory 1859

14   1861 census return for Thurnham
           NA reference RG9 504

15   Messuage and nine acres at Ware Street, 1883
          CKS reference U1644 T188b

16   i   An equivalent sum today would be just over £1,080.

          ii   Parish Rate Book for Thurnham 1862
                 CKS reference Q/GFr12/102 and 103

17   Entry for Thurnham
          Kelly's Trade Directory 1874

18   1881 census return for Thurnham
          NA reference RG11 0933 121

19   *op.cit.* Messuage and nine acres at Ware Street, 1883
          CKS reference U1644 T188b

20-23   i   *ibid.*

          ii   An equivalent sum would be £18,783 today.

24-26   Registers of Licences 1927-1952
          CKS reference PS/BL3-4

27   Entries for Thurnham
          Kelly's Directory, incorporating the Kent Messenger Directory for Maidstone and surrounding villages, 1956
          Copy in the Centre for Kentish Studies

Ware Mead and the farm in Chapel Lane

1   *op.cit.* Codex de Kent
          1/46   Manor 1374-1374
          1/91   Manor 1411

2   A Survey of Boxley and Thurnham, drawn by John Watts, 1709

3   i   An equivalent sum would be £97,000 today.

          ii   Indentures 2 November 1742 & 27 December 1764-5
                 Manor of Thurnham 1542-1844
                 CKS reference U348 T1/1

          iii   Agreement for sale of Manor of Thurnham 1842
                 CKS reference U348 T1/3

4   Plan of Methodist Chapel, c1818
          CKS reference N/MS/369/19

5   pp.89-91, A *History of Bearsted and Thurnham*

6 i Historical appraisal of Chapel Lane farmhouse by Julian Swift, of Rockhill Farm, Egerton, Ashford 1 November 1995. Copy in papers held by Deborah Evans

  ii *A Survey of Chapel Lane Farm, Chapel Lane, Bearsted*
Rupert Austin
Canterbury Archaeological Trust Annual Review 1995-1996

7-16 *op.cit.* Historical Appraisal by Julian Swift
Survey by Rupert Austin

17 i Messuage at Ware Street 1721-1883
CKS reference U1644 T389

  ii 1797 Land Tax Return for Thornham
CKS reference Q/RP/383

  iii The value of this tax payment is around £184 today.

18 It is possible that this property is the one named as Ware House, Thurnham in an auction advertisement which appeared in the *Maidstone Gazette*, 26 August 1823. See page 203.

19-21 i Entries cover 1797 to 1824, Parish Chest Constables and Overseers of Poor Accounts
CKS reference P369/9/1-2

  ii Marriage and Baptism registers for St Mary's church
CKS reference P369/1/1

22 *op.cit.* Parish Chest Constable and Overseers of Poor Accounts
Entries for 1823

23-24 i Bidingfield Wise was admitted to the copyhold on 30 October 1822
Particulars and conditions of sale of some freehold estates 1858
CKS reference U1569 T15

  ii Ned's occupation was recorded in the *Maidstone Gazette and Kentish Courier*
21 August 1827

  iii Account for Edward Hart 1822-1823, Parish Chest Constables and Overseers of Poor Accounts
CKS reference P369/11/2

25 i *op.cit.* Baptism register for St Mary's church

  ii *op.cit.* Parish Chest Constable and Overseers of Poor Accounts
CKS reference P369/9/1-2

26 *op.cit.* Baptism register for St Mary's church

27 I am indebted to Steve Finnis of the Queens Own Royal West Kent Regimental Museum for this information.

28 i Edward Hart's trial was number 54
Kent Gaol Calendar for Summer Assizes 16 August 1827
NA reference ASSI 94/186

  ii The duration of Ned's stay at Maidstone gaol was recorded as costing 5s 8½d
Entry for Edward Hart 1827, PC/N Convict Book 1805-1833
CKS microfilm reference Z87

   Ned's stay would cost £595 today.

29 i Research undertaken by June Fancett and Malcolm Kersey
Home Office: Convict Prison Hulks, Registers and Letter Books Index to *The Retribution* 1802 to 1834
NA reference HO 9/6 and HO 9/7

  ii Sentencing report in *Maidstone Gazette and Kentish Courier*, 28 August 1827

30 i It has been estimated that approximately one third of all convicts that received similar sentences at this time did not subsequently fulfil their transportation orders and were eventually released. Information supplied by Wesley Harry, former historian at the Royal Arsenal, Woolwich.

  ii See Appendix Two for further information about transportation to Australia and other penal colonies.

31 Briefing and records of trial proceedings for John Dyke:
NA reference TS 11/943 folder 3412

32 p.21
To Fire Committed: the history of fire-fighting in Kent
Harry Klopper
Kent Council of the Fire Services National Benevolent Fund 1984

33-34 *op.cit.* Briefing and records of trial proceedings for John Dyke:
NA reference TS 11/943 folder 3412

35 Papers in Thurnham file, Gordon Ward Collection

36 *op.cit.* research undertaken by June Fancett and Malcolm Kersey

37 i   *op.cit.* Messuage at Ware Street 1721-1883

    ii   Equivalent sums would be £265 and £1,260 today.

38 Tithe Apportionment Map and Schedule for Thurnham 1843
    CKS reference IR 29/17/39

39 i   Will of William Akehurst 1846
       NA reference PROB/11/282

    ii   An equivalent sum for William's estate would be £11,832 today.

40 1851 census return for Thurnham
    NA reference H107 1618

41 1861 census return for Thurnham
    NA reference RG9/504

42 i   An equivalent sum today would be just under £4,800

    ii   Parish rate book for Thurnham, 1862
       CKS reference Q/GFr12/102 and 103

43 Ordnance Survey Map 1866

44 Recital and schedule of previous owners included in the Conveyance of Freehold land situate and known as Chapel Lane Farm, Bearsted. Lieutenant Colonel A J Trousdell and another, to Miss K V Seager, 28 July 1954. Copy in papers held by Deborah Evans.

45 1871 census return for Thurnham
    NA reference RG946 10 133

Chapel Lane in later years

1   i   Parish rate book for Thurnham, 1874
       CKS reference P369/4/1

    ii   An equivalent sum would be £3 today.

2   Parish Rate book for Thurnham 1873
    CKS reference P39/4/1

3   1881 census return for Thurnham
    NA reference RG11 0933 123

4   Messuage and 9 acres at Ware Street 1883
    CKS reference U1644 T188b

5-6 i   *ibid.* Draft Conveyance 11 July 1883

    ii   An equivalent sum would be £29,181 today.

7   p.55
    Vinters, the story of Kentish estate
    Vinters Heritage Project, undated

8   *op.cit.* Recital and schedule of previous owners, 1954

9   Order of Chancery 7 August 1890
    CKS reference U1833 T29

10 *op.cit.* Recital and schedule of previous owners, 1954

11 1891 Census return for Thurnham
    NA reference RG 12 691 208-209

12 i   Baptism entry for Alexander Henry Goodwin Kemp, 1896
       Baptism register for St Mary's church
       CKS reference P369/1/1

    ii   1901 census return for Thurnham
       NA reference RG13 770

    iii Tom Gilbert's memories of Ware Street which formed part of transcribed oral history contributions during the 1980s:
        James Moore and Thurnham History Group Project

13   i   Papers from Whatman estate
           CKS reference U1289 E12 and U1289 E16

       ii   An equivalent sum would be £1,530 today.

       iii   Agreement Walter Fremlin Esquire with the Mid Kent Water Company, 29 November 1907
           Copy in papers held by David Pearce

       iv   An equivalent sum would be £115 today.

14   *op.cit.* CKS reference U1289 E15

15   i   An equivalent sum would be £4,956 today

       ii   *op.cit.* CKS reference U1289 E12

16   Catalogue of sale for Sandy Mount, Bearsted 24 January 1944
       Copy in author's possession

17   i   Personal recollections of Deborah Evans, 22 June 2005.

       ii   *op.cit.* Recital and schedule of previous owners, 1954.

18   i   Entry for Thornham in *Kelly's Trade Directory for Kent, 1954*

       ii   p.156
           Boxley: the story of an English parish
           Daevid Hook & Robin Ambrose 1999

19   i   Conveyance of Land, part of Chapel Lane Farm, Bearsted, 20 April 1976
           Copy held in papers of Deborah Evans

       ii   *100 years of golf at Bearsted 1895-1995*
           Clive Horton 1995

20   National Monuments Record listing for Chapel Lane Farm:
       Monarch Uid 503560
       NBR Number 8674

Bell farmhouse, Bell Lane and the Bell Inn

1   *passim.* p.122
       An Illustrated History of the Countryside
       Oliver Rackham
       Phoenix Illustrated 1997

2   i   Entry for Thurnham
           p.8b
           The Domesday Survey of Kent
           Phillimore 1983

       ii   For fascinating information about providing pannage for pigs and other uses of acorns see:
           Oak: the Frame of Civilisation
           William Bryant Logan
           W W Norton 2005

3   *passim., op.cit.* p.122, *An Illustrated History of the Countryside*

4   1841 census return for Thurnham
       NA reference HO107 463 2

5   1843 tithe map and apportionment schedule for Thurnham
       NA reference IR 29/17/39

6   1861 census return for Thurnham
       NA reference RG9 504

7   1871 census entry for Thurnham
       NA reference RG10 946

8   Parish rate book for Thurnham 1880
       CKS reference P369/4/1

9   1881 census return for Thurnham
       NA reference RG11 0933 122

10   1891 census return for Thurnham
       NA reference RG12 691

11   1901 census return for Thurnham
       NA reference RG13 770

12   *op.cit.* pp.11 and 21, *'Dutifulness and Endurance' Bearsted and Thurnham 1914-1918 and 1939-1945*

13   i   Entries for Thurnham
         Electoral Roll for Maidstone, 1939
         Held at CKS, Maidstone

     ii Entry for Thurnham
         Kent Messenger Directory of Maidstone and surrounding neighbourhood 1933 to 1934

14   *op.cit.* Electoral Roll for Maidstone, 1939

15-16   *op.cit.* pp.130-131, *'Dutifulness and Endurance' Bearsted and Thurnham 1914-1918, 1939-1945*

17   i   Entry for Thurnham
         Kelly's Directory of Maidstone and surrounding neighbourhood 1933 to 1934
         Kent Messenger

     ii Entries for Thurnham 1955, 1956
         Kelly's incorporating Kent Messenger Directory of Maidstone and surrounding neighbourhood

18   Register of Alehouse Keepers
     CKS reference Q/RLv4 1-3 Z186

19   Security for replacing £4000, 24 July 1801, Deeds relating to The Bell, Thurnham, and The Target, Maidstone
     CKS reference U896 T15

20   Will of John Seager, brewer of Maidstone, 1801
     NA reference PROB 11/1355

21   *op.cit.* Deeds relating to The Bell, Thurnham, and The Target, Maidstone

22   Land Assessment Tax for Thurnham, 1801
     CKS reference Q RP 383

23   i   *op.cit.* Deeds relating to The Bell, Thurnham, and The Target, Maidstone
         Bond as collateral security for £2000 and interest, 12 August 1825

     ii Register of Alehouse Keepers
         CKS reference Q/RLv4 3-6 Z187

24   Abstract of Title as to Piece of Copy Hold land at Thurnham 1828, documents re Armstrong sale, 1858
     CKS reference U289 T43

25   i   Entry for Bearsted and Thurnham
         Pigot & Co National Commercial Directory 1839
         Facsimile Text 1993, Michael Winton

     ii Entry for Thurnham
         Kelly's Trade Directory for Kent 1859

26   *op.cit.* Entry for Thurnham 1841 census

27   *op.cit.* Tithe map and apportionment schedule for Thurnham 1843

28   i   Deed of appointment 4 January 1853 re The Bell
         CKS reference U896 T150

     ii Transfer of mortgage 4 January 1853 re The Bell
         5 April 1855 re-conveyance of mortgaged hereditaments
         CKS reference U896 T1 156

29   *op.cit.* 1881 census for Thurnham

30-31   i   Register of Licences 1903-1906
            CKS reference PS BL/3

     ii Entries for Thurnham, Electoral Roll for Maidstone, 1939
         Held at CKS, Maidstone

     iii Entries under Thurnham
         Kelly's Directory, incorporating the Kent Messenger Directory for Maidstone and surrounding villages 1949 and 1956

32   January 1944 Holy Cross parish magazine
     CKS reference P18/28/20

33   By December 2006, when this chapter was under preparation, the ownership of The Bell Inn had passed from Isherwood and Stacey through Fremlin Brewery to Greene King.

Ware Street in the twentieth century and more recent times

1   List of Connections 29 November 1907, Agreement W T Fremlin and The Mid Kent Water Company
        14 November 1906 and 29 November 1907
        Copy held in private papers of David Pearce

2   An equivalent sum would be £13 today.

3   p.42
        Villages around Old Maidstone
        Irene Hales
        Meresborough Books 1980

4   i   p.xi, *A History of Bearsted and Thurnham*

        ii   1881 census return for Bearsted
                NA reference RG 11 0926 54 and RG 0926 48 7

        iii   In March 1938, the parish magazine for Bearsted published an article concerning the memories of the sand
                quarry and donkeys by Mr Card. Although his age is not given, Mr Card had been born in Bearsted. He recalled
                that he often helped to fill bags with silver sand before setting out on the long delivery rounds. Each donkey
                carried six or eight bags and the price ranged from 1s 6d to 2s 6d. The sand was purchased by gentleman's
                gardeners, innkeepers, and shopkeepers. Demand was steady but it was not a lucrative trade. There were
                occasions when the donkeys were not adequately fed so they browsed for forage locally. One of the owners was
                regularly prosecuted for neglect. Upon the journey for home, as soon as they reached the top of the hill above
                Hollingbourne, the donkeys and their drivers would make a bee-line for home, regardless of roads and hedges.

                Holy Cross parish magazine, March 1938
                CKS reference P18/28/18

5   *ibid.* p.127

6-7   Unpublished correspondence from Paul Ashbee dated 12 February 2004

8   i   Equivalent sums would be £1,880 and £15,764, respectively

        ii   No report about the official opening of the chapel in 1877 could be found in any local newspaper

9   pp.19-26, *100 years of Bearsted Golf Club*

10   This information is largely based on an article about the process of making bricks published in 1864, published in *The
        National Encyclopaedia*, and a series of undated recollected conversations between Joseph Crane and Kathryn
        Kersey. Joseph's eldest brother had worked in a Kent brickfield in the early years of the twentieth century.

11   Entry for Thurnham
        Kent Messenger trade directory for Maidstone 1937-1938
        Copy in the Centre for Kentish Studies

12   This property was wrongly identified as the medieval hall house in Ware Street demolished during the 1950s
        p.18 *Bearsted and Thurnham Remembered*

13   i   *op cit.* National Monuments Record listing for Stocks House, 70 Ware Street

        ii   Entry for Stocks House, Thurnham
                Medieval Houses of Kent – a survey conducted by the Royal Commission on the Historical Monuments
                of England
                HMSO 1994

14   There is one document in the Centre for Kentish Studies which mentions a fifteen year lease for a Stockwell Farm in
        Bearsted and Thurnham dated 1745, agreed between Lord Romney and William Randall. Although the farm was
        substantial; the land holdings were estimated at fifty three acres, unfortunately the description does not include a
        location or any details which would directly link it to Ware Street.
        CKS reference U1515 T195

15   i   Robert Shornden left his son, also called Robert, some lands in Ware Street believed to be opposite, what is
                today, the site of the Methodist chapel, and a property called The Stockhouse.
                Will of Robert Shornden 1599
                CCA reference DCb-PRC 17/51/371

        ii   See William Shornden holdings in the Manor of Ware Court Book entries for 1648
                CCRc reference M5 folios 5-6 and folio 14 169401

16   Entries for Thurnham, Electoral Roll for Maidstone, 1939
        Held at CKS, Maidstone

17   Conversation between Jean Jones and Kathryn Kersey, 12 February 2004

18-19 i   An equivalent sum would be £26,909 today.

      ii   1742 Memorandum concerning the purchase of a house and two acres of meadowland adjoining Ware pond by Henry Rand.
CKS reference U1401 Z4

20-21 i   Tithe apportionment map for Thurnham 1840
CKS reference Dcb/TO/T6B

      ii   Tithe apportionment schedule for Thurnham 1843
CKS reference IR 29/17/39

22 i   An equivalent sum would be £107,141 today.

      ii   *op.cit.* 1742 Memorandum

Appendices

Appendix Two

1 i   Entry for Edward Hart 1827
PC/N Convict Book 1805-1833
CKS microfilm reference Z87

      ii   An equivalent sum would be £595 today.

2 *ibid.*

3 Entry for *The Retribution:* www.answers.com

4-6 Information about prison hulks on the River Thames: www.portcities.org.uk/london

7 i   Details from: www.medway.gov.uk/index/leisure.localhistory.timeline/17905/prisonhulks.htm

      ii   pp.89-90
The English Prison Hulks
W Branch Johnson
Phillimore 1970

8 *ibid.* p.32

9 *ibid.* pp.101-102

10 *ibid.* pp.98-99

11 *ibid.* p.33

12 *Account of the Hulks System in England 1834*
Originally published in the Sydney Herald, New South Wales republished J Fawcett 2000-2005
For further details see: www.genseek.net

13 i   An Edward Hart is listed as sailing on the *Roslin Castle* to Australia which left Cork on 8 October 1832 and arrived at Sydney in New South Wales on 5 February 1833 but this is a different man, convicted in Dublin. Details of *Roslin Castle* sailing 1832 to 1833: www.convictcentral.com

      ii   Research undertaken by June Fancett who checked the Australian Joint Copying Project details for convict records.

14 E-mail correspondence June 2006 between Wesley Harry and Kathryn Kersey.

15 i   Details of Samuel Jarman's trial: *Maidstone Journal*, 7 January 1834
On this occasion he received a life sentence and was transported, arriving in Sydney on 9 July 1834.

      ii   Details of *Susan* sailing and arrival 9 July 1834
www.convictcentral.com/

16 Home Office: Convict Prison Hulks, Registers and Letter Books 1802 to 1836
Convict Hulks moored at Woolwich: Index to register of prisoners on *The Retribution*, 1802 to 1834
NA reference HO9/6

17 Home Office: Convict Prison Hulks, Registers and Letter Books 1802 to 1836
Convict Hulks moored at Woolwich – *The Retribution, Bellerophon* Register of prisoners
NA reference HO9/7

18 Home Office: Convict Prison Hulks, Registers and Letter Books 1802 to 1836
Convict Hulks moored at Woolwich: Index to register of prisoners on *The Justitia*
NA reference HO9/5

19 Research in Bermuda undertaken by Judy Corday has found no record of Edward Hart arriving at the island.

20 Information from the website: www.portcities.org.uk/london

21 E-mail correspondence June 2006 between Wesley Harry and Kathryn Kersey

22 *op.cit.* www.portcities.org.uk/london

23 Article *for The Illustrated London News 1856*, subsequently published in:
The Criminal Prisons of London and Scenes of London Life
Henry Mayhew and John Binny
Griffin, Bohn and Co. London 1862

Appendix Three

1 Thomas Hendley's Book
CKS reference U1044 F1

2 Manor of Ware Court Book including 1613-1647, 1637-1647, 1661-1671
CCRc reference M5 folios 5-6 and folio 14 169401

3 i *ibid.*

 ii An equivalent sum would be £6 today.

4 Messuage at Ware Street 1721-1883
CKS reference U1644 T389

5 Tithe Apportionment Schedule for Thurnham 1843
CKS reference IR 29/17/39

6 i Messuage at Ware, 1703
CKS reference U1823 T70

 ii Despite the inclusion of Elizabeth Dixon's name here, there is no further evidence to link her with the lands shown in the Survey of Boxley and Thurnham, drawn by John Watts, 1709

7 Messuage and Shop at Ware Street, 1760
CKS reference U229 T270

8 Transcript of advertisement
26 August 1823, *Maidstone Gazette*

Glossary of some words and terms used in this book

Note: This is not an extensive glossary but it is hoped to contain the majority of obscure terms found in the court rolls for the manor of Ware and other associated documents.

ALIENATION	Transfer of a holding by sale rather than by inheritance. A feudal tenant was unable to alienate without licence from the lord who would collect a fee for granting the transfer.
AFFEEROR	A person appointed by a court to advise on the scale of amercements.
AMERCEMENT	A fine paid for a minor infringement of court rules or manorial custom.
APPURTENANCES	The rights connected to a piece of land.
BEADLE	Officer of the court or parish.
COMMON SUIT	Attendance at the manorial court was described as 'paying suit 'Sometimes found in the phrase 'default of common suit': failure to fulfil manorial court obligations, usually attendance of the manorial court when required unless specifically excused or not summoned.
COMMUTATION	Money paid instead of services.
COPYHOLD	Land held by a copy of the entry in the court roll.
COPYHOLDER	One who holds land by right of a copy of a court roll entry.
CROFT	An enclosed piece of land frequently close, or adjacent, to a dwelling and often used as a garden.
COURT BARON	A court held by each manor to deal with matters on an estate. This included minor infringements of the rights of the lord and local customs, disputes of tenancy and changes of tenancies. Courts Baron also held rights to listen to civil pleas to the value of forty shillings.
COURT ROLL	A formal record of a manor court. Usually in the form of a continuous roll of parchment membranes or paper, but also extended to separate sheets of paper. If the separate sheets are bound into a volume, they are sometimes referred to as Court Books.
CUSTUMAL	A formal record also called a survey or rental, which notes the details of the rents, services and customs.
CUSTOM	A scheme or framework of local rules, practices, expectations relating to economic or social activities.
DAY-WORK(S)	The amount of work that could be undertaken in a day, so 'six day-works' was the amount of work carried out over six days.
DEFAULT	The failure to meet a requirement of the court such as paying a fine.
DEMESNE	A section of a manor directly used by the lord.
DISTRAIN	If a sum of money that was due remained unpaid, the Lord of the manor or his agent could apply a process of distraint. This involved collecting goods to the value of the unpaid sum. If this was unsuccessful, and the sum remained unpaid, the Lord of the manor could reclaim the property. As most sums were paid, the distraint clause was rarely executed.
DOMAIN	All the land belonging to the manor. Sometimes called DEMESNE.
ENFEOFFMENT	Legal term for the process of possessing a property.
ENTRY FINE	A payment made upon formal admittance to a property, usually the sum of a year's rent.
ESCHEAT	A reversion of land or an estate to a lord or the crown when there were no heirs.

ESCHEATOR	A legal officer of the crown whose duty is to oversee and note what escheats have occurred.
ESSOIN	An excuse given for not attending a court. Also used to indicate those people named in the roll summoned to attend the court, but excused.
FEALTY	Sometimes described as 'act of fealty' or to 'swear fealty'. Either process involved a new tenant swearing an oath of loyalty and a promise to conform and uphold customary service and payments of the manorial court.
FEOFFEE	A trustee.
FINE	A payment of money paid to the lord or court for a specified concession.
FREEHOLD	A free tenancy of a manor held in perpetuity. Such land was not subject to the customs of the manor.
FREEHOLDER	One who holds a free tenancy.
FULL AGE	The age at which heirs were recognised as adults and therefore able to inherit.
GAVELKIND	The custom of equal inheritance between heirs. Also known as PARTIBLE INHERITANCE.
HOMAGE	An act of submission in which a tenant acknowledges a superior, or lord, of the manor.
HUNDRED	An administrative division of an English county. The manor of Ware was part of Eyhorne Hundred.
INTER ALIA	Latin phrase used to indicate 'amongst other things'.
LABOUR SERVICES	A duty to work for the lord, frequently on the demesne of the manor. It was often included as a condition of a tenancy in the manor.
MANOR	An estate, usually comprising the lord's property and his tenants' holdings.
MESSUAGE	A house, but also including associated outbuildings and land.
PANNAGE	The right to, and practise of, feeding animals, usually pigs, on acorns or beech fruits or mast.
PERCH	A linear measure, standardised as $5\frac{1}{2}$ yards or $16\frac{1}{2}$ feet.
POLE	Alternative name for Perch.
PRESENTMENT	A matter or accusation brought before a court for consideration by a tenant or tenants, made under oath.
QUITCLAIM	The release and disclaimer to all rights, and interest in a property. Sometimes a quitclaim fee was also payable.
RECOGNISANCE	A legal bond agreed in court for a tenant to undertake an action.
RELEASE	The act of conveying a property or rights to another person, sometimes this includes a legally recognised document which confirms the conveyance.
RELIEF	A payment made by all freehold tenants. It was normally levied when a new tenant took possession of land on the death of his parents or another relative. Occasionally it became liable if it was deemed that the tenant had taken possession as a minor but had then reached adulthood. The amount paid depended on the custom of the manor but was usually an amount equivalent to half, one or two years rent.
REMAINDER	A residual interest from a legal estate.
RENTAL	A record of a list of tenants which also includes the amount of rent which is payable.
REVERSION	A future interest in a property.
ROD	Alternative name for Perch.

ROOD	A measure of land equal to one quarter of an acre or forty square perches.
SEISED	A term used for the legal ownership of a property.
SEISIN	Legal possession of a property.
SUIT	Obligatory attendance of the manorial courts by tenants, so 'to do suit' was to attend the manorial court, sometimes phrased as SUIT OF COURT.
SUITOR	Person appearing at court.
SULUNG	A measure of land. In the Domesday book, the sulung was usually twice the area of a hide or carucate: around 240 acres. It is thought that the name partially derives from the Old English word for a plough.
SURVEY	A description of a manor and which includes the boundaries, customs and details of each land holding.
TENEMENT	A property holding but consisting of a dwelling and land. Sometimes included in the phrase 'messuage and tenement' indicating the property included a house, outbuildings and associated land.
TITHE	A payment to the church, usually one tenth of all produce.

Bibliography and Further Reading

The Allotment Chronicles – a social history of allotment gardening
Steve Poole
Silver Link Publishing Limited 2006

Ancient Woodland: Its History, Vegetation and Uses in England
Oliver Rackham
Castlepoint Press 2003

The Bishops and Monks of Rochester 1076-1214
Colin Flint
Kent Archaeological Society 1997

Bound for Botany Bay: British Convict Voyages to Australia
Alan Brooke and David Brandon
National Archives 2005

The British Oak: Its History and Natural History
M G Morris and F H Perring
The Botanical Society of the British Isles 1974

Captain Swing
Eric Hobsbawm and George Rudé
Phoenix Press 2001

The Codification of the Customs of Kent
C L Sinclair Williams
Archaeologia Cantiana Volume XCV 1979
Kent Archaeological Society

The Compleat Court Keeper
Giles Jacob
1713

Continuity and Colonization: the evolution of Kentish settlement
Alan Everitt
Leicester University Press 1986

The Court Baron: Precedents of Pleading in Manorial and other local courts
Edited by Professor F. W. Maitland and W Paley Baildon
The Selden Society 1890

The Criminal Prisons of London and Scenes of London Life
Henry Mayhew and John Binny
Griffin, Bohn and Co.
London 1862

Discovering Green Lanes
Valerie Belsey
Green Books 2001

Documents Illustrative of Medieval Kentish Society
Edited F R H Du Boulay
Kent Records Volume XVIII
Kent Archaeological Society 1964

Early Modern Kent 1540 to 1640
Edited Michael Zell
Boydell Press and Kent County Council 2000

The English Alehouse: a social history 1200-1830
Peter Clark
Longman 1983

The English Manor 1200-1500
Edited Mark Bailey
Manchester University Press 2002

The English Prison Hulks
W Branch Johnson
Phillimore1970

Forty Years of Convict Labour in Bermuda 1823-1863
C F E Horris Hallett
Bermuda Maritime Museum 1999

The Hundred and the Hundred Rolls: An Outline of Local Government in Medieval England
Helen M Cam
Methuen 1930

The Intolerable Hulks: British Shipboard Confinement 1776-1857
Charles Campbell
Heritage Books 1994

Lost Rents, Vacant Holdings and the Contraction of Peasant Cultivation after the Black Death
John Titow
Agricultural History Review, Volume 42, 1994

Jack Cade's Rebellion of 1450
I M W Harvey
Clarendon Press 1991

John de Berwyke and the Consuetudines Kancie
Felix Hull
Archaeologia Cantiana Volume XCVI 1980
Kent Archaeological Society

Kent Hearth Tax
Duncan Harrington, Sarah Pearson, Susan Rose
Kent Archaeological Society & British Record Society 2000

The Manor Court: A Bibliography of Printed Sources and Related Materials and Vocabulary
CJ Harrison
Keele 2005: www.keele.ac.k/depts/hi/resources/manor courts/index.htm

Manorial Records 16th to 19th Centuries
Rosalyn Bass
Borthwick Institute of Historical Research and University of York 1998

Medieval Society and the Manor Court
edited Zvi Razi and Richard Smith
Clarendon Press, Oxford 1996

Nineteenth Century Church Registers of Bermuda
Indexed A C Hollis Hallett, updated, C F E Hollis Hallett
Juniperhill Press and Bermuda Maritime Museum Press 2005

No Return Tickets
L Grace Dibble
Stockwell Books 1989

Oak: the Frame of Civilisation
William Bryant Logan
W W Norton 2005

Registrum Roffense
John Thorpe
London 1769

The Social Structure of Manorial Freeholders
M A Barg
Agricultural History Review Volume 39, 1991

Some Medieval Records for Family Historians
Peter Franklin
Federation Family History Societies 1994

The Stripping of the Altars
Eamon Duffy
Yale 1992

A Treatise of Gavelkind
William Somner
(Second Edition) London 1726

Using Manorial Records
Mary Ellis
Public Record Publications 1997

The Voices of Morebath
Eamon Duffy
Yale 2001

The Woodland Economy of Kent 1066 to 1348
K P Witney
Agricultural History Review Volume 38, 1990

Index

Index

Places mentioned in Early Manor of Ware section

Later Manor of Ware – specific properties named in this section but see also Ware Street

Index

Robert Morrell	5, 7, 9, 13, 17, 37
Henry Morris	152
James Morris	142
John Mortimer	53
Martin Moss	vi, 63
Muddle	43
Henry Muddle	26
Nicholas Muddle	25, 26
John Mumford of Sutton at Hone	94
Samuel and Elizabeth Murton	61
Alfred, Sarah, Mynn and their children, Mary, Suzannah, Sarah and Laura	95-98
Charlotte Mynn	95
Walter Mynn	95
Joseph Nealby	113
George and Ann Nelson	152
George Newton	70-71
Henry Nichols	26
Charles Noakes	103
Richard and Charles Norman	161
Sir John de Northwode	132
Joane, Lady of Northwoode	8, 14
Lady of Northwood	5, 7, 38
Lady Joan de Northwood	15, 17
Lady Joan de Northwoode	15
Lady Joan, the Lady of Northwoode	12, 41
Jane Norton	95
Richard Obee	127
Mr and Mrs Ollett	172
Thomas and Suzann Oliver of Maidstone, husbandman	202
Baroness Orczy	92, 172
Thomas Packham	78
George Page	21, 47
John Pandhurst of Teston, bricklayer	202
Dr Frank Panton	vi, vii
Parks family	97, 172
Michael Patterson	110
Pawley family	97, 105
John Payn	54
Edmund Peachey	112
David Pearce	vi
Rosemary Pearce	vi
Mr Pearson	159
Mr Perrin and Perrin family	160
E L Pemberton	201
Michael Perring	v, vii, xi, 77, 89, 102, 127, 132
Richard Pett	78
Edgar and Emily Pettipiere and their daughter, Norah	141
Luke Phillips	168
Elizabeth Philpott	79
Thomas Philpot	50, 78-79, 80, 152
John Pixe	53
Margaret Plowright	vi
John Pokyll	74
Thomas, William and Elizabeth Pokyll	74
John Pollard	112
John Portyngton	54
Pound family. also Harry, Daisy and Albert	97, 166
James Price of Hollingbourne	112
John Prisot	54
William Pound	97
Nurse Beeton Pull	63, 65, 120
Thomas Punnett	112
Elisabeth Rackham	vii
Rev Henry Rand, vicar of Bearsted	168
James ,Rachel and Amy Randle, also Randall	61-62, 141
Elizabeth Reach	94
Charles, Douglas and Perry Redgrave	94
Sarah Richards	94
William Roades	26
Richard Robasar	15

Index